THE NEXT STEP IN STUDYING

The Next Step in Studying Religion

A Graduate's Guide

Edited by Mathieu Courville

continuum

Continuum

Continuum International Publishing Group
The Tower Building
11 York Road
London SE1 7NX
www.continuumbooks.com

80 Maiden Lane
Suite 704
New York NY 10038

© Mathieu Courville and Contibutors 2007

First published 2007

Grateful acknowledgement is made to the following for permission to reprint previously published poetry:
Harcourt, USA: Excerpts from T. S. Eliot, 'Burnt Norton', *Four Quartets*
Faber & Faber, UK: Excerpts from T. S. Eliot, 'Burnt Norton', *Four Quartets*

British Library Cataloguing-in-Publication Data
A catalogue record for this book is available from the British Library.

ISBN: HB: 0-8264-9842-6
        978-0-8264-9842-7

        PB: 0-8264-9843-4
        978-0-8264-9843-4

Library of Congress Cataloging-in-Publication Data
A catalog record for this book is available from the Library of Congress

Typeset by Fakenham Photosetting Limited, Fakenham, Norfolk
Printed and bound in Great Britain by Cromwell Press Ltd, Trowbridge, Wiltshire

To '*Gurus*' (teachers),
In their infinite varieties,
In all times and all places.

Contents

Preface

This is a book for graduate students, written by people who would wish to see them do their best, aided by the best assistance possible. The book is the result of the work of professors. Aside from the editor's brief introduction (and this even briefer preface), the book is a collection of practical as well as theoretically minded work by professors for current and future graduate students pursuing studies of the various facets of religion with hopes of remaining in this field once their MA and PhD degrees are completed. It is a book full of hopes, yes, but hopefully realistic ones. The book's simple aim is to help current and future students at a time when a little guidance and understanding, a helping hand, is most welcome.

Mathieu E. Courville
Val-des-Monts, QC
March 2007

Introduction: Reaching the Other Shore

MATHIEU E. COURVILLE (UNIVERSITY OF OTTAWA)

In a recent column in the *Chronicle of Higher Education*,[1] literary and cultural critic Stanley Fish concluded that since the high water mark of 'theory' is past its peak, the next hot-button topic will be religion. One might wonder if our state of purportedly being 'post-theory' is not itself the great question (i.e. what is post-theory?) and the relation between the fall of high theory and a purported return to religion an obvious extension of it. Many quite worldly reasons could be enumerated to begin explaining why the likes of Stanley Fish think religion will be the next centre of an academic craze; the next 'academania'. Not all of these worldly reasons are laudable. A sound corollary, to counter Fish's new found interest in religion, might be Hannah Arendt's still true epigrammatic observation that it is no blessing, but rather a curse, to live in interesting times.[2] This also holds true for current students of religious studies and/or theology and those of the foreseeable future.

Some signs of this trend's emergence (or re-emergence) could be easily enumerated.[3] However, anyone with a keen critical awareness of the history of the study of religion and theology is likely to think in terms closer to Ibn Khaldun – 'the future is to the past like water is to water' – than in the terms of Stanley Fish, who seems to discern something radically novel about religion and theology as foci of intellectual work and interest.

It is true that, in a certain sense, the degree of our acute self-awareness of religious pluralism is a relatively recent phenomenon. One can here point to, for example, the esteemed work of W. C. Smith, *The Meaning and End of Religion*,[4] in which he writes that 'the prevailing conceptions on such fundamental matters' of this purported thing some attempt to identify, isolate, objectify, reify even, and call religion, 'are of relatively recent origins', and 'that only slowly and of late have our minds become prisoners to the kind of thinking that has proven itself inadequate to deal with the phenomena before us'. One can affirm this at least partial truth and yet also affirm the fact that religious pluralism is itself not a novelty, drawing for example on Henri Pinard de la Boullaye's magisterial work on the history of the comparative approach to the study of religions, in which he writes that although a would-be science of religions is of recent pedigree, '*la simple comparaison des religions remonte beaucoup plus haut dans l'histoire*'.[5] He goes on to write the following:

> *Elle a dû s'imposer à quelque degré, dès que des cultes distincts se sont trouvés côte à côte, dès qu'un voyageur sortant de sa bourgade (ou dès qu'un indigène*

mis en contact avec un voyageur) a pu constater des conceptions et des usages différents de ceux auxquels il était accoutumé. Quelle conduite tenir à leur égard ? Pourquoi rester fidèle aux uns et se désintéresser des autres ? Ces questions sont si naturelles et si graves, qu'il était impossible de ne pas leur donner une réponse.[6]

What has become more frequent is the rate of inter-religious and inter-cultural contact as well as the rate at which politicians, policy wonks and mass media pundits can blame such contact for many of our time's deeply rooted problems. That these problems might largely or in part result from processes which need not be thought of mainly or exclusively in religious or theological terms are matters that students of religion and students of theology have and must continue to address. Still in regard to this 'multiplicity of religious traditions', and the rise of sustained exposure to one another, in *The Meaning and End of Religion*, W. C. Smith wrote the following:

> In addition to a myriad of lesser groups, [population-wise that is] there are on earth not one but at least four or five major religious communities each proclaiming a faith with a long and impressive, even brilliant, past and with the continuing creative allegiance of mighty civilizations. This is known in theory; the knowledge is today supplemented in practice by personal contact and widespread social intermingling. Any adequate interpretation of a Christian's faith, for instance, must make room for the fact that other intelligent, devout, and moral men [and women], including perhaps his [or her] own friends, are Buddhists, Hindus, or Muslims.[7]

Although these words were consigned to paper long before Samuel P. Huntington penned his 'clash of civilization' thesis,[8] they still have some relevance today in that many feel this task is still largely unfinished business. Moreover, secular humanists also need to make room for themselves at the proverbial 'table of the gods' and this via making more room for themselves as yet another 'Other' within their interlocutors' worldviews.

Indeed, the likes of Wilfred Cantwell Smith, not to mention Mircea Eliade, Ninian Smart and Paul Tillich, to name but a few quasi-titanic scholars of the mid- to late twentieth-century religiological and theological academic scenes, would not have been surprised or bewildered by the early twenty-first century's developments, encapsulated in Fish's observations. Many of them, I am sure, would feel they had in fact foreseen it and predicted it in various ways.

Students of religious studies or theology should nevertheless take at least some pleasure in Stanley Fish's comments. Fields of study or disciples – depending on where one situates oneself within that debate – such as theology and religious studies have and continue to be seen and feel themselves to be marginal at best within the overall academic edifice. It is to be hoped that the would-be trend described by Fish, among others, can serve to not only solidify the secular positions and critical roles that theology and religious studies occupy within modern universities, but also enable students of these fields to become still more confident about some of *le bien fondé* of their respective collective endeavours, engaging both the rest of the modern university as well as the greater modern world beyond it with that much more aplomb. Moreover, it is to be hoped that this trend Fish describes will also draw more young students to fields that consider religion to be of central intellectual concern. In a parallel, though modest manner, this book aims to help young students of religious studies or theology to successfully pursue graduate degrees, working toward establishing themselves as the professional scholars for coming generations. The editor and the contributors to this volume also hope that in an equally modest way, this work will help graduate student's mentors as well, since they play such a pivotal function in this process.

This book's title, *The Next Step in Studying Religion: A Graduate's Guide*, describes what the volume attempts, i.e. to furnish graduate students with guideposts, with signs along the way, in making this 'next step': that step being transmuting one's 'scholar self' from graduate student to professional scholar. As many students of religion will have observed, convocation, as a ceremony, still maintains the well-known structure of a rite of passage, marking the end of a much longer rite of passage; a much longer process of self-transformation, which the convocation serves to symbolically complete. Graduate school is very much a passage, literally from studentship to professional scholarship; for many, the envisaged end being professorship. My title to this brief introductory chapter also utilizes another image to describe this process, a well-known Buddhist teaching about 'Reaching for the Other Shore'; moving from one state to another. This book then largely concerns 'the raft', a necessary object and yet one too few are invited to glance back at once discarded.

The essays collected were written specifically to help graduate students of religious studies and theology in their quest to become professional scholars and professors. In fact, many of the essays may be thought of as open letters to young scholars of religion. This aptly describes the spirit in which many were written. The book itself is made up of more than a dozen essays written by an interesting variety of scholars. The great majority of the contributors to this endeavour are well established, but in the selection I have also asked for and received contributions from relatively younger, though nevertheless also well-established, scholars. I requested that all of the contributors write to today's and tomorrow's graduate students of either religious studies or theology, to tell them what they would have wanted to know back when they themselves were graduate students. To borrow a phrase of Professor Patriquin, I have asked for their 'pearls of wisdom'. I invited the scholars to be creative and not overly formal in their writing; the aim being to provide a candid and yet practical guide for graduate students of their fields. The contributing scholars were invited to reflect on the processes by which they themselves became scholars, to utilize their own experience, their own narratives, as a means of grounding their recommendations, thus avoiding the 'voice from nowhere' pitch. Many of the scholars are historians of religions, yet perspectives were also solicited from social scientists and theologians, and so, it is hoped that in the collection as many graduate students as possible within these cognate fields will find something of lasting use to them in their respective scholarly quests.

THE NEXT STEP'S 'GENESIS'

I should also like to very briefly explain how this book came about. While a PhD student of religious studies myself, I was elected the Graduate Student Representative of Canadian Corporation for the Study of Religion (CCSR), the consortium of Canadian learned societies concerned with the study of the various facets of religion and theology. Professor Peter Beyer, then President of the CCSR Executive Board had recommended me for the position, which I gladly accepted. The initial plan had been that the contributed essays be published as a special issue in the Canadian journal *Studies in Religion/Sciences Religieuses*. The journal's editors had accepted the project and yet, even from its inception, members of CCSR executive and the journal's editorial board expressed their opinion that a collection of essays such as this would be best served if published as a book, so as to ensure that it enjoy a larger, more lasting circulation. Moreover, I thought it best to attempt a more global book, with contributions from scholars from beyond a strictly Canadian context.

ITS STRUCTURE AND CONTENTS

The first part of the book, 'Part I: Practicalities', is most explicit in its practical approach. Part I begins with a piece contributed by Larry Patriquin, entitled 'How to Complete a Doctoral Dissertation in This Lifetime: Some Marbles of Wisdom'. Students and scholars who have searched the web for this sort of wisdom may already be familiar with Professor Patriquin's wit and wisdom: this piece, in an earlier form, had been made available on the internet. Although the piece was not originally written for this book's discipline-specific audience, it is, in my own estimation, one of the best texts of its kind, a natural complement to that of Professor Michel Desjardins, which immediately follows it. Moreover, Professor Patriquin has revisited the text, neutralizing discipline-specific language where possible and therefore making even plainer its relevance for graduate students of many fields of study, religious studies or theology included. Where Patriquin discusses research that is not religion or theology oriented, readers can however easily imagine how his recommendations would nevertheless apply to these fields. Patriquin's text is gritty and commonsensical, and for these reasons invaluable.

The second text of Part I is Professor Michel Desjardins' 'Netting a Job in Religious Studies: Some Notes from the Field' (a text which also had been available on the internet and has since been revised to be included here). Of this text, my colleague Timothy Pettipiece likes to say that it is a religious studies graduate student's virtual 'bible'. Whereas Patriquin's text can be applied to many fields (ours included), Desjardins' text narrows the focus via discipline-specific suggestions. The complement of these two first pieces should be obvious. Through Patriquin's piece one gets to grapple with that which is more generally expected throughout the humanities and social sciences; via Desjardins' one must grapple with our own fields' specific frames of reference.

The third text of Part I, again a punchy one, is entitled 'Theses on Professionalization', contributed by Professor Russell T. McCutcheon. Some of McCutcheon's theses cover, in their own way, areas broached in the first two texts, though each with their own distinctive 'slants of light'. The 'Theses on Professionalization', however, also shifts the discussion's centre of gravity slightly, looking onward toward some of what newly minted PhDs need to consider if and when they land their first academic positions. This concern dovetails well with those of the fourth and final text of Part I, by Professor Kay Koppedrayer, in that her text asks the reader to consider matters such as the tone and style of their first publications. Drawing on her own experience, both as a scholar and as a journal editor, Koppedrayer leads one to see that such things as a published piece's tone and style is often what separates that which reads like a first piece and that which does not. Koppedrayer's essay is a discerning look at academic publishing, specifically aimed at letting graduate students know some of what one may otherwise only come to learn by trial, and yes, by error. Anthropologically speaking, she describes for us much of the 'emic' perspective, the point of view of the editors on the receiving end of our would-be professional work. Insofar as graduate students want and need to publish, Professor Koppedrayer's text charts the course toward a kind of 'going native', i.e. learning to think and write more like a journal editor would want authors to think and write, thus saving younger scholars from much uncertainty as well as the resulting anxieties and frustrations. All four pieces of Part I are invaluable resources.

In 'Part II: Reflections', the reader will find more overtly reflexive essays from scholars aiming either at drawing on their experiential storehouses in hopes of providing orientations for younger scholars, or drawing on what the scholars would have wished to know (practically and/or theoretically) when they were graduate students earlier in their own academic careers.

Sometimes, even oftentimes, the reader will find a mix of both: past personal insights to guide oneself by, or current theoretical interests to go forward from.

Professor Harold Coward's contribution makes a strong case concerning the crucial sense of time and place that graduate school occupies in the overall life course of the scholar. Coward's essay also introduces themes such as interdisciplinarity, worldly engagement and the longstanding influences of graduate student mentors; themes that subsequent essays also develop. One of the themes Professor Klaus Klostermaier's essay places emphasis upon is that of dialogue, specifically inter-religious dialogue. Klostermaier also makes a strong case as to why religious studies, properly conducted, needs the secular university setting; possibly more importantly though, Klostermaier affirms that the converse is also the case: for the sake of its own secularity, a secular university needs to house religious studies. Professor Klostermaier's and Professor David Chidester's texts, although distinctive, share an emphasis on not only the role of location but also history (and all about it that is potentially meaningful but also actually *'aléatoire'*, i.e. arbitrary, contingent). Professor Chidester emphasizes how one's awareness of one's location may not only change the foci of our studies, but may also impact how we look at our own discipline's history and how we define our so-called object of study. His essay also examines how progressive political leaders in South Africa during its historic struggle against apartheid were themselves astute students of symbolic form and of what may be called a dialogue of secular religions, which is also a form of inter-religious dialogue, though less obviously so. Like Coward, both Klostermaier and Chidester emphasize how life and work influence one another in many ways that deserve our attention, not to be wholly ignored or demeaned. This common thread (one which I do not wish to overemphasize in that the contributions are all very distinctive, reflecting each scholar's individual experiences) is uncovered further in Professor Marc H. Ellis' work, in which he calls attention to some of the field's less easily acknowledged political tensions. If the graduate student reading this volume thought they might find a comforting bedtime story here, they should avoid reading Ellis' essay first. Ellis' essay is not a bedtime story. It can only be appreciated as the dark coffee of criticism in the metaphorical early morning light of daybreak, when the mind might let fall some of its idols of the marketplace. And appreciated his essay should be, since it attempts to 'tell it like it is' regarding some of the most conflicted areas of what might be called, in part borrowing and adjusting a phrase of Edward Said's, religious studies' 'politics of knowledge'.[9] Indeed, the graduate student reader should be thankful for Ellis' frank attempt to make obvious issues that are not yet discussed openly enough in religious studies' quarters. It is also true that many advisers will feel ill at ease faced with this piece's presence in such a volume. Is it not sound academic advice to advise graduate students to avoid all politics, even contentious methodological issues, until, well, until they are safely tenured? There is some wisdom in this, but a wisdom that serves only the student's quest for safety in the 'other-worldly' ivory tower, and not the creation of his or her actual safety in the 'real world' where politics should and do matter. Underlying Ellis' entire piece is the humane desire to warn graduate students about what they are getting into: should we look into these waters, we might be forced to admit that, as the 'Wicked Witch of the West' informs Dorothy in *The Wizard of Oz*, we are 'not in Kansas anymore'. Such thoughts are indeed quite timely.

Professor Vern Neufeld Redekop offers the reader a piece on the act of 'blessing' as an actual and potential site of research; much needed in our all too *un*blessed, strife-riddled world. Redekop's contribution also picks up a thread from earlier essays in this volume, namely that of interdisciplinarity, since his work fuses theology with conflict resolution and peace studies. This fusion dovetails well with the synchronicity of Professor Carolyn Sharp's essay, which brings together many themes that crisscross the boundaries between the other essays that make up this volume: different lands and our conceptions of space, the politics and the epistemologies of these categorizations, the overlapping mappings of gender, ethnicity, language, culture, class, nation, civilization, etc. and the ways engaged scholarship has begun developing for the sake of standing up to such oppressive systems in the hope of beginning to subvert these, thus creating the preconditions of true independence, emancipation and liberation.

In the spirit of interdisciplinarity of the previous two chapters, Professor Darlene Juschka's essay offers the reader another sustained reflection from a location shot through with structures of power, namely the interdisciplinary interface of religious studies and women's studies. Juschka's essay also exemplifies well what may best be understood as deconstructive approaches to the notion of 'religion' itself; indeed, Juschka's essay, as well as recent work akin to it, may lead one to think that the moment of theory in religious studies is of a more 'spacious present' (to borrow from William James' lexicon) than elsewhere in the academy; religion may provide theory its greatest resistance, and theory provide the greatest intellectual resistance to previous conceptions of religion.

The next essay, Professor Jon R. Stone's, is also essential reading for students of religion who would understand the impact of postmodernism upon religious studies. In this it shares a common theme with Juschka's essay. It is indeed important to keep in mind that postmodernism had already deeply impacted the minds of many professors when many of today's PhD candidates attended their very first university lectures. Postmodernism, for this volume's intended audience, is like 'mother's milk'. For this reason alone, Stone's contribution is most helpful for the sake of reflecting more critically about the supposedly anti-dogmatic dogmas that went into generating the 'post-postmodern' generation of scholars that his essay and this volume as a whole seek to address. Professor Charles H. Long's essay also moves the discussion in this direction. Building his case on previous work, Long reaffirms that religious studies (or, more specifically, the history of religions) might be better conceived of as a 'serious human discourse' rather than a not yet fully established would-be science. This leads Long to reflect on the Enlightenment foundations of the human sciences, more specifically their view of matter. Long suggests that two fascinating foci of human religious history are crucial for religious studies as it attempts to renegotiate itself in light of both postmodernism and postcolonialism; when examined as Long does, these two foci enable the constellation of many suggestive inroads; the two foci are the notion of the 'fetish' on the one hand and on the other that of the 'cargo cult'. Professor Long makes a strong case for understanding these two notions, that of the fetish and that of the cargo cult, as core concepts with much mileage left for the emergent disciplines that would wish to better understand some of the interconnected dimension of the worlds that produced them (and still implicitly do). The insight to be gained from reflecting on these concepts and the worlds that generated them is not lessened because they are crossroads between overlapping and contested worlds, both in space and time. The final contribution, that of Professor Donald A. Crosby, also puts forth a strong case for interdisciplinarity in the study of religion, arguing convincingly that philosophy and religious studies are better when conducted in tandem, one not wholly free of tensions and yet one in which much mutual benefit is found. Crosby's essay makes most explicit a critical position in which many of the prior essays are implicitly couched: that the fuzzy boundaries between theology and religious studies, philosophy of religion and philosophy are crucial areas of interest to best understand the reasonable accommodation of religion and secular civilization.

It is worth noting that these contributions provide the reader with overviews *in media res* to some of the themes and questions most prevalent in contemporary studies of religion and, in so doing, provide ways of entering or deepening such themes and questions, thus complementing existing scholarship. Once again, this is but a modest contribution to a crucial area of concern for students of religion and of theology, far from even beginning to exhaust such areas of concern. However, here the reader will find many core issues, arising in various ways throughout the various contributions to this ongoing discussion, i.e. of the best way or ways of becoming a better student of religion or of theology.[10]

Part I: Practicalities

1

How to Complete a Doctoral Dissertation in this Lifetime: Some Marbles of Wisdom[1]

LARRY PATRIQUIN (NIPISSING UNIVERSITY)

It has been rumoured that about 50 per cent of those who enter a doctoral programme in the social sciences and the humanities never finish. It is common knowledge that it is not necessarily the brilliant who survive; it is the persistent. The information in this chapter is designed to turn you into one of those persistent folk: to help you complete the process of writing a thesis while avoiding forever remaining ABD ('all but dissertation'). I wrote this piece because, when I was completing my PhD, I found only a few works to guide me through the doctoral minefield. However, even these were helpful only in a limited way. Most published advice, as it turned out, was not particularly enlightening, often something like: 'If you've had a bad day, go home and take a bubble bath.' In the end, I had to discover most of these lessons myself, through a process of trial and error. My hope is that this chapter will assist you in moving expeditiously toward your goal while reducing visible scars to an absolute minimum.

Before we begin, I would like to draw your attention to the phrase 'some marbles of wisdom' in the subtitle. It was placed there as a reminder that you have to consult many individuals if you want to collect 'pearls'. In other words, these are one person's suggestions. Feel free to disagree with what I have to say. There is always more than one way to complete any job.

1   OVERCOMING THE OBSTACLES

There are a number of obstacles to obtaining a doctorate (particularly in North America), though they are all useful to some extent. Learn what you can in the process of moving past these barriers, but do not drag them out to ridiculous lengths. In chronological order, the obstacles are:

(a) *Courses*: Many students take forever to finish a course because they will settle for nothing less than an A+. 'A-pluses' are great for scholarship applications, but they mean little if you never finish the programme (you can always frame your transcript). They still mean little even if you finish, because no one is going to look at your grades; they want to see what you have accomplished in your dissertation. In fact, they do not even want to see that; they just want to read your published work. So do not spend a lot of effort on your course papers; do only what is required to get by. For instance, full-year courses typically run from September to April – and that is it. In these cases, your papers should be written by the end of May at the latest. If you are unable to do this, you already have a canary in your coal mine (and it is weaving back and forth on its perch). If you are regularly handing in course papers six months or a year after they are due, it is unlikely that you will ever complete a dissertation. Do not try to compose impeccable works of art. My papers ended up in the recycling bin, right where they belonged.

(b) *Major research paper (MRP)*: Many programmes have an MRP. If yours does, beware; this seems to be a major obstacle for students who do not finish. It may sound cynical, but my advice is to slap a couple of your course papers together, with a paragraph joining the two in the middle, and hand it in. OK, that is probably not acceptable. You are required to do a bit more work than that, but you get the point. At least take advantage of the opportunity, typical in many graduate programmes, to make the MRP (usually around 50 pages) an extension of a course paper. Completed papers and MRPs should be viewed as rough drafts of *possible* dissertation chapters, so do not waste much time on them.

(c) *Comprehensive exams*: Doctoral students typically write two comprehensive exams, in 'major' and 'minor' fields. This is a great opportunity to undertake a careful study of the key texts in your area, while considering possible dissertation topics. I spent about a year and a half preparing for my comprehensives. It may have been overkill on my part, but if there is one area of your programme where you can proceed slowly, paying attention to details, this is it. Also, if you have any say in the matter, I recommend that you focus more on theoretically oriented works than empirically oriented ones. If you are planning to examine a 'case study' you may change your mind. This means that you will have spent a lot of time reading material you will not use. Reading theory is never wasted time. You can focus on the empirical case at the thesis proposal stage.

(d) *Thesis proposal*: Your graduate programme will probably have instructions for writing proposals and you should take these seriously. They will typically emphasize that a dissertation proposal is not expected to incorporate a thorough analysis of the literature, have definitive conclusions, and so on. It is a *plan* of work. Do not 'freeze' when faced with an obstacle like this. Write it, hand it in, and get your rubber stamp of approval. In a doctoral programme, you need to arrive at the official stage of 'working on the dissertation' as soon as possible.

(e) *Language skills*: If you do not learn a new language as a graduate student, you will probably never find the time to do so. On the other hand, this can be time-consuming. You need to think about whether or not there is room for this in your schedule.

In sum, get past these obstacles as fast as you can. There seems to be a fear of doing so, perhaps because as you progress you leave the comfort of the classroom, with all your friends, and move to increasingly isolated work. After your courses, you are on your own. You have to be self-motivated, which means that in the process of completing the MRP, the comprehensives and the proposal, you have to mark the dates in your calendar, write them and get them over with. Psychologically, it is important to see yourself progressing up the steps of the ladder. Otherwise, you will get to the sixth year of the doctorate and you will still have much work to do. At that point, finding the time, energy and money to finish the thesis could prove difficult.

2　WHAT IS A THESIS? OR, WHY ALL BOOKS ARE NOT THESES AND WHY ALL THESES ARE NOT BOOKS

A book with a title such as *Theories of the Media: An Introduction* is not a thesis. The purpose of this text would be to introduce undergraduate students to a topic. An admirable objective – but not a thesis. Obviously, this work would be written from a certain perspective, but that does not qualify it as a dissertation. So not all books are theses. Conversely, not all theses are books. The vast majority of them are not published as books. I have heard a thesis described as a 'bad version of a good book', though, more often, it is a 'bad version of a series of good articles'.

The main criteria of a dissertation, and what differentiates it from, say, an introductory text, is that the author (namely you) has to add to knowledge. 'Adding to knowledge' means saying something that no one else has said before. You are not merely translating difficult works into everyday language for an audience of novice students, as the textbook would do. Your 'thesis' (that is, your argument) is the new piece of knowledge you have created. The question you must be prepared to answer is: 'So, what do *you* have to say that is *new?*'

What qualifies as 'new'? I am not sure. For example, a critique of the assumptions behind neo-classical economics may come as a shock to a liberal, but a Marxist would say, 'In my paradigm, that's old hat.' Always be discussing this with your supervisory committee. Ask them: 'Do I have an adequate argument, one that meets the criteria of a doctoral dissertation?' The answer may not be so obvious depending on the type of thesis you are writing.

In moving toward something new, you need to reflect carefully on what you will be arguing. You have done two or three years of reading at the doctoral level. Now ask yourself: 'Where is there an intellectual problem or a void? Why is it important to address the problem or fill the void? What are the openings/absences in the literature that I can step into?' So you have to say something original. At the same time, you are not obligated to shake the disciplines to their foundations. ('The world is round, not flat.') You have to push knowledge forward by an incremental step. At the end of the day, the dissertation is an *exercise* to ascertain whether or not you qualify as a researcher. The dissertation will not be your masterpiece. You will write that 20 years after you graduate.

3   TYPES OF THESES

I have surmised that there are four thesis 'types'; though do take this list with a pinch of salt, as it is by no means 'scientific'. It is meant to show you that there is more than one way to meet the dissertation requirement. Of the four types, there are two I like: (a) *Critical*: In this case, you have enemies who will be subjected to your trenchant critique. Tell us why everyone else's (or almost everyone else's) interpretation of a theorist, a theory, a concept or an event is 'wrong' and yours is 'right'; and (b) *Original*: In this case, you conduct primary research. Unlike a 'critical' thesis, which enters a hotly debated area, this work explores a topic where hardly anything has been said. It might go something like this: 'The so-and-so people of such-and-such island are interesting because blah-blah-blah, and I am going to be the first one to explore them in detail, and from this study I will comment on some aspect of religion, society, politics, history, etc. (or, more precisely, I will alter the way we think about citizenship, violence, community, narrative, ontology, policing, health – or whatever)'. This kind of dissertation, I believe, is a requirement in disciplines like history and anthropology. (Obviously, this type of thesis has to be 'critical' in the sense of 'challenging claims to truth'.)

There are two further dissertation types I do not like, but they seem to be acceptable: (c) *Exploratory*: In this case, the student 'explores' something. A reader can wonder: What was the objective of this work? What did the author have to say? In a thesis like this, at the end of 300 pages, the student still has not found much, but the exploration was so breathtaking it is deemed worthy of a doctorate; and (d) *Studies in (fill in the blank)*: In this case, you find an overarching theme, combine everything you have written, usually a gaggle of course papers, and hope it works ('Studies in the Postmodern'). I have seen a few of this type. It seemed rather obvious that they were bits and pieces of papers tacked together.

So what does a dissertation look like? There are plenty at hand, ready to inspect. Visit your university library's Archives section to see what other students in your programme have done. This will give you a good impression of what the standards are and what will be expected of you. Then relax, because most people overestimate what they have to do (though you do not want to underestimate the requirements either). In addition, check *ProQuest*

Dissertations and Theses (online).[2] Type in some key words, say, 'Christianity and violence'. In this instance, you will come up with about 90 'hits'. The full text (PDF) is available for almost all of these going back to the mid-1990s and a handful before then, going back to 1980. Read about nine or ten of them. You can peruse about one a day, skimming through most of them while in each one carefully reading the introduction, the conclusion and the key chapter(s). As well as getting a 'feel' for a dissertation, you will also gain an appreciation for how long a standard bibliography is in your discipline. Once you have completed this task, you will have a solid idea of what passes for 'adding to knowledge'. Believe me, no matter what key words you use, you will not be overwhelmed by feelings of inferiority.

4   CHOOSING THE TOPIC: OR, THE DIFFERENCE BETWEEN A THESIS AND YOUR LIFE'S WORK

Supervisory committees do not provide much direction on choosing a topic. They tend to say 'looks great' to just about anything. But there is a good reason for this. You are the person most familiar with the material, so you need to focus the topic yourself. Start thinking about what you might study from the day you enter your programme. In doing so, develop 'mini-proposals', two or three pages long with a table of contents and a bibliography, and discuss these with your supervisor. If you do this, you will eventually end up where you need to go. My original objective was to examine the reaction of the Canadian state to the Great Depression. I wrote a paper on this topic and compiled a large bibliography. As a result of further coursework, however, I went off in a different direction. My 'Canadian' past-life was part of the process of discovering what I am interested in. Do not begrudge the fact that you have found something new and fascinating. That is what a doctorate is for, so do not look at such changes-of-heart as misspent time.

At the beginning of their graduate careers, most students tend to assume that a dissertation involves mastering a huge breadth of knowledge (after all, we are always being told to think big). Many students select as a dissertation topic what is in fact their life's work ('Liberalism from Hobbes to Rorty'). However, a thesis is a *narrow* project. Accordingly, you have to go back over your proposed life's work and choose a small portion of it to examine in depth. My life's work is 'Capitalism in Theoretical and Historical Perspective'. Define your own – using an equally catchy phrase – and then focus. To focus means to narrow the subject matter extensively, because a dissertation can grow into a many-headed monster. Aim for 200 pages, minimum. I wrote on poor relief in England, yet I ended up suggesting that capitalism and welfare be redefined, I entered a number of historiographical debates, and so on. I had not planned to do this. I eventually went over 360 pages, excluding the bibliography.

Focusing means more than making minor changes to the topic you are proposing to undertake. For example, once I had moved down a new path, I first planned to write on 'The Origins of English Capitalism: Wage Labourers and Private Property, 1350–1780'. There was supposed to be a chapter on capitalism and one on historical materialism, a middle chapter on feudalism to capitalism: theories of transition, and two further chapters that accounted for the relationship between the state and the economy over the period under study. One problem that can be immediately identified (in hindsight!) is that the proposed middle chapter could be the subject matter for an entire thesis. You need to watch for this. Do you have what are, in effect, 'mini-theses' hidden within the heart of the thesis? If you do, this is potentially dangerous, because it probably means you are trying to cover too much ground. In the fifth chapter of this never-written dissertation, one of the seven sub-headings was 'Poor laws'. This section of a proposed chapter eventually became the thesis itself. But before I made it to that other shore, as it were, my next proposal was 'Poverty in English Political Economy: From the Elizabethan Era to Adam Smith'. This project was soon abandoned because it seemed there was little to add to the existing literature. I could have argued that the ideas of the writers of this era should be viewed in the context of a transition to a peculiarly capitalist economy. However, it did not seem worth the time to make this point; it had already been more than adequately made elsewhere in the literature. In other words, I would not have been contributing much to knowledge. Moreover, preliminary reading led me to believe that the existence of poor relief in England was a problem/puzzle that had not been adequately explained, and hence was a more interesting topic. My next proposal became the title of the dissertation: 'The English Poor Laws in Capitalist Context'.

On the matter of choosing a topic, the best advice I ever received was that you should be able to state the thesis (that is, the argument) in a single sentence. The rest of the work is a 300-page defence of that sentence. In other words, your dissertation must take a position and must be a sustained argument for that position. Try to frame your thesis as a response to a 'why' question (this is not the only acceptable form of a question, though I believe it is the most interesting).

Be on guard for potential problems in choosing a topic. For one, think seriously about primary research and why you might want to avoid it. Archival work, interviewing and so on may prove to be time-consuming with lots of dead ends. If possible, save this type of work until after you graduate (or after you receive tenure). For another, be careful of bringing together areas of thought that traditionally have made strange bedfellows, for example Marxism and psychoanalysis. This could create hostility among your supervisory committee, especially if you have members who sit on separate sides of the fence. This can work, but it probably will not. If you sense that it may be problematic, do not be so arrogant as to think that *you* will be the one who will convince a committee of the validity of the project. You will receive severe bite marks (and they will not be love bites!). Again, save this type of work for later.

5   THE BIBLIOGRAPHY AS A SIGN OF A VIABLE PROJECT

A comprehensive bibliography, leaving no stone unturned, is a superb way to judge the viability of a project. Count the number of books and articles you have read over two or three years, listed in your course outlines, the bibliographies of your papers and MRP, and your comprehensive reading lists. Project that number on to the next few years, knowing that you probably breezed through some course readings, which you cannot do for the thesis. Now, if your proposed thesis bibliography has far more entries than you can possibly read in the time you have left, then (all together now) narrow, narrow, narrow. To remain on track, start developing a thesis bibliography, as part of a mini-proposal, as soon as the project begins to take form. Divide it into five or six sections that reflect the different aspects of the work. This helps you to stay organized and enables you to prioritize your book list (which includes: those that must be read, those that should be read and those that might be read if there is enough time). Also, in compiling your bibliography, be careful that you have recorded all information correctly from books and articles. I am amazed at how many mistakes I found in the bibliographies of other writers. Spend the extra pennies to photocopy the cover and the copyright page of a book or the table of contents page from a journal.

I also suggest you maintain an 'Extra Bibliography Book'. I received one address book too many somewhere along the way and I converted it into a 'one-stop' spot for references. In it, I hand-scribbled information on works that looked interesting but did not quite fit the thesis topic and hence did not make it into the main, typed bibliography. I cannot count the times I went back to that book saying, 'Where's the reference for that article on ...' and hey presto.

6   THE THESIS PROPOSAL

Among other things, the thesis proposal should elaborate on the following: (a) What is the problem/question and why is it important that it be addressed/answered? (b) What kind of contribution to knowledge will the dissertation make? The answer to the question of 'contribution' does not have to be something like, 'With my dissertation, humankind will join together in one big, happy family; the bells will ring out; and ABBA will finally reunite for a farewell tour.' It will probably be something a bit more mundane, along the lines of: 'Our understanding of John Locke's chapter "Of property" will be blah, blah, blah.'

7   THINKING ABOUT THE TABLE OF CONTENTS: CHAPTERS AND SUB-HEADINGS

I spent many hours searching for a work that gave an adequate account of English poor relief. In this search, I would always have a certain table of contents in mind. But then the light bulb finally went on, and it dawned on me: *I* am the one who has to write this. Another way of conceiving the dissertation, then, is this: *You have to write the book that you are always looking for in the library – but can never find.* In setting out what you have to do, think in terms of an introduction, five or six chapters (perhaps four long chapters), and a conclusion. Do not begin with ten or twelve chapters – that is a recipe for disaster.

Give plenty of thought as to how to organize the entire work. In my case, I proposed to answer the following question: Why was England the only European nation to have poor relief in the period c.1550–1800? My answer was that England at this time was the only country that was being transformed into a capitalist society. I asked myself: What do I have to do to make this point? I then worked *backwards* from the thesis statement. In my proposal, I suggested that I would provide an account of the evolution of poor relief in the first capitalist country (Chapter 3). In order to convince the reader of my claims in Chapter 3, I would draw out a detailed history of the transition to capitalism in England (Chapter 2). Finally, so that readers would see the uniqueness of English capitalism, in contrast to the peasant-based economies of the Continent (described in Chapter 2), I proposed discussing the nature of capitalism and the state from a theoretical perspective (Chapter 1). In other words, you could not understand Chapter 3 without reading Chapter 2, and you could not understand Chapter 2 without reading Chapter 1. Keep this 'backward step' method in mind when you are trying to organize your thesis. Also, note how skewed the table of contents was. Only one of the three proposed chapters was on poor relief and poverty – and that is what the dissertation was supposed to be about. In the end, Chapter 3 turned out to be three separate chapters on the old poor law, the new poor law and historiographical questions. A sixth chapter on poverty and poor relief outside England was also added. The moral in this case is that you have to be constantly reworking your chapter titles and the sub-headings within each chapter as the thesis becomes more focused. I know this sounds obvious, but it is easily overlooked.

8   HOW TO TAKE NOTES

I have a terrible memory. So I gave plenty of thought to the question of note-taking when I was preparing for the comprehensives. Given that I often do not know what day it is, how was I going to take exams on books that I had read as much as one year ago? In meeting this challenge, I came up with the idea of employing 'scribblers' (the 8½ x 11 inch notebooks, containing around 32 pages, that schoolchildren use). I handwrite my research notes in these but I also photocopy select pages from the texts I am reading, then later on I 'cut and paste' in the key passages I want to save. I make sure to leave the appropriate space in the scribbler for the photocopied passages. I hold the book up against the scribbler, mark off a space with my pen, then continue taking notes. This is a fair bit of work. It takes about 30 minutes to cut and paste a scribbler. This looks time-consuming, leading a friend to tell me, 'You should patent this method, but no one else would be crazy enough to use it!' It is something monotonous to do during down-time, late at night. It takes time to be organized, but it takes much more time when you are disorganized.

With this method, you can empty out whole drawers of your filing cabinet. All my notes, ranging from my preparation for the comprehensives to the completion of the doctorate, can be found in scribblers that fit into five or six magazine boxes. Combined, they take up less than three feet of shelf space. (When my time started to run out, I abandoned this method and copied everything.) If this sounds like too much work, an alternative would be to photocopy the pages and place them at the back of the scribbler; that is, forgo the cutting and pasting and perhaps highlight the key passages.

A major benefit of this method is that it is not necessary to engage with the author while reading. You are simply 'mining' the text for information. The cut and paste method is an efficient way of mining. One does not have to mull over difficult material, thinking about how to synthesize it; that can be done later. (I do not use the 'scribbler method' for complicated, theoretical books. As a graduate student, you should own a copy of these works, because you will need to read them carefully more than once.)

If the scribbler method sounds onerous, do give serious thought to how you are going to take notes and keep them in order. You are embarking on a major project, unlike anything attempted before, and if you are not well organized it will become frustrating. Note-taking for a thesis has to be comprehensive. You have to go back over the notes after a long period of time and be able to get the 'full flavour' of the authors' arguments. If 'cryptic', point-form notes are taken, you may not understand them after a year or so. Having high-quality notes is especially important when your supervisory committee asks you to expand on or modify a point. You can often find the required information in the scribblers, because they contain wonderfully condensed versions of the books you have read.

Finally, keep a 'Pearls of Wisdom' book. Purchase one of those thin, hard-cover books, full of blank pages that can be used for recording your thoughts. This is where you keep those flashes of brilliance, the major breakthroughs, those wonderful things that pop into your head while you are chewing on a muffin at the local coffee shop. It may be the introductory sentence to your conclusion. You recognize that immediately, but you are still in the middle of Chapter 3. You quickly scribble the pearl on to a paper napkin. But where do you keep these little gems? That's right. In the book, which never leaves your home. Transfer each pearl from the napkin to the book, and then return the book to its sacred spot – propping up the short leg of your dining room table.

9   THE IMPORTANCE OF THE INTRODUCTION

At one point, my introduction was a slightly rehashed version of my thesis proposal (written three years previously). Given the vast changes that will undoubtedly take place after you first formulate the proposal, when you have finished a draft of the dissertation, it is crucial to go back and thoroughly rewrite the introduction with the purpose of making it clear to even the thickest dullard how you have limited the scope of your topic. This should help avoid questions as to why you didn't do *this* or why you didn't do *that*. The following few paragraphs, from the revised introduction to my dissertation, serve as a sample of what you should do.

> Assistance to the poor is just one aspect of what often gets termed 'social reproduction'. I want to make clear at the outset that I am not, in this dissertation, interested in all things having to do with this issue (such as family formation, sexuality, etc.), despite their importance in explaining the complex whole of any given society. My particular focus is on the question 'how do people manage to feed, clothe and house themselves and why, in some important ways, was the English way of ensuring these basic human needs different?'
>
> I should also provide two more caveats. First, I have no intention here of dealing with all the state activities which come under the rubric of the 'poor laws', including vagrancy, begging, 'dangerous occupations', bastardy, imprisonment, and so on. I do touch on some of these issues, but only tangentially. They are of course related to the question of social reproduction (as are the division of labour, birth and death rates, the role and rights of women in society, patriarchy, ideologies, etc.). However, within the limits of this dissertation, I have chosen to narrow the focus to strictly a 'bread and butter' issue of how people obtained the resources they needed in order to survive.

The second caveat is that while this thesis has a lot to say about class relations, it does not pretend to be an extended discussion of class struggle per se, though, again, this is something I will touch on from time to time; for example, when I take note of opposition to the new poor law. Detailed works on class conflict usually include protracted analyses of the involvement of the various classes, prominent state officials, and so on. This is typically the work of archival historians, like E. P. Thompson and Rodney Hilton. I should stress that my objective here is not to deal with every aspect of English poor relief, but rather to contribute to a body of social-theoretical literature, in particular a reassessment of our understanding of 'welfare'.

10 WRITING THE CHAPTERS

Spit out words. At some point, you have to stop reading and start writing. Take heed of the wiseacre who once said: 'Don't get it right; get it written.' Writing takes a long time, especially rewriting, revising and reorganizing, so get this ball rolling as soon as possible. If you are a self-described perfectionist and hence have 'problems writing', you are in deep trouble. I suggest you simply excise the perfectionist side of your personality and get on with the task of climbing the dissertation mountain. In doing so, accept the fact that there is no such thing as writer's block. There is, however, such a thing as 'ideas block'. So, if the writing is not flowing, you need to do more thinking and planning.

When writing, do not get involved in controversy where you do not have to. Keep the controversy focused on the narrow area of knowledge you want to challenge. In my case, in the original draft of my first chapter, I had about 50 pages on Marxian economics (exchange value, use value, the commodity, and so on). That was unnecessary. It was too much (this was not a thesis on Marxian economics, after all) and it was too contentious. This is an area where much blood has been spilt. In explaining what I saw as the origins and nature of capitalism, then, I rewrote it, discussing how capitalism is grounded in competition; how it has a unique division of labour; how it involves the buying and selling of labour-power; and so forth. Even the School of Business types would find little to disagree with in this 'generic' description, except, of course, for that little matter of 'exploitation'.

In my process of composition, I make further use of scribblers, within which I collect 'crib notes'. I use one scribbler per chapter, leaving five or six blank pages for every section I plan to write. For instance, in the scribbler for Chapter 3 ('Poor Relief Under the Old Poor Laws'), I had three sections covering the years 1530–1601, 1601–1662 and 1662–1790. I would go through my research notes and, in the appropriate section(s) of the crib-note scribbler, I would jot down points or quotations under a sub-title for each author (for example: *Oxley, 1969*). When this task was completed, I would then type the chapter into the computer. I would begin with the first section (in this case, 1530–1601), crossing out the hand-written lines in the crib notes once they had been entered somewhere in the text. I would compose one section of the chapter, make some revisions so that the text was readable, then I would move on. This method minimized the time I spent in front of the computer and enabled me to churn out chapters quickly and still be semi-coherent. Working out the finer details would occur later, when I was editing the printed text, covering it in red ink. By the way, do not type research notes into your computer. This is a lot of work and you end up with a big mess, not to mention a bad back. Type only the chapters of your thesis.

When writing, do not waste space. If something does not need to be in the thesis, then drop it. 'Before we look at X, we *must* have a 50-page survey of Y.' Do we, in fact? Take the amount of space required to make your argument – and no more. The same advice applies, perhaps even more so, to material that is not part of the main text. For instance, there is always the odd bit of information that does not fit in the narrative, yet you need to mention it somewhere. That can go in an endnote. For everything else, put it either in a chapter or in a trash can. Maintain a (close to) zero-tolerance policy for explanatory notes. If you are one of those footnote-fetish folks, you have my sympathies. But remember, long, chatty notes are just more junk that you are going to have to reorganize, rewrite, spell check, proofread and defend.

I recommend that you hand in each chapter for comments to all the members of your supervisory committee. I let my committee know that I planned to read their suggestions, put them in a file, then continue with writing the next chapter. Once I had a draft of the whole thesis, I went back and made extensive revisions from beginning to end. Do not wait to perfect each chapter. You need to see a version of the entire work, and you need to receive feedback, as soon as possible. It can have gaps and problem areas – that's OK. Remember what we tell students who are new to university: 'It's only a draft. Don't get so uptight about it.'

In order to avoid having a mental breakdown, I also recommend that, before you write your first sentence, you decide which stylistic conventions you will use. Will it be percent, per cent, or %? Old Poor Law or old poor law? Single 'inverted commas' or double "quotation marks"? And so on. Most graduate faculties will publish a document with a title like *Guidelines for the Preparation and Examination of Theses and Dissertations*. These guidelines will provide instructions on proper format, font size, margins and so on. Read your faculty's guidelines at the beginning of the process so you do not have to go back at a later point and correct mistakes. Choose a style guide, such as the *Chicago Manual of Style*, *MLA Handbook for Writers of Research Papers*, or the *Publication Manual of the American Psychological*

Association, and be consistent. Learn the difference between British and American conventions (for instance, "percent" is American while 'per cent' is British). This will allow you to prepare your work properly, depending on where you plan to publish it.

11   THE CONCLUSION

Tell us how your subject area has changed as a result of your work. In doing so, squeeze out every drop of knowledge from the topic. Put some of your sharpest phrasing in the conclusion. Obviously, you are not dropping a bomb on the reader. After all, you stated your argument in the introduction, and you defended it all the way through, but do save some of the best for last. Go back and pluck out the gems from your 'Pearls of Wisdom' book. Also, do not have a conclusion that is four or five pages long. This would suggest that you have not discovered much of importance. Aim for 15 to 20 pages.

12   HOW TO ORGANIZE COMPUTER FOLDERS AND FILES

You should have a folder for general materials, each chapter of the thesis, and the bibliography. Begin each folder with 'THESIS' so the folders appear together on your computer screen. I recommend you use a version of the following: (a) THESIS GENERAL, with files for your Proposal, Cover, Contents, List of Tables, Abstract, Acknowledgements, Introduction, Conclusion, Speaking Notes for the Defence, and a 'To Be Read' file, which is always being revised based on your time and priorities; (b) THESIS1, with files for Chapter 1 (notes to the chapter are included here), Extra Material (if required), and other files titles as needed. Repeat THESIS(NUMBER) for every chapter you have; and (c) THESIS BIBLIOGRAPHY, with a file, Bibliography A–Z, and four or five files organized by topic, for your personal use.

If you use a 'Note Style', do not have a separate file for the notes. Insert a page break at the end of each chapter and place your notes there. Do not place them at the bottom of the page. Putting them at the end of the chapter is what journals want when you submit articles to them (if they use Note Style). Do it now so you will not have to make changes later.

Use an 'Extra Material' file for sections you have written which you later determine are not required in the thesis (yet you want to save them). I did this for the first chapter, but as I progressed I quickly learned what was superfluous, and hence no longer required this garbage-can file.

Think of how you want to set up the bibliography: first, for your own organizational purposes; and second, how you will present it in the thesis.

For the latter, you will typically have one large file, containing all materials, organized alphabetically by the authors' surnames.

13   EMERGENCY PREPAREDNESS PLAN

What happens if your house or apartment building burns down? Computer disks and photocopies of your notes must be stored at a location that is not your primary residence. Most people think only about computer disks. But ask yourself: Of all the work you have done in the last three or four years, how much is on disk and how much is on paper? Unless you are a computer-geek, I will bet it is 20 per cent for the former and 80 per cent for the latter. In preparing for an emergency, you will discover that the 'scribbler method' is a blessing, because virtually all your research notes can be photocopied, easily and relatively cheaply.

14   THE SUPERVISORY COMMITTEE

The supervisory committee is the (typically) three individuals who read your thesis, give you feedback and sign the form declaring it 'ready to go'. Digging for information on your supervisory committee is the most critical research you will undertake as a doctoral student, because these people can make or break you. If possible, get three individuals who like each other and who see eye-to-eye ideologically on most things. Do not say to yourself, 'Professor X is a Marxist; Professor Y is a Liberal. That's good. I will get a diversity of opinion.' This might be OK, but it might not. This kind of 'diversity' (the cat and dog variety) is best to avoid. Begin by choosing a supervisor then work your way out. In other words, ask your supervisor if so-and-so is acceptable, then ask your two committee members about your proposed third. For all three choices, take personality over intellect (take both if you can get them). Do not work with jerks or prima donnas; writing a dissertation is difficult enough. Equally important, you need to find people who understand what a thesis looks like. In other words, they are not overly demanding, constantly asking for revisions, nor are they too lenient, saying 'looks fine' to anything you give them.

   How do you locate committee members? This is not always easy. I suggest you (a) take courses with them; (b) listen to the student grapevine, though do get plenty of opinions because someone's 'ranking' can vary depending on who you talk to; (c) ask faculty about other faculty. Do this in a subtle manner. You will receive a discreet – or not so discreet – reply; (d) check dissertations that are similar to your topic to see who has served as committee members on these projects. If the same names keep cropping up, chances are that those professors will be good candidates for your committee, because it demonstrates that they are capable of guiding students through the process. At the same time, do not ignore new professors who are enthusiastic and interested in your work.

15   THE EXAMINING COMMITTEE

You defend your thesis in front of the examining committee. It usually consists of six people, generally (but not necessarily) the three members of your supervisory committee, and (typically): (4) *The Dean's representative*: This person does not have to know the topic. He or she is the official representative from your Faculty of Graduate Studies (FGS). Get someone with a reputation as a decent person. You do not want any 'loose cannons' within a mile of the defence; (5) *The external/internal*: This individual is external to your programme, but internal to your university; and (6) *The external*: This is someone from outside your university. This person should be geographically close, especially if the defence is in winter and he or she lives in an area where travel delays can occur as a result of bad weather. Call on a faculty member from a nearby university.

The voting procedure is complicated and will vary from university to university. In general, you can have only one person in the room who is against you. Given that your committee (of three) will vote for you, and you have a nice Dean's representative (one), it all comes down to the (two) externals. Externals, then, have considerable power. Avoid people who, by definition, are going to be hostile to the project. To give only one example, I heard of a sociology student who had to make major revisions because the external/internal was from psychology. The student did his thesis on male violence, so the 'social' and the 'individualistic' interpretations were in conflict.

Externals should be 'known' to one of your supervisory committee members. These externals, one hopes, will not blindside you. The external from outside your university must be at 'arm's length' to you and your committee. At the very least, get some 'intelligence' on a few individuals before recommending a name to your FGS. There are many ethical academics who do scholarly work. Find them. Once again, take personality over intellect (of course, both if you can get them). Furthermore, in hunting for the right people, do not feel guilty because you are apparently tampering with the rules of justice. Justice is not supposed to be arbitrary. The judgement of a dissertation, however, can be extraordinarily arbitrary, depending on who is reading it. Do not for one minute believe that externals have to carefully read your material and develop an intelligent, rational critique. They, especially the ones with a personal or ideological axe to grind, can write two or three pages of incoherent blather, portraying trivial issues as 'major drawbacks', demonstrating in the most obvious way that they have barely cracked the spine on your work. And, yes, they can get away with this type of behaviour. So avoid professors who take pleasure in devouring graduate students (these 'twerps in tweed' are a small minority, thankfully).

16   THE DEFENCE

The defence date will probably be about six months after you finish a draft of your last chapter and conclusion. At the latest, you should be at the point of writing your conclusion shortly after you enter the sixth year of the doctorate; that is, if you want to have this completed while you still have a teaching assistantship or some other form of official financial support. Before setting the date, make sure the final, pristine copy of the dissertation has rolled off the printer. Do not say, 'Sure, I can have it ready in three months,' only to find out later, for whatever reason, that that is not possible and you miss your FGS's deadline (in general, everyone on an examining committee must have a copy of the thesis four weeks before the defence). And note that 'pristine copy' means *perfect*. Go over areas where errors can easily creep in – especially the notes and the bibliography – and try to catch as many gaffes as possible. We are all human and are entitled to make a typo or two, to fail to capitalize a letter here and there, etc. But a whole host of mistakes, which might point to an approach that is sloppy overall, could begin to put doubt in the minds of your readers (especially the external examiners). Do not give anyone an opening to criticize you. Proofread until your eyes bleed. Lastly, when setting the date, choose the room and let your programme assistant know so it can be booked. I wanted to be in an environment that had natural light. It is your show, so choose the time as well, depending on whether you are a morning or an afternoon person.

It is important to note that your academic rite of passage is not called a 'party' or a 'coronation'. It is a *defence*. Be psychologically prepared to provide a defence of what you have done. Go in with an aggressive mindset. Hopefully, you will not need to use it, but do be ready to fend off an attack.

Here is how it typically works. You leave the room while the examining committee discusses whether or not the thesis is ready to be examined. This is normally a formality since everyone is supposed to have indicated their agreement to proceed at least one week in advance. You return to the room and you speak for no more than 15 minutes. The first round of questions goes from 'farthest' to 'closest' (that is, from the external examiner to your supervisor). Each person on the committee should take around 15 minutes on average, with the externals usually above the average. The first round will take about an hour and a half in total. There is a briefer second round. You leave the room, then you are invited back after the committee makes a decision. You want to escape with, at most, *specified* revisions (which means adding a paragraph here and there, clarifying a point or two, and so forth).

And don't worry. You know the material inside out by now, and you have been given the green light to proceed. Just pop some anti-nausea pills before you walk in and don't forget to breathe. If all goes well, you will be a doctor in a couple of hours.

2

Netting a Job in Religious Studies: Some Notes from the Field[1]

MICHEL DESJARDINS (WILFRID LAURIER UNIVERSITY)

What follows are suggestions on how to increase the chances of getting a permanent academic position. The suggestions are based on my own job-seeking and candidate-seeking experiences over the past 20 years in Canada, and those of my North American friends and colleagues in the field during this period. I offer these suggestions not as a 'how to' guide but as a basis for dialogue, and with the belief that the unemployment and underemployment of recent graduates represents the greatest challenge now facing the academy.

1   GENERAL ADVICE

1.1   Insist on the best possible graduate school training

- Training includes courses, advisers, graduate student cohort, professional development workshops (how to teach, how to prepare syllabuses, etc.); if your department isn't supportive, seek broader university help to ensure that you graduate with the best possible training.
- Take/make the time to learn what needs to be learned (e.g. enough German to read fluently for years to come; enough about pedagogy before you teach that first course).
- Strive for excellence in everything you do (take the time to do things well, seek expert guidance): this includes teaching apprenticeship (TA) responsibilities, teaching that first course, preparing papers for oral delivery and publication (letters of recommendation that note these points of excellence will later catch the search committees' attention); a memorable first conference presentation in the third year of one's doctoral programme is more valuable than three respectable ones before that time; one 'outstanding' publication is worth half a dozen 'good' ones; a 'This was my most impressive TA in my last ten years [followed by specific reasons]' on a letter of recommendation is worth four 'The applicant performed her TA duties admirably for us'.

1.2   Develop a broad support base

• Support will come from graduate students, faculty (inside and outside your institution) and others (extended friend and family base) – the graduate and postgraduate road is often narrow and rough, and others can help carry the burden, facilitate the process and share the delights.

1.3   Build breadth alongside depth

Systematically aim to be well rounded circa five years after beginning your doctorate (recognizing that there are many ways to achieve this balance, that 'life' will inevitably confound even the best-laid plans, that economic and social circumstances cannot be ignored, and that many doctoral programmes now encourage completion in four years). One sample plan (based on sound pre-doctoral training, a supportive department, good financial support and the help of the gods) is the following:

• Year 1: Complete course requirements; work closely with one new professor; attend one conference late in the year as an observer (e.g. the regional American Academy of Religion (AAR) meeting, an academic society meeting such as those at the Canadian Congress of the Humanities and Social Sciences); early in the year, send out feelers to a few journals regarding the possibility of doing book reviews for them (mention this to your advisers and ask for their advice), and late in the year (or early in Year 2) attempt your first review; begin developing a strong 'minor' area; keep a journal of your TA experiences (what works, what doesn't) in order to build expertise in this area. (Teaching is what most of us do most of the time; best to begin working on it as soon as possible.)
• Year 2: Prepare for, and take, general/comprehensive (and language) exams; prepare a dissertation proposal; continue expanding TA and research skills; attend two academic conferences (e.g. the AAR or SBL regional meeting, and the annual meeting at the Congress if it's at an affordable location); present a modified form of your best Year 1 paper at a university colloquium or local conference; in the summer, work with your adviser on revising that paper/presentation, then submit it for publication.
• Year 3: Fill in glaring gaps (e.g. languages, field work); enrol in a professional development workshop (teaching); continue to expand and chronicle TA and research skills; throw yourself into dissertation research, carving off a small section that can be completed in eight months, presented at an academic meeting in the spring, then polished and submitted for publication; in the second term, consult with adviser and department chair on applying to teach a course the following year; recognize who your dialogue partners are across the world and begin to interact with them (email talk, letters, conference sessions) – get to know your peers

and soon-to-be-peers; in March submit a proposal to deliver a paper in November of the following year at the AAR or SBL annual meeting (based on dissertation work; consult with adviser on this).

- Year 4: Your first independently taught course (spend time on it; do it well; ensure that it gets properly evaluated by students and that you keep a record of this); your first presentation at an international conference (in the US, e.g. AAR or SBL) or one abroad (e.g. IAHR); more dissertation work, taking another small piece you worked on in the summer and turning it into another presentation at the following year's Congress.
- Year 5: By mid-year, begin to apply for jobs (and a post-doc), and by year's end complete your dissertation; early in Year 5 you'll truly be 'ABD' ('All But Dissertation'), with good teaching experience (three years as TA, at least one independently taught course), good conference experience (regional AARs, at least three Congresses and one international conference and several presentations), publications beginning to emerge (one or two book reviews out, the first article about to emerge, with another to come), close working relationships with a handful of academics and a larger group of student colleagues and the likelihood of finishing by year's end – the challenge is to finish that dissertation and to work closely with your adviser on job-hunting strategies.

1.4   *Learn (through close friends, partners, therapists, etc.) to see yourself as others do; take steps to build on your strengths and work on your weaknesses*

- Departments hire people, not just 'intellectuals'; to be sure, different personalities will appeal to different people, but it is fair to say that self-centred, arrogant individuals, for instance, on the whole will have a harder time finding and keeping employment (as will someone who is painfully shy and cannot look others in the eye, however brilliant they may otherwise be).

1.5   *Find ways to 'make beauty necessary ... [and] necessity beautiful'*[2]

- The lives of graduate students/adjunct professors include their share of frustrations; appreciating their wonders, though, will help your work shine and will facilitate the process of landing you a permanent job (besides letting you keep your sanity).
- If you're burned out, bitter and depressed when you graduate, nobody's going to want to hire you, or live with you.

1.6   *Diversify without compromising your specialization*

- 'Diversification' means more than adding 'Psalms' to 'Prophets', or 'Ethics' to 'Philosophy of Religion'; it entails adding to your specialization, for instance, 'Modern Judaism', 'Western Religions', 'Method and Theory in the Study of Religion', 'Postmodernism' or 'Media Studies' – and doing it rigorously (courses, exams, TA duties, private reading).

- Consult Harold Remus' *By the Skin of our Teeth*[3] for his emphasis on versatility and flexibility – not only to increase the chances of getting a permanent academic position but to increase the chances of getting other types of fulfilling jobs.
- Most departments will want a colleague who develops a specialization that will lead to an outstanding reputation, but they will also appreciate someone who is able and willing to teach a broad range of courses and interact with a wide range of issues and people.
- Diversification will also broaden your pool of jobs (inside and outside academia) and perhaps unearth something better suited for you; look *between* your specialization and another – like reading between lines; figure out how to facilitate the traffic/communication between those two domains.

1.7   Acquire a clear sense of what that academic 'job' entails

- Most commonly, it includes a frenetic mix of teaching, student counselling, departmental and faculty committee work, research and publications, community involvement, grant applications: which of these can you develop now?
- Departments/universities will emphasize certain aspects – e.g. a large research university will expect its faculty to publish more and be more successful at acquiring grant money: what would your ideal location be, and what can you do to increase the odds of getting hired in such a place?

1.8   Be realistic

- Permanent academic jobs *do* exist out there, but in the near future there will not be enough to go around: not every well-trained and deserving candidate will get an academic job; fewer still will get one in a department of their choice.
- Job-hunting is enormously stressful, all the more so when one is not successful; expect the process to take its toll on you physically and emotionally – to be successful in the end usually requires a two-pronged attack: a refusal to lose hope too quickly (keep developing your skills accordingly), balanced by a willingness to keep looking for alternative types of jobs should that academic position not come around.

1.9   Develop a professional-looking curriculum vitae

- Seek advice (repeatedly, as you revise) on your CV's format and content; ensure that it can be read easily, has clear categories, accurately reflects and positively promotes your career; also ensure that there are no gaps (e.g. if you've left out four years, search committee members will wonder what you're hiding), typos (I've seen over 300 CVs over the past ten years and about 25 per cent of them quite amazingly had spelling and typographical problems) and over-representations (e.g. research work for a professor that gets listed under 'publications'; a 'publications and presentations' category that mixes eight presentations, from high school to international conferences, and one book review, in order to make it seem as though someone has published extensively when they have not).

1.10   Work closely with at least two academic advisers, and allow others in the field to get to know you

- The professors will be able to serve more effectively as mentors (they'll know you better), as referees (detailed letters of recommendation by people who know you well are generally worth more in the eyes of the search committee) and as supporters in your searches – attend the yearly Congress meetings on a regular basis if possible; give others the chance to get to know you. (If a one-year teaching position comes open in a department, for instance, the people who will immediately come to mind are those whom people have seen give papers, or with whom they've shared a coffee or a lunch – there's nothing mysterious about this process.)

1.11   Be aware of aids that exist in the academy

- University jobs are typically advertised in Canada in the Association of Universities and Colleges of Canada's *University Affairs/Affaires universitaires*[4] and the *CAUT/ACPPU Bulletin*;[5] in the US a good source is *The Chronicle for Higher Education*;[6] for religionists, job advertisements can be found in the AAR's *Openings*, though one needs to be an AAR member to gain early access to the electronic version,[7] on the Canadian Society for the Study of Religion (CCSR) website,[8] on electronic lists related to the field, and on the bulletin boards of the graduate departments.
- Course syllabuses can be found online at the AAR Syllabi Project Website.[9]
- A must-read (for both women and men) is Mary E. Hunt (ed.), *A Guide for Women in Religion: Making Your Way from A to Z*, which is a revised version of the *Guide to the Perplexing: A Survival Manual for Women in Religious Studies*, prepared by members of the Committee on the Status of Women in the Profession of the American Academy of Religion.[10]
- The rights and dignity of adjunct professors are highlighted, for example,

in 'Workplace': a publication of the Graduate Student Caucus of the Modern Languages Association.[11]

1.12   Introduce yourself to department chairs nearest to you when you're in Year 3 and beyond of your doctoral programme

- On a yearly basis, send a copy of your CV and follow up with a phone call; let them know that you're interested in teaching, and be clear on your specialization; last-minute departmental teaching decisions sometimes need to be made, some departments hire without advertising, and one can sometimes get an adjunct position by being known; once 'in', further teaching duties (on contract, and permanent) are easier to obtain. (Departments are more apt to hire someone they know and who has taught exceptionally well for them in the past than they are to take a risk on someone who is untested.)
- Make it your job to get a job …

2   MAKING THE SHORTLIST

2.1   Apply when you're ready, and only to positions for which you are qualified

- Departments are not eager to hire someone who is likely to remain ABD during the first year of employment (the completion could take longer than expected, reducing that person's effectiveness in the department, in the end jeopardizing the individual's chance of tenure and the department's chance of keeping the position); unlike 'the good old days', there are now enough qualified candidates to render it fruitless for someone having just done their dissertation on a chapter in the Gospel of Matthew, for instance, to apply for a position in Modern North American Christianity – if you pretend to be someone you're not you'll be caught somewhere in the process (it's a small world, and you don't want to be leaving bad impressions in too many people's minds).

2.2   Discover as much as you can about the department to which you're applying

- Relevant resources include: departmental web pages, people who know about the department in question, faculty publications.

2.3   Prepare a brief (1–2 pages) cover letter that personalizes your interest in the position

- Flag relevant elements from your CV, connect your qualifications with those in the advertisement; aim for a collegial tone.

- Keep in mind that a US position will have five to ten times the number of applications (in comparison to positions in Canada), so if you're preparing a cover letter for a US position, make it especially clear, professional and accessible.
- Generic applications sent out to every conceivable position are annoying to those who receive them, and a waste of time and money for the sender and the referees.

2.4   Make it clear in your letter and on your CV how you can be contacted

- Provide an email address; if you don't have a telephone answering machine, rent one; decisions often get made quickly, and search committees can seek additional information (e.g. teaching evaluations, copies of published articles) from attractive candidates.

2.5   Have someone review your application before you send it

- Especially for those first few applications you send, have your adviser (or an experienced colleague) read your application package. (Have you presented yourself clearly and accurately? Could it be improved?)

2.6   Follow up on your application shortly before the closing date

- Letters get lost, mail gets diverted, etc. A week or so before the closing date, contact the chair of the search committee to ensure that your file is complete.

2.7   Be kind to your referees

- Give them sufficient time to write letters; give them a copy of the advertisement and whatever additional information you might have about the position; provide them with an updated CV (if they've not written for you in over a year), highlighting your recent work and accomplishments; keep them informed of the results.

2.8   Be aware that Canadian citizens can apply for US jobs (Americans usually are not given the same privilege), and that the majority of jobs that went to Canadian graduates over the past ten years have been in the US

- Canadians not used to American public and college-level curricula might want to familiarize themselves with the particulars before they apply; applications should indicate citizenship, and note explicitly that as a Canadian one is eligible to work in the US (some search committees don't realize this and can reject an application).

- Differences between the countries need to be appreciated – e.g. (I generalize, of course): (a) US positions in religious studies typically receive five to ten times the number of applications than their Canadian equivalents; (b) US search committees often expect a 'dossier' (organized and sent out directly by the applicant's university), whereas Canadian search committees are used to receiving dossiers but often consider them glitzy, so if you're going to apply for US jobs, set up a dossier with your university, but don't send it to Canadian positions; (c) US search committees typically expect more self-confidence on the part of the candidate – a 'Some of my courses have not been as successful as I would have liked', when backed by excellent teaching evaluations, will be interpreted as welcome modesty by most Canadian search committees but is likely to get one excluded directly by the US counterparts.

3   CREATING A SUCCESSFUL ON-SITE INTERVIEW: AAR AND SBL CONFERENCE MINI-INTERVIEWS ('THE MEAT MARKET')

3.1   *Arrive on time*

- Interviews are short and the search committee handle many in one day, so it's important to observe their schedule.

3.2   *Be prepared to talk about your dissertation and further research*

- Practise with an academic friend who is outside your area: can you explain succinctly and energetically what you've been doing, what you expect to do over the next few years, and why any of this might matter to others in the academy?
- Add context to the discussion; e.g. What got you started on your dissertation topic? Why are you interested in the upcoming research area and how does it fit into your overall work?

3.3   *Try to avoid thinking: 'What are they looking for?' or 'I'm not a serious candidate'*

- Each hiring situation is complex; it's usually best to be yourself and let the committee decide whether you fit their needs.
- If the committee has any integrity, they will have asked you to come (impinging on their time and yours) because they are interested in you (that is not always so, but worrying about this can only lead to madness).

3.4 Bring extra copies of your CV, and some sample course syllabuses (of courses you've taught and could teach for them)

- They might not have brought your complete file with them; pointing to something on paper and leaving something with the committee can augment your chances of being remembered.

3.5 Imagine the shoe being on the other foot

- The interviewers (who are also typically tired and uncomfortable in these settings), in the short span of time they have, will want to make you feel comfortable while gathering as much information as possible. How you relate will suggest to them something about the type of colleague and teacher you would be; your ability to describe your work clearly will tell them something about your intellectual abilities; your energy will tell them something about your interests (little sleep and heavy drinking the night before is usually *not* a great idea).

4 UNIVERSITY/COLLEGE/SEMINARY VISITS

4.1 Ensure that you understand with utmost clarity what's expected of you when you visit

- Do they want a 45-minute talk? Then keep religiously to that limit. If the audience mix will be postgraduate students and faculty, engage them at the highest level; if it includes undergraduate students, ensure that you reach out to the entire group (your talk will be seen as an example of your teaching style).
- Do they want you to teach a class? Then know the level, what's been taught already and how it's been taught.

4.2 Prepare your talk(s) diligently

- The talk often gets the widest audience; members of the audience are likely to give their feedback to the search committee.
- The department is looking for your style, your method, your pedagogical skills – and they're looking for intellectual stimulation. Make the talk exciting; choose an engaging topic and present it with flair and intellectual sophistication.
- Talk about something familiar; practise it once or twice before you arrive on campus (have one or two colleagues listen and provide feedback).

4.3   Assume that people are interested in you as a person and as an academic

- Aim for a spot between naivety (this is all great fun and everyone loves me) and paranoia (everyone's out to get me; they're asking me trick questions): the whole process (from arrival to departure) is quite serious and everything you do and say will become part of their experience of 'you', but everyone is aware of the stresses and strains that each candidate faces, and the over-determined nature of these visits.

4.4   Assume that the committee members (usually including student members) like to have the candidate show some interest in them and their department

- Before the campus visit, read some of the members' published works to acquire a sense of who does what. This will allow you to ask better questions in order to get a sense of whether it's a department you'd like to join ('getting a *good* job' should be the goal), to connect your own interests more creatively with theirs and to express simple politeness to your hosts.
- Make an effort to avoid favouring some members (e.g. the senior faculty): this usually aggravates both those favoured and those ignored.
- Find out ahead of time what courses you'd be likely to teach there in the first year, and come to the interview with sample syllabuses (showing respect for that programme, for the process and for yourself). Take the situation (the department and its members) seriously and act professionally; come ready to talk about teaching, and come ready to listen to how people in that department teach.

4.5   Talk about what you know best and don't hesitate to admit your limitations

- Be positive about the job, the department and your chances. (If you don't think you can do that, it's only professional to decline the invitation; nobody likes to have their time wasted and departments usually agonize over creating shortlists.)
- The committee will be interested in your interests and expertise; they don't expect you to be an expert in everything.
- Claiming false expertise ('Yes, I could easily teach a course in Islam since I took one undergraduate course and visited the Middle East last summer') will likely get you into trouble, and can elicit awkward questions (e.g. 'You say you're interested in postmodernism – wonderful, that's an area that increasingly fascinates me too, as my recent publications show; can you tell the committee what you've read on the topic recently and how you'd position yourself in this field?').

4.6 Expect the experience to require a huge amount of energy

- Being on stage for a day or two, however well that process is facilitated, usually leaves a person drained, on edge and worried. This can be easier to take knowing what will happen ... or if you're an extrovert ...

5   SURVIVING A NON-SUCCESSFUL INTERVIEW

- Learn from the process afterwards by asking the chair of the search committee, or the chair of the department, for feedback (Do you have any advice? What could I have done better?). Appreciate that these people may not always be forthcoming with much information (for reasons of confidentiality; because they typically do not have much experience with such matters, and often express themselves awkwardly to those they've turned down), then keep the information to yourself: email notes that now typically fly furiously across the world during and after job searches ('You wouldn't believe how terrible that department is ... how badly I was treated ... what a terrible choice they made ...') can be unfair and unprofessional, and can also hurt a person's chance of getting another interview (messages bounce around ...).
- Remember that most people go through several interviews before landing a job, and that the 'adjunct professor' stage is becoming the norm after graduation; all those who make a shortlist, and many who do not, are eminently 'qualified' – the department's decision reflects their specific needs and interests, and almost always should not be interpreted as a slight against the unsuccessful candidates, however frustrating (understandably) it may seem to the candidate at the time.
- Filling in the gaps can make the difference. If your publications are weak, work doggedly on them for a year; if your teaching experience is sparse, talk to as many people as possible to advance your chances of part-time employment; if your speaking skills are slight, enrol in public speaking courses; if you are less and less attracted to an academic life (not just as a counter-reaction to job woes) consider other options (there *is* life beyond academia).
- Recognize that academic meetings provide a superb opportunity for reminding the religious studies community at large of your presence, qualities and present employment status – despite frequent appearances to the contrary, people in the field, and within individual academic societies, *do* care about their colleagues who are unemployed and underemployed. Most care deeply; we are in this together.

3

Theses on Professionalization[1]

RUSSELL T. MCCUTCHEON (UNIVERSITY OF ALABAMA)

1   Academia is unlike other professions in that the pre-professional period of training – which includes coursework, dissertation research and writing and teaching assistantships – is not akin to an apprenticeship. Accordingly, there is no direct linkage between the accumulation of credentials and admission to the profession, no necessary relationship between feeling oneself to be qualified and the ability to obtain full-time employment as a university professor.

2   A PhD is awarded not only as a mark of intellectual competence and disciplined method but also as a professional credential that signals one's eligibility for employment as a researcher and teacher within academia. Although these two aspects of the degree can complement one another, they can just as easily conflict, as in when one's research expertise fails to overlap with ever-changing employment needs.

3   Pursuing a PhD purely for the 'love of learning' is one among many legitimate reasons for graduate studies. Pursuing such studies for both intellectual stimulation and eventual employment requires candidates to be as intentional as possible about opportunities to increase their competitiveness on the job market.

4   Applying for full-time employment prior to being awarded the PhD degree (i.e. when, after successfully completing comprehensive or general exams, one holds the status known as ABD [All But Dissertation]) is not uncommon; however, failure to gain employment at this stage must not undermine one's confidence. Apart from extraordinary circumstances (e.g. the so-called 'fit' between your expertise and a department's needs), the doctoral degree remains a necessary condition for entrance into the profession.

5   Whether as an ABD or after having been awarded the PhD, some candidates accept year-to-year work as a full-time instructor or lecturer (sometimes also called a sessional position or a part-time temporary instructor). Such positions often entail teaching loads that are heavier than tenure-track or tenured faculty members and, depending on the salary offered, may necessitate supplemental teaching (e.g. evening or summer courses) for one to earn a sufficient income. Although the

benefits of teaching experience and an academic home can be invaluable to an early career person, the costs such temporary employment entails for one's ability to carry out research and writing can be high. Navigating these costs/benefits is no easy task; for instance, one might learn that, sometimes, time is more valuable than money.

6   Although it is necessary, the doctoral degree alone is hardly a sufficient credential for being admitted to academia as a full-time employee because most of the other applicants also possess this credential (i.e. it is the level playing field onto which ABDs have yet to be admitted). There was a time, prior to the early 1970s, when the job market was such that merely possessing a PhD would lead to multiple tenure-track job offers; in the humanities that time has long past.

7   For some of those who will be judging candidates' credentials to determine their admission to the profession, the reputation of the school from which they have earned their PhD plays a significant role in assessment of applicants' skills and future promise as colleagues. Although one's Alma Mater does communicate with whom one has trained and what traditions of scholarship one may pursue, yet for others the reputation of candidates' schools is secondary to the quality of their current research, the places where they have published their work and the experience they have had in the classroom.

8   Like all institutions, academia provides a case study in the complex relationship between structure and agency; for, although there are a variety of things that one can do to increase one's competitiveness, job candidates must recognize that there are also a host of factors of which they are unaware and which are therefore beyond their control (e.g. the unstated needs, interests, goals and even insecurities of the hiring department; the number of other candidates qualified at any given time in your area of expertise; the impact of world events on the perceived need for scholars in your subject area, etc.). Success probably requires one to learn to live with the latter while taking control of the former.

9   A structural element that must be taken into account is that departmental search committees often fail to entertain the difficult questions in advance and, instead, go on 'fishing expeditions' by defining their open positions far too broadly and vaguely, such as looking for the 'best qualified' applicant. Making explicit their implicit and often competing preferences may strike members of a department as being too costly an exercise. It is into this mix of unstated disagreements and long-standing rivalries that job applicants can be thrust, affecting such things as how their letters of application are read, their credentials judged, and their performance during campus interviews measured. While one cannot control such factors, when representing oneself one at least ought to be aware of their potential presence and impact.

10   Whether working at a publicly or privately funded institution, profes-
      sors are comparable to self-employed entrepreneurs inasmuch as they
      can increase their social capital (i.e. reputation) by seeking out new
      books to read and review, unique topics on which to research and write,
      novel and timely courses to develop and teach, and different profes-
      sional service opportunities to provide them with additional experience,
      as well as new national and international contacts. Graduate students
      are in much the same position and the additional qualifications that
      result from their entrepreneurial pre-professional activities can serve to
      distinguish one job applicant from another. Documentation from such
      activities, as recorded on one's CV, communicate to the hiring com-
      mittee that one is already skilled at participating in the many aspects
      of the profession that will surely be required of a tenure-track assistant
      professor.

11   While higher education is organized so as to train ever increasing
      specialists – a process that begins with surveys and broad coursework,
      examines candidates on their knowledge in general areas, and then cul-
      minates in writing a dissertation on a highly technical topic – eventual
      full-time employment can just as easily depend upon one's ability to
      contribute lower-level, so-called core or general education introductory
      courses to a department's curriculum. Because many departments of
      religious studies justify their existence not simply by appealing to the
      number of their majors or graduates, but also the number of core or
      general education courses that they offer to students pursuing degrees
      in other areas of the university, gaining early experience in such courses
      as a teaching assistant is an important step toward being able to per-
      suade future employers of one's ability to be a colleague who helps to
      teach their department's 'bread and butter' courses.

12   Many doctoral students do not realize that finding authors willing to
      write book notes, book reviews, etc. is sometimes difficult for journal
      editors. As a first step in professionalizing themselves, graduate students
      should become aware of the journals in their field and write to their
      book review editors, suggesting that the journal allow them to write
      and submit a review (especially for books that they are already reading
      for their courses or research, thereby minimizing on work additional
      to their class and dissertation research). Besides providing experience
      in writing and a much-needed line on one's CV, one never knows who
      will read the review or what other opportunities might follow upon it.

13   Because there is no direct relationship between seniority and the quality
      of one's writing, one's familiarity with the literature or the novelty of
      one's ideas, graduate students ought never to refrain from submitting
      their work to a scholarly journal for possible peer review publication
      simply because they understand themselves to be novices. Even if
      rejected, the comments that result from the blind review process will

be of benefit to students who have so far only received feedback from professors already familiar with their work.

14   Depending on the type of institution into which one is hired (i.e. its teaching load, service obligations, emphasis on research, sabbatical opportunities, etc.), the dissertation may constitute one of the few, or quite possibly even the last opportunity a candidate has to devote an extended period of time to one, focused project, free from the many obligations routinely expected of an assistant professor. Given the pressure to publish that, for some time, has attended academic careers, graduate students would be wise to write their dissertations while keeping in mind their eventual submission for possible publication – whether as a monograph (which, depending on a department's 'tenure and promotion' requirements, may be preferable) or as separate peer review essays.

15   Having successfully defended the dissertation, the manuscript does candidates no good in their desk drawer. However, before making revisions (unless they are dissatisfied with its argument or quality), graduates should create a prospectus containing a brief cover letter, annotated table of contents, and sample chapter (e.g. the introduction) and submit it to a select number of top-tier publishers in their area of expertise. Obtaining an outside expert's assessment of the manuscript – a step often essential to a publisher's process of evaluation – provides the best place to begin one's revisions of a manuscript with which one is intimately familiar and, perhaps, too closely tied.

16   Apart from professionalizing themselves through research and publication, candidates should consider the cost of regularly attending regional and national scholarly conferences simply as the price of being a graduate student. Waiting until one is on the job market is therefore too late to consider attending and trying to participate in such conferences – especially when one learns that being placed on the programme of such annual meetings often comes about gradually, over the course of several (or more) years. Whereas regional meetings are often useful places to try out one's research, become accustomed to speaking in public, and learn the rituals of the question/answer sessions that follow the presentation of papers (knowledge especially important during on-campus interviews), national meetings play a crucial role in efforts to integrate oneself into networks of colleagues at other institutions who share one's interests.

17   National scholarly conferences and professional associations often host on-site job placement services and publish employment periodicals. Becoming thoroughly aware of such services and resources, long before actually being on the job market, may not only assist one's decision-making when it comes time to select an area of expertise (i.e. judging national employment trends over time may shed light on areas likely to

require staffing in the coming years), but also prepare one for the eventual time when one is on the market and seeking campus interviews.

18 Despite being the primary, and sometimes even the exclusive, focus of candidates' attention during the last years of their PhD, once hired into a tenure-track position a variety of other, just as time-consuming, tasks compete for their attention. Learning to juggle many balls simultaneously – knowing which will bounce if dropped and which will break – is therefore an essential skill for early career professors who wish to continue carrying out original research while also teaching a full course load and serving the needs of their departments and the profession at large.

19 Although it can be intellectually stimulating, developing new courses is time-consuming. Depending on the needs of their department, teaching multiple sections of the same course provides early career professors with fewer course preparations, helps them to quickly establish their area of expertise in the curriculum and among students, and allows them to gain teaching competencies far more quickly, thereby enabling them to devote more time to their research and writing.

20 Despite what some maintain, teaching and research are complementary activities, inasmuch as teaching, somewhat like publication, constitutes the dissemination of information gained by means of prior research. Based on one's strengths, candidates can understandably emphasize one over the over, but declining always to carry out both, integrating them when possible, is to shirk one's responsibilities as a scholar.

21 As with the effort to enter any profession, a price must inevitably be paid – economic as well as social – in terms of the other activities and goals one might instead have worked toward and possibly attained. Candidates must therefore not only be as deliberate as possible in determining which costs they are willing to pay and which they are not, but they must also learn to trust their own judgements when, regardless of how their job search turns out, they someday look back on the decisions they once made.

4

Some Thoughts and Advice on Academic Publishing

KAY KOPPEDRAYER (WILFRID LAURIER UNIVERSITY)

The university where I teach subscribes to a software program that allows instructors to check students' papers for illicit use of others' work. I routinely use this service in part because it saves me or one of my teaching assistants some work. But vigilance and whatever deterrence its mere presence offers are not the only reasons I use it. Seeing how much coding appears on students' papers sometimes prompts me to think about how stale some of my assignments have become. Occasionally, the coding prompts me to call students into my office to talk about their presence or their voice in what they have produced. In these cases, the issue is not plagiarism; even when the assignment has lit up like a Christmas tree, the sources are almost always meticulously documented. Instead, the problem is that 30, 40, 50, maybe even as much as 60, per cent of the writing is someone else's. Such students are not claiming the work to be their own – their citations are all in order – rather, hiding behind others' thoughts and expressions, they have proved themselves to be good scribes.

In the conversation that ensues, I flash their now colour-coded assignment across my computer screen and we talk about how a thinker becomes a writer. For sure, the thinking part has to precede the writing part, and for some students neither is compelling. But for others, something is occluding the process. Insecurity, lack of time, laziness, bad habits, intimidation in the face of what they perceive to be great thinking, satisfaction in another's expression, or a sense that the idea, so well formulated by another, can be rendered no further and certainly not by their hands: these and a complex of other reasons reduces much of their work to transcription. Sometimes it is good transcription, sometimes mediocre, but in the end it is mostly but transcription. So we talk about how one finds their own place in their work and also about the hard work that involves.

These are undergraduates whose academic writing is at a certain stage of development and whose audience is generally quite restricted. Apart from whatever they may post on a blog and perhaps an op-ed piece in a local newspaper, their scholarly output is read by very few. This is not the case for graduate and post-doctoral students for whom survival in the academic world depends upon seeing their work through to publication. While it may seem that their concerns are quite different from what I have been describing, I suggest that finding one's academic voice and finding suitable outlets for that voice are more closely connected than may first appear. While all graduate students are presumably well beyond the stage of transcription, many are still establishing their scholarly style as well as learning the art of getting published. In the paragraphs that follow, I offer some thoughts on scholarly style, some advice and some information on the nuts and bolts of publishing.

1   GOOD SCHOLARSHIP, YOUR SCHOLARLY VOICE AND ITS AUDIENCE

We all know what makes up good scholarship: meticulous research, impeccable use of evidence, well-honed research questions, thorough knowledge of the field, understanding of theoretical nuances, good application of analytical and methodological approaches, solid argument and a coherent presentation. All through your university years you have been trained to think of the process of doing scholarship and writing it up as interconnected. From early on you have been producing papers, grinding them out, as it were. Done as course requirements and in the dissertation, your writing has been supervised, sometimes quite closely, sometimes not, but produced under a state of supervision nonetheless. Once you get to the other side of your degree programme, the relationship you have to your research and writing changes. The work is now yours, not that it is without the traces of the people you have worked with and studied under and also of your graduate cohort – those influences will always remain – but it is yours in a way it has not been before. Some graduate students have already begun to experience this shift while still in graduate school; their activity on the conference circuit and their forays into publishing testify to this. Others become more cognisant of it in their first job.

It involves, among other things, recognition of your own scholarly style. How you teach, how you think, how you supervise your own graduate students, the research you choose to undertake and how you choose to do so, the principles and ethics that guide you along the way, and certainly how you choose to write are all part of this style. If you go to a conference and attend to the ways scholars present their work, you can discern different styles. Some relate to their audience as if they were holding a machine gun; other adopt a more reflective mode, some are argumentative, others use a narrative voice to seduce their listeners. Dialogue partner, opponent, co-conspirator, projection screen, target are among the roles we assign to our audiences. Our style relates to our public face and also to reputation: the imprint you leave on your work as well as the impression it leaves on others.

Think of someone who is known to be pugnacious and here you are thinking of style. As we mature as scholars on our own, we settle into particular styles; moreover, most of us freely move among several styles, depending upon circumstances and what we seek to accomplish in a particular setting.

Classroom and seminar teaching, conference presentations and our publications are the places where we develop and exercise our scholarly voice. Our publications are also where we find our largest audience. Think of the scholars whose work you know. You probably could read an unidentified paragraph by any one of them and recognize the voice immediately. Some fine thinkers are known for their narrative voice, others for their obscurity. Literary qualities, analytic voice, cautious scholarship, exploratory approaches and rigorous proofs are among the intonations you hear. Reflect on the qualities of those voices and what they represent as you develop your own. How you write is as important as what you write, so take the time to develop your writing.

2 DEVELOPMENT OF THE CRAFT

Writing is a craft; done well, even an academic piece can take your breath away. Think of A. K. Ramanujan's 'Is there an Indian way of thinking?'[1] Although you might not agree with his playful claims, you cannot help but appreciate the power of his writing. Look long and hard at examples of academic writing. While holding your reactions to their contents in suspension, look at the way they have crafted their arguments. Go back and reread William Strunk Jr and E. B. White's *Elements of Style*.[2] The work's first edition dates to 1911, but the common sense and guidance it offers have never gone out of date. Consult Rolf Norgaard, *Ideas in Action: A Guide to Critical Thinking and Writing*.[3] Make the *Chicago Manual of Style*[4] your sacred scripture. Take pride in its quality as you fine-tune your writing.

While you are developing your craft, think also about the relevance of your work. Ask yourself whether you would be interested in reading the piece on which you are working. Would anyone else want to read it? Who? Where would that readership be found? Is the piece really intellectually stimulating or is it merely following the current trend of fashionable denunciations? Articles of the former type have staying power; these are the ones that continue to be cited and reprinted, the latter are but flashes in the pan. They glitter, but have little real substance. After you have read enough journal articles, you can recognize almost immediately certain ones written by junior scholars. They are often full of an inflated sense of self-importance, written by someone a little too captivated by his or her own cleverness. Journal editors sometimes propose changes of wording in the hopes that the author will soon grow out of that state. Some, however, never do. Do yourself a service by tempering any tendency to posture; printed words have a staying power that outlasts the insular moments of graduate seminars where posturing is sometimes part of the game. Learn instead to trust yourself while refining your skills of analysis, presentation and argument.

When critiquing another scholar's work, choose your method and style carefully. One can launch criticisms in all manner of ways, gracefully as well as aggressively. A slight change of wording can make all the difference in reception. The scholarly world is very small and individuals' memories can be quite long. Slights and insults, real and perceived, can come back later to haunt you. A danger is not simply that you make an enemy, but also that you lose control over your work. Embroiled in academic disputes, you can end up writing in an attack and response mode, a reactive mode, rather than one in which you are producing or generating new ideas. Think long and hard here: do you really want to devote your scholarly career to such work?

Arrogance is one extreme among newly minted PhDs, lack of self-confidence is another. This trait is a harder to spot when reviewing journal articles, mainly because it hardly shows itself. Junior scholars – and, for that matter, senior ones too – who doubt their worth rarely subject themselves to scrutiny. They resist sending their materials off to editors, sometimes devising all sorts of elaborate diversions to prevent their work from moving to publication. A piece may remain suspended in a state of revision or maybe there is just a little more work to do before it is ready, or maybe the immediacy of the demands of teaching and departmental work always take precedence. Resting in a state of occultation, these works speak of some promised future, but that promise is rarely fulfilled. If you recognize your-self in this description, develop the means to address it. Set aside one day a week or whatever to write and, no matter what, send something out. Your scholarly life depends upon it.

3   PRACTICAL CONSIDERATIONS: SOME NUTS AND BOLTS OF PUBLISHING

Journals abound in all fields of the humanities and social sciences. The *ATLA Religion Database* gives you a good idea of the range of journals that specialize in religion.[5] The *Journal of the American Academy of Religion, Numen, History of Religions, Studies in Religion/Sciences Religieuses, Method and Theory in the Study of Religion* are among the better known, but these are not the only journals to consider. Also worthy of consideration are jour-nals in cognate fields and those that specialize in topics corresponding with your work. These you often discover through electronic database searches when undertaking literature reviews. Many are possible destinations for your work. What is of prime consideration is the quality and reputation of the journal as well as the fit between your work and the journal's reader-ship. To adjudicate that, ensure that submissions are peer-reviewed, that the journal is known, and that the material a journal publishes matches your standards of scholarship. A quick check in Ulrich's *Periodicals Directory*, available online, will indicate the scope of the publication and whether it is a refereed journal.

Equally important is the relative weight of a refereed publication in a reputable academic journal as compared to a chapter in a book. Certain publicly funded granting agencies, including the Social Sciences and Humanities Research Council of Canada (SSHRC), set little value on book chapters when adjudicating an applicant's record of publications. The logic behind this weighting relates to the question of the extent to which the work has been refereed. It is believed that a chapter in an edited volume of essays receives much less scrutiny than a stand-alone journal article, hence for some granting agencies, refereed journal articles count, while book chapters do not. Hiring committees and tenure and promotion committees do not necessarily make that same distinction. Still, it is something to consider as you deliberate on what to do with your material. Also bear in mind that some journals routinely grant authors republishing rights. Permission to republish an article in an edited volume can be obtained or negotiated with the journal. You might find it useful to check into the journal's policy prior to submission.

4   SUBMITTING WORK TO AN EDITOR

Even a finely crafted and brilliant piece will get nowhere unless you submit it somewhere. Left in a drawer to languish or locked in an electronic file that you can no longer access because the software has become obsolete, these pieces rot away. What was once cutting-edge theory is now considered trite, fresh data are now sadly out of date and your interests have turned to other domains. It is possible that a friend or colleague might give you a call looking for a contribution to an edited volume, with the piece you have stashed away a perfect fit: a fortuitous moment, but one that will not happen unless your work is already known, and to have your work known is to be published. To do that, you need to send your material out. You have to brave the possibility of an editor saying revise and resubmit or, worse, an outright rejection. If you do not, you will never know what might have become of that languishing manuscript.

Pertinent here is another side to the world of academic publishing. Younger scholars may not realize that their relationship to academic journals and academic presses is symbiotic: university presses and journals need materials to publish as much as scholars need to see their work published. Manuscript editors need submissions. Some actively seek these by putting out a call for papers or, if with an academic press, a call for book-length manuscripts. Announcement digests posted on academic discussion groups and databases such as *PapersInvited* and *Humanities and Social Sciences Online* can inform you of journals and presses seeking submissions on special topics.[6] Both lists call for papers issued by professional bodies, journal editors and other conference organizers in all disciplines. Journal and series editors may also network by attending conferences or by contacting colleagues to meet potential contributors. Quite often journal and book editors run sessions on how to publish. Make it a point to attend such sessions and ask questions.

5   JOURNAL ARTICLES

As already mentioned, the first step in submitting an article to a journal is to choose the journal carefully. You have read issues of the journal and you are confident that your article fits the mandate of the journal. You know its readership and reputation and you feel it offers a good fit with your subject matter, approach, writing style and ideological slant, so you settle on that journal. The next step is to prepare your article in accordance with its protocol; information about submitting an article is generally posted on the journal's website. The accepted length, method of citation, spelling preferences, use of endnotes, format for references, the use abbreviations, font size, spacing and other requirements related to the article's presentation are usually spelled out in some detail. Follow those instructions: if a submission looks like a journal article it is more likely to be treated as one. Carefulness and attention to detail convey the message that you care about your work and respect the work of the editors and reviewers.

Once the manuscript editor determines that your submission is suitable for consideration, he or she will send it out to readers for a blind review, along with some instructions about the criteria with which to evaluate the piece. Policies vary among journals as to how readers are selected. Some journals rely on a regular set of reviewers; others seek specialists in the area of research. If it is the latter case, the editor has sent the abstract you prepared when asking a reader to do the review. Because the abstract will help convince someone to consider the piece, and later, if it is published, the abstract serves to catch a reader's attention, take extra care with it. You might also want to ensure that it contains precise information to make it electronically searchable by potential readers. While electronic search capacities are continually increasing, key words – names, locations, terms, and so on – should be present in the abstract so other scholars working in the same area will be able to find your article. In the same way, catchy titles can be wonderful so long as they do not completely obscure the subject matter of the article.

Some reviewers send back pages of comments on an article, others barely a paragraph. Their reaction to your essay may be caustic, supportive, laudatory. Some may have given the article a careful read, others but a cursory look. It is up the editor to sort the reviews out and get a response back to you. If the reports are widely divergent, the editor will usually seek a third, and sometimes even a fourth reader. The amount of time it may take an editor to get back to you on an article can be surprisingly rapid or tediously long. I have had editors get back to me with readers' reports in a matter of weeks and I have seen the review process drag out for over a year. I suspect that well-crafted articles see a quicker turnaround; in my own writing, articles I have been most satisfied with came back sooner and with more positive reports than pieces I did not like as much. There is also a matter of fit: an experimental piece will not suit a stodgy journal, just as more conventional scholarship may not be as well received in a journal specializing in cutting-edge theory. Unless the review process is taking an unseemly amount of time, do not hound editors about the status of an article. Their work is usually unpaid service, done above and beyond an already heavy workload. Sometimes, though, one does have to query to make sure the piece is somewhere in the review process. Do not, however, send emails after six weeks saying that you figure the article should be through the review and that you would like to know the decision. After an email like that, your piece might just remain a little longer in the process.

Editors have the responsibility of getting a report back to you that includes readers' comments. Along with the report will be a decision: no go, go (with or without conditions), or try again. This last category is a revise and resubmit; here the biggest mistake is rushing the piece back to the editor. Though not always the case, the editor should have included some recommendations along with the ambivalent verdict of 'Maybe yes, maybe no, let's see just what you can do'. Scrutinize those recommendations and take the time to make the article a better article. Sometimes, however, the editor simply sends along the reports to let you sort it out. Worse, the comments may be all over the map, demanding that this or that be done. Here you have to exercise judgement as to how to proceed; consultation with the editor might also help provide direction. If the recommendations are out of order, explain why in a cover letter or in email correspondence with the editor. Keep in mind that a resubmission is no guarantee of an acceptance.

Acceptance notices often come with conditions and readers' recommendations. Use your scholarly instincts to determine what you will change, rewrite or add to fulfil those conditions. Unless stated as a requirement of the acceptance, the recommendations may be for your consideration, and are not necessarily prescriptive. Your objective should always be better scholarship. Upon receipt of your final piece, editors find an accompanying cover letter explaining what you did by way of changes useful.

If your article has been rejected, do not take it personally. Go over the reports and learn from the experience. Even the most seasoned and well-published scholars receive rejection notices. When I was a manuscript editor for *Studies in Religion/Sciences Religieuses* I sometimes received notes from

authors whose articles had been rejected. They would be offering explanations on why their piece was not accepted, sometimes in angry tones
bordering on paranoia. In all cases their conjectures were wrong; their
articles were just not up to par. All the energy they wasted on conspiracy
theories could have been put to more fruitful outcomes. Learn the art of
drawing constructive advice out of criticism. Even a scathing report gives
you something to work on. Learn what to attend to and what to ignore.

At any rate, somewhere along the line, an article you have written has
been accepted by a journal and you have sent off what you expect is the final
copy. What you do now is add a line to your CV that reads 'Forthcoming'
and wait. Sometimes you wait and wait and wait. The production schedules
of journals can run like Swiss clocks; however, they can also be very erratic.
Sometime within the next year or two proofs should arrive. These days
they are mostly sent electronically. No matter how long it has taken to get
your article to press, the editor will want it back within days. Honour those
wishes. The extra work involved in contacting dawdling authors is not only
aggravating, but it also causes further production delays.

When going over your proofs, you will find that copy editors can do
wonders with your prose, but at times their changes have resulted in egre-
gious errors. Know when to stand your ground and know when to back off.
Some battles are worth fighting and some aren't. Resolve any disputes and
get changes and corrections back to the editor. It may seem silly to say this,
but write clearly when making corrections. Do not expect the editor to read
your mind. Then, at a certain moment after proofs have gone back and forth,
like magic, your article appears. It is a satisfying moment.

6   LOCATING AND CHOOSING AN ACADEMIC PRESS

Journal articles are only part of your work. The larger goal is to see a book
in print. Similar to what you do with articles, only on a larger scale, getting
a book published involves choosing and then working with a press. At one
time you would have needed to head to the reference section of a library to
look through a directory of academic presses to find a suitable publisher; this
information is now available online. The Association of American University
Presses posts a comprehensive directory of presses; a listing that includes
Canadian and West Indian presses.[7] The site also includes information about
available grants and a bibliography of works relevant to scholarly publishing.
Another place to locate prospective publishers is the conference venue. At
the book displays at the large conferences such as the annual meetings of
the Canadian Society for the Study of Religion (CSSR) and the American
Academy of Religion (AAR) as well as at more localized conferences, acquisition editors are present and usually more than willing to field questions
about manuscripts' possible fit with their presses' mandates. They will walk

you through the process of how to prepare a manuscript for submission. It is in their interests as much as yours to publish good work.

All good presses post information online as to how to field a book proposal and what the proposal needs to include. The extent of the work's readership, its relationship to a field of study, table of contents, approximate size, expected date of completion, and possibly a sample chapter are among what a prospective publisher expects to see in a proposal. This is your letter of introduction to a publisher; give it the attention it deserves. Do not hesitate to contact a press or the editor of a book series as you are in the early stages of deciding upon a press and preparation of a manuscript. Also, consult with colleagues who are actively publishing for recommendations.

The unwritten ethics of submission allow you to consult with as many presses as you want in the preliminary stages of deciding upon a press, but once you move to the proposal stage, and certainly at the manuscript stage, the rule is only one press at a time. Both proposals and manuscripts are sent to recognized scholars in the field for appraisal; to squander their resources by working clandestinely with more than one press is bad form; to opt for another press midstream is unacceptable. If you do, the press may be disinclined to consider future work from you. As for the amount of time it takes to turn around a manuscript, this varies from press to press, but an editor should be able to provide you with a reasonable estimate. For a proposal, the rule of thumb is to allow at least three weeks between its submission and any follow-up queries. The review of a complete manuscript takes months longer.

The fit between manuscript and a suitable press relates to the kind of publishing it does. For example, while suited for a press handling liturgical and confessional works, a book on pastoral counselling might be panned at a press oriented towards social scientific approaches to the study of religion. Presses have specializations: native studies, life histories, gender studies, post-colonial thought, Asian studies, Christian studies, American religious life, and so on; get familiar with these specializations. Check to see what a press is publishing in your area. Professional ethics will keep editors from discussing manuscripts under review, but an editor can provide an overview of the types of works the press deals with. Also check the types of works a publisher handles. Some are known for textbooks, others publish general interest and trade works along with their scholarly specializations.

Included in your deliberations about which press to choose should be information about the distribution mechanisms a press uses. Find out if the press works with library subscriptions, direct mailings, whether it has export capacities and any reciprocal distribution agreements with other publishing houses. You will want the comfort of knowing the monograph on which you worked so hard will actually be read by someone. Ask for estimates on how many books might be sold and how they will be marketed. Discussion of royalties should be part of these discussions. Most presses offer around 3 to 6 per cent net on the list price in addition to offering a number of complimentary copies and discounts on additional purchases. The amount of royalties increases with volume of sales, though scholarly works are rarely bestsellers. Some works do have lasting value, as evinced by continued print runs of works such Durkheim's *Elementary Forms of Religious Life* and Rahula's *What the Buddha Taught*.

Once you have settled on a press and have submitted a manuscript, the next stage is the review process. Policies can vary from one press to another, but in some instances, names are obtained from the executive committees of learned societies. Areas of expertise, gender, geographical location and languages may all be taken into consideration when a reviewer is chosen. These individuals are in effect both gatekeepers and gate-openers; the role of learned societies and of manuscript reviewers in publishing should serve as a reminder to become active and remain active in professional organizations during your career. A press will send the manuscript to two readers; they will decide whether it is suitable for publication. Among their considerations are questions of the soundness of the scholarship, whether it is up-to-date and original, whether the work makes a contribution to the field, and its readability. The readers will also provide their judgement on whether the work is publishable as it stands or whether revisions are needed. If so, the reader is expected to provide specific recommendations. If the two reader reports are divergent, the press will seek a third reader.

Once all reports are in hand, the acquisition editor contacts the author for a response. If you are the author in question, you will recognize that your immediate response can be quite a personal reflex. You have busted your gut on this manuscript and now you are confronted with reports that may include some very untoward comments. Your first response may be to come out slugging, but this is one moment when a first response is not necessarily the best response. Take a deep breath, pause and gather your thoughts. In the end, how you write your response is up to you, but here are some suggestions.

Begin with a reiteration of the positive points that the readers have noted. Though the reiteration may seem redundant, it is useful as it again draws attention to the work's merit. Then address the criticisms and recommendations the readers have made. It is possible that their suggestions will make your work much better. If so, note that, but be realistic in what you are able and willing to do by way of revisions. If among the criticisms there are some you find irrelevant or invalid, say so by drawing upon evidence and sound argument. Here you may want to return to your manuscript to ensure that what you have written is clear. The problem may be in your presentation, in which case you would explain how you can clarify what appears in the work. However you approach what you deem to be unwarranted criticisms, do not turn to denunciation. Maintain your professional standards.

Upon receipt of your response, the acquisition editor ranks the manuscript based on both the reports and your response. Decisions can include readiness to publish, rejection or revise and resubmit. For scholarly publications in Canada, an application to the Aid for Scholarly Publications Program (ASPP) is needed. In some instances, the reports may deem the work to be of high quality, meriting publication, while the application for funding is rejected. A press may decide to go forward with the publication anyway if they believe the work warrants publication. In such cases, applications to other funding sources, such as an internal book preparation grant, may be in order. Further, depending upon the policy of the particular press, the final decision on whether or not to publish the work may rest with the editorial board of the press, a group of scholars from the university that houses the press who review all reports and vote on whether or not the publication proceeds. If the decision is favourable, an advance contract is signed setting out the conditions. Conditions can include the receipt of a satisfactory manuscript and the securing of funding. Finally, how long might it take from initial proposal to the release of the book? At least two years, often longer. Once a work moves into production stage, the author or volume editor will have some input as to layout and design, limited by the capacity of a press and its production schedule. If you are under deadline for a tenure or contract decision, the press may be willing to provide documentation that the work's publication is pending.

7   PUBLISHING YOUR DISSERTATION

For most academics, the revised dissertation is their first book-length publication. The question facing many newly minted PhDs is whether it is better to establish a publication record by producing articles drawing upon sections of the dissertation or to wait to see the revised dissertation go to press. In part, personal circumstances will dictate the response. If you are coming up for tenure, you might need to go the quicker route of seeing several articles in print rather than waiting the longer period of time that it will take to get a book manuscript through. However, one thing to consider is the danger of publishing too much in article form so as to render it no longer possible to see the full-length work in print. An acquisition editor will not be likely to consider a revised dissertation if more than a third of its contents have been previously published in article form. And, even if it is less than a third, but the core of the work is already published, it is unlikely the manuscript will be considered. Another question an acquisitions editor will ask is whether there is readership for the topic.

In revising the dissertation for publication you may be faced with what appears to be a project of undoing or dismantling some of its scaffolding. The literature review will be among the first sections to go. Likewise, a reworking of the introductory chapters will probably be in order, as you no longer have a captive audience – your committee – reading the work. Instead, now you have to prove the work to be an engaging piece. A convincing introduction that clearly lays out what a reader will gain from reading the work will help engage the reader. As well, the revision may demand of you a shift of posture: you no longer have to prove your expertise; you are now writing for peers. And, throughout, the tight writing of the thesis can be opened up. Your work can become more thoughtful, rather than argumentative. Where technical terms are used, they should be explained completely and accurately. No sloppiness here. Provide a good conclusion. Paginate, double-space, and ensure that the editor receives a clean copy. Here, as in all publishing endeavours, the key is to submit well-prepared material where finely honed scholarship is complemented by attention to the guidelines and style a press or journal uses. Such work respects the dignity of the academic enterprise. Presumably, as graduate students, you value that enterprise; otherwise you would not be a participant.

Part II: Reflections

5

Graduate Education: A Place Where Past and Future Meet

HAROLD COWARD (EMERITUS, UNIVERSITY OF VICTORIA)

> At the still point of the turning world.
> Neither flesh nor fleshless;
> Neither from nor towards; at the still point,
> There the dance is,
> But neither arrest nor movement.
> And do not call it fixity.
> Where past and future are gathered ...
>
> (T. S. Eliot, 'Burnt Norton'[1])

When asked to reflect on my approach to graduate education in religious studies, my mind takes me back to T. S. Eliot's poem, 'Burnt Norton'. There Eliot suggests that to see the pattern of the changing world we need to step into a 'still point'. Graduate education, it seems to me, has exactly that as its purpose – to provide a reflective point, a moment out of the usual treadmill of time, from which to find a fresh perspective on the future, informed by the wisdom of the past. Hence my title: 'Graduate Education: A Place Where Past and Future Meet'.

In this article, I will reflect first on my approach to graduate education, second on how this has been shaped by the McMaster Religious Studies Graduate Program, where I completed my PhD, by the Calgary Department, which I helped develop, and by the University of Victoria Centre for Studies in Religion and Society of which I am the founding director.

1   THE 'STILL POINT' OPPORTUNITIES OF GRADUATE EDUCATION

Those of us who have had the privilege of graduate education recall its special quality. Once class requirements are met and comprehensive exams are over, there is that marvellous block of time for thesis writing that is for many a once-in-a-lifetime experience. To have a lengthy clear period devoted to thinking, reading and writing opens the way for the development of an intense consciousness which is the special creative experience of graduate studies. We become caught up in the thesis writing with an intensity and single-mindedness that allows for the discovery of new insights. From this 'still point' we see the pattern of the world in a fresh way, and that is our contribution to knowledge. It is the kind of contribution that cannot be made from the midst of the busy round of life, for to see the pattern one has to pause and reflect. At that still point, says Eliot, there is 'neither arrest nor movement. And do not call it fixity …' It is the creative moment where the wisdom of the past and the possibilities of the future are gathered. In this pregnant moment, says Eliot:

> Time present and past
> Are both perhaps present in time future
> And time future contained in time past.[2]

Insights are born and with great struggle written down in a thesis that frequently becomes the basis for a lifetime of scholarly contribution – a lifetime of teaching and research.

The 'thesis moment' encapsulates the original purpose of the university: to reflect deeply on life and to contribute that knowledge and wisdom back to society. Pure curiosity-driven or basic research has been the mainspring of graduate education in the past and should remain so in the future. It gives free rein to the imagination of the graduate student with only the requirement that the research produce a focused and significant result as a contribution to knowledge. Such basic curiosity-driven research in the humanities and social sciences, as well as in the sciences, has produced the most profound knowledge. It is at its best when the promising graduate student is given financial support and secure supervision and is set free to follow his or her own quest. This has been the model for the best graduate education of the past and is still valid today.

The pragmatic push for more accountability and speed in the completion of graduate programmes has some merit, but must not be allowed to reduce the time and support provided so that the creative still point for thesis writing disappears. The other obstacle which sometimes gets in the way of graduate student curiosity-driven research is the limiting action of disciplinary methodologies which are too narrow and too inflexible. Rather than serving and fostering the scholarly search, such scholasticism suffocates creative imagination. In my view, methodology should simply serve to maintain a standard of critical excellence in search for knowledge, in whatever direction that search should lead the scholar. Too often, today, methodology becomes a dogma that blocks the path to knowledge rather than helping to open the way. I include here as well our reluctance to admit different approaches to knowledge such as we find among women, aboriginal and non-European cultures – approaches that nowadays claim the interest of many graduate students. My first point, then, and one I emphasize strongly, is that curiosity-driven or basic research should remain the mainspring of graduate education.

But there is also our responsibility as scholars to reflect in a more strategic way on the major problems facing society; for example, health-care provision, the environmental crisis, population pressure, the over-consumption of the earth's resources, migration, the need for peace-building, to name only a few. Such problems demand both an interdisciplinary approach and an engagement in applied research. While many graduate students today are drawn to these problems, the requirements for good work in interdisciplinary applied research are daunting. Usually two disciplines have to be mastered before serious work can begin. For example, a thesis project in religion and medical ethics will require a comprehensive base in both medicine and religious studies before the graduate student is qualified to begin research. Similarly, work on environmental issues requires expertise in science, geography, economics and religious studies as prerequisites. And in all of these problems, questions of public policy in the realms of public administration, political science and law come constantly to the fore. Because it is so difficult, the wisest course may often be to provide interdisciplinary graduate training, but not to give interdisciplinary degrees. At McGill University, for example, a person in medical anthropology will be exposed to medical history and sociology, but he or she will get the degree (and a thorough disciplinary education) in anthropology. This is a far better approach than that typically found in many, if not most, interdisciplinary graduate programmes. Too often, such programmes lack the necessary rigour in admission prerequisites and depend on inadequate supervision arrangements. Successful supervision requires scholars who themselves have conducted and published interdisciplinary research. Such research is usually more, not less, demanding than work in a single discipline. Careful supportive supervision is most important if a significant result is to be achieved. Too often interdisciplinary graduate programmes are treated as ad hoc, with the student being left to sink or swim on their own – an approach which seldom produces a significant result. For most students the wise course may well be the completion of a strong disciplinary graduate degree as a base for the later development of interdisciplinary research.

During the past two decades, some graduate programmes have developed successfully in areas rather than disciplines – one thinks of comparative literature and our own field, religious studies. Much of the work is interdisciplinary in nature. While some scholars are unusually brilliant, it must be admitted that in such areas it can be easier to do poor work and get away with it. This certainly happened, for example, in psychology of religion where much nonsense was produced by faculty and graduate students with no solid grounding in psychology.

In my experience, those who have demonstrated excellence at the highest disciplinary levels make good interdisciplinary researchers. This is why I mentioned earlier that the most promising students for interdisciplinary research are often mature students who have already demonstrated excellence in one of the disciplinary areas required. They have the disciplinary rigour and self-confidence which allows one to launch into study of a new discipline that also must be mastered before interdisciplinary research can begin. Starting interdisciplinary research too early in one's education, or before firm grounding in the required disciplines has been established, is a recipe for failure or at best a mediocre result. Yet, today, this often occurs, especially when the enthusiasm for openness to interdisciplinary work results in ad hoc approaches in graduate programme regulations and supervision. It is not acceptable, in my view, to name supervisors with only disciplinary research expertise (from the disciplines involved) to supervise a student in an interdisciplinary thesis project. Yet one finds this being done in graduate faculties where the desire to respond to students wishing to do interdisciplinary work on difficult problems in health care or environmental ethics results in ad hoc and less than carefully thought-out arrangements being accepted. Let me repeat my earlier statement that significant interdisciplinary research is often more demanding than disciplinary work, and thus requires more stringent requirements and supervision to be successful at the graduate level.

In the future, problems will be more interdisciplinary and global in nature, often necessitating a team approach involving not only scientists, social scientists and humanists working side by side, but also researchers from government and industry. I myself have had success in directing such research teams. Together with Thomas Hurka, I directed a Social Sciences and Humanities Research Council of Canada (SSHRC) and Shell Canada funded project: 'An ethical analysis of possible scientific and social responses to the greenhouse effect', now published under the title *The Greenhouse Effect: Ethics and Climate Change*.[3] In that project, no graduate students were included, as I then held the view that there was no role for them in such a project. Since then, however, my thinking has changed. In subsequent interdisciplinary team research projects that I have directed,[4] graduate students were included as full team members with considerable success. They contributed increased energy and at times fresh perspectives to the research. For them it was an excellent *training experience* in interdisciplinary team research. They found themselves having to work side by side with scientists, social scientists, humanists and persons from industry and government. The focused disciplinary perspective of their home departments, valuable as it was, was seen to provide only a portion of the knowledge needed to deal with the problem. They came to see the necessity of gaining an understanding, however rudimentary and incomplete, of the methods and technical terminology used by others, so that an atmosphere of trust and communication could be established between team members. Finally, they realized that interdisciplinary team research is not the patching together of a series of disciplinary contributions but rather an approach in which each team member must take account of all the data (from all perspectives) in making a contribution to the problem's solution. In the end, when they returned to their home departments to take up their disciplinary thesis research, they did so with a changed consciousness: a wider awareness of other approaches to knowledge and the valuable contributions they make. In short, they were now much better educated graduate students. I am confident that this change reflected itself in the problems they selected for thesis research, and the way in which these questions were formulated. And after completing graduate work, this team research training will have provided a basis from which they are more likely than other graduates to involve themselves in interdisciplinary work in the future.

2 MY EXPERIENCES AT MCMASTER, CALGARY AND THE UNIVERSITY OF VICTORIA

The above approach to graduate education evolved out of my own graduate experience at McMaster (1970–73), my time as a Professor at Calgary (1973–92) and my work as Director of the Centre for Studies in Religion and Society at UVic (1992–2001). McMaster in the early 1970s was a very large department with over 70 in the PhD programme alone. We came from across Canada, the United States, the United Kingdom, India, China and Japan. What attracted us? Money helped, but more important was the quality, diversity and energy of the faculty, along with the unique vision that the McMaster programme introduced into the new academic field of religious studies (biblical studies, Western religious thought, religion and society, Eastern religions or philosophy). For me and for many others of that period, what attracted us was the combination of:

- rigorous specialization using the best of humanities and social science approaches (including appropriate languages);
- comparative study in both Eastern and Western religious traditions;
- anthropological, sociological and psychological approaches to the study of religion and society;
- the chance to study and work with persons of other religions and culture.

Harold Remus in *Religious Studies in Ontario* reports that a rationale for an even-handed treatment of Eastern and Western religions was given early on by George Grant's vision that students must acquire some knowledge of the religious history of the West, but must also investigate some other great tradition such as Hinduism or Buddhism. Reductionism was to be avoided – religions were to be allowed to speak in their fullness. Eastern religions were to be approached without assumptions of Western superiority. Study was to be interdisciplinary as well as comparative. At the graduate level, we were to balance the need for specialization against the need to think comprehensively about religion. To help achieve these goals, Grant stressed the principle of having first-hand contact with the religious traditions one is studying.[5] One of the greatest strengths of the department then was the opportunity for students to interact with faculty and students from other cultures and religious traditions. This was long before Canadian society and universities were as diverse as they are presently. We were taught by faculty from India, China and Japan, who represented a variety of religious and philosophical perspectives. We were in seminars with students from a great variety of backgrounds. This was both intellectually stimulating and personally enriching.

When I started in at McMaster in the autumn of 1970, I almost missed out on much of this. You see, the thesis research I had proposed to George Grant, and on which I was accepted, was 'A psychological, philosophical and theological analysis of the Christian reception of scriptural revelation'. However, after a couple of months and a few discussions about this thesis project with George, he called me into his office one day and told me, 'You can't do this.' When I asked why, he said that when it came time for the oral exam, because I was including psychology in my analysis, the Psychology Department would put psychologists on the examination and, since they were all 'rat psychologists', they would fail me – which was true. And since I was also including a philosophical analysis, the Philosophy Department would put someone on my committee and, as they were all positivists, they would also fail me. So, said Grant, 'You just can't do it.' You can imagine I was quite shattered. Here I was, having moved my wife and children 2,500 miles across the country to do this project only to be told, 'You can't do it.'

As I left George's office and started down the hall, head down in shock, I had to suddenly stop, as I was about to run into a short Indian gentleman dressed in a Nehru suit standing in front of me. Now, I knew there were a lot of students and faculty at the other end of the hall studying Eastern religions, including a famous visiting professor from India, but I had never studied Indian religion or even taken a single course in comparative religion. Professor Murti simply fixed me with his sharp eyes and asked, 'What's the problem?' I blurted out what I have just described. He said, 'We have been studying the reception of scriptural revelation in India for about 3,000 years and we don't have this separation into psychology, philosophy and religion, so why don't you do your thesis on the Hindu experience of the Veda and then after you get your PhD, you can write your book on the Christian reception of revelation.' That is what I did: I completed my PhD in Hindu philosophy and religion and many years later wrote my book on the

Christian experience of revelation, *Sacred Word and Sacred Text: Scripture in World Religions*,[6] but including all the world religions.

I remember going back down the hall with Professor Murti to his office, where he told me what I would have to do: learn Sanskrit, start attending his seminar on Indian philosophy, and come to his apartment three afternoons a week where we would read texts line by line *guru-sishya* style for two hours a time, after which he would make me tea and teach me about the culture. It took us two years to read Patanjali's *Yoga Sutras* this way, but in so doing, I learned most of the schools of Indian philosophy. I then read Bhartrhari's *Vakyapadija,* or 'Philosophy of Word and Sentence', on which I wrote my thesis published in 1976 as *The Sphota Theory of Language*, the Hindu philosophy and theology of the reception of revelation.[7] After meeting with Murti, I went home and talked with Rachel, my wife, about what we should do. It seemed right, yet, given my background, an impossible challenge. The next day I knocked on David Kinsley's door and asked what he thought. I told him, given our finances and young family, I had to be done in three years. His advice was 'Don't do it', but I went ahead anyway and finished in three years. George Grant continued as my official supervisor because Murti was returning to India – although when it came time for my oral and he read my thesis, he called me up and said, 'This is all Sanskrit – I don't understand it.'

The high points for me at McMaster from 1970 to 1973 include the following:

- The chance to read Plato's *Republic* and the *Laws* with George Grant in his seminar, where a part of the excitement was to see if George would set himself on fire with the cigarette ash dribbling down his front;
- The chance to study Kant and experience the pure joy of scholarship in John Robertson's seminar which for me became the model for how to teach a seminar;
- Learning Indian philosophy, especially *Advaita Vedanta*, from John Arapura;
- Learning from David Kinsley how to teach Indian philosophy and religion to large classes of undergraduates;
- Watching Ed Saunders' masterful way of teaching about the New Testament to large undergraduate classes in which I was a TA.

Most important of all, however, was the opportunity to study with Professor T. R. V. Murti in his seminars on Sankara, Ramanuja and Nagarjuna or at his apartment in traditional *guru-sishya* style, by myself or with others of his students from India, such as Bibhuti Yadav or Braj Sinha. As his students, our relationship with him was like a father–son relationship, a commitment from him to us and from us to him that lasted for life. It meant that I ended up as his senior student, editing his collected works and, together with Krishna Sivaraman (also his student), editing his Festschrift which we presented to him at the University of Calgary in 1978.[8] Even though he is now dead, this lifelong relationship still continues with his family through his eldest son, a professor of physics, who spends half his time at Princeton University and the other half at the technical institute in Bangalore.

Coming back to McMaster days, one event that vividly brought home the problems of translation was a special seminar that Professors Murti and Jan jointly offered on the Buddhist text, the *Abhidkarma Kosa* – Professor Jan and his students reading the Chinese text and Professor Murti and his students reading the Sanskrit text. Although the Chinese text was held to be a translation from the Sanskrit, the difference between them was so great, especially as read and interpreted by Jan and Murti, as to make them seem like two quite different texts. I remember Murti afterwards confiding to us that that demonstrated the inability of Chinese to convey the sophisticated and subtle philosophical concepts of the Sanskrit texts. For Murti, there was absolutely no doubt that Sanskrit was *Davi Vak*, the divine language!

The final high point I will mention from being at Mac in the early 1970s was not just the large group of truly fine and challenging faculty (Saunders, Coombs, Craigie, Meyer in Biblical; Grant, Robertson, Greenspan and Weeks in Western Thought; Arapura, Murti, Younger, Kinsley and Jan in Eastern Religions; and Mol and Lane in Religion and Society). This truly fine collection of faculty attracted large numbers of excellent students to study with them, especially since the financial support offered by McMaster was better than anywhere else at that time. So as students we found ourselves caught up in a field of study that seemed worthwhile, challenging and important in itself – well worth the sacrifice that our family was going through to be there. One of the greatest contributions was the opportunity to study with and socially get to know faculty and students from other cultures and religious traditions. The unique nature of the programme requirements ensured that those of us specializing in India and China did not hide away with our professors at the far end of the hall and not mix at all with biblical or Western thought faculty and students (as was usual in other programmes). So, in addition to my seminars with Murti and Arapura, I ended up doing courses with Grant, Robertson, Lane and Weeks, and TA-ing for Saunders as well as Kinsley. I had to write comprehensive exams for Robertson as well as for Murti and Arapura. I remember being in John Robertson's seminar with a wonderful group of students, including Greg Schopen (now a leading Buddhist scholar at UCLA), Lance Nelson (now at San Diego) and myself from the Eastern side as we read Kant's major texts – and had to perform at a level equal to the leading students in Western thought. It was a wonderful educational experience. Of course the same thing was happening in the opposite direction, with students in biblical or Western thought sitting with me in Arapura and Murti's seminars. In this we really did live out George Grant's founding vision that at the graduate level, one needs to balance the need for specialization against the need to think comprehensively about religions, and have first-hand contact with representatives of the religious traditions one is studying. The requirement of gaining familiarity with both Eastern and Western religious traditions in addition to our own specialism was not happening elsewhere in Canada or abroad at that time. And McMaster was the only place in Canada in the 70s and 80s where one could get a credible education in social scientific approaches to the study of religion from a religious perspective working with faculty like Hans Mol and later Ellen Badone.

For Rachel and me, as young people who had grown up in the homogenous WASP environment of Southern Alberta, McMaster was wonderfully enlarging. At the same time as I was entering into the Indian worldview of *karma* and *samsara* in my studies, we were being invited for dinner with the Grants, Arapuras, Kinsleys, Robertsons and of course with Professor Murti. Dinner with Murti was a special experience, for he was cooking for himself in his own apartment (his wife and extended family being back in Banaras). Not only did he invite Rachel and me, but also our three children whom he came to regard as his grandchildren. He cooked a fine meal of simple Indian food and a big bread pudding filled with raisins and Indian spices. To keep the children busy while we talked, he took down his portable typewriter with lots of paper and put it on the floor for them to play with. We had many faculty along with other students such as Bibuti Yadav, Braj Sinha, Ed Babineau, David Hawkin and Robert Forest to our home for dinner. Before coming to McMaster, Rachel and I had experienced life in the graduate psychology degree which I completed partly at University College London, England, and partly at the University of Alberta in Edmonton, where I also studied Christian theology. While the graduate seminars were quite good and we had good colleagueship with faculty and students, our experience at McMaster was at an altogether different level. The high quality of the graduate seminars, the unusual breadth and depth of the academic programme, the special stimulus of studying with faculty and students from India, China, Australia, the UK and US, as well as Canada, made for a wonderfully stimulating scholarly three years that far exceeded anything I had previously experienced. The McMaster graduate programme powerfully shaped me along with many others into a way of studying and teaching about religion that, through us, has had a major impact upon the development of graduate work in religious studies in Calgary and Victoria – to which topic I now turn.

Both Calgary and Victoria have been modelled on the McMaster vision as it existed in the early 1970s. For both, I drafted many of the course descriptions and programme requirements. At the University of Calgary, we based ourselves on the McMaster vision but sought to improve it. We collapsed biblical into Christianity and ended up with three streams: Western (Judaism, Christianity and Islam, missing at Mac), Eastern (Hinduism,

Sikhism, Buddhism and Chinese) and in the middle the McMaster Religion Society was reconceived as 'The Nature of Religion', (involving the application of philosophical, psychological or sociological analysis to the basic data of both Eastern and Western religious traditions). So we had three streams of study – Western, Eastern and Nature of Religion, and we tried to balance faculty appointments across all streams so that no religious tradition or method of analysis was favoured over the others. At both the undergraduate and graduate levels, we copied McMaster's breath and depth requirements. In the BA programme, students had to specialize in one area but complete breadth requirements in the other two. Someone specializing in Judaism would have to complete at least two years of Hebrew language and minimum requirements in both Eastern religion and nature of religion. If someone was focusing on Buddhism, for example, they would have to do at least two years of Sanskrit and/or Tibetan and minimum requirements in both Western religions and nature of religion. Someone specializing in the Nature stream (philosophy, sociology or psychology of religion) would have to complete language requirements as well as breadth requirements in both Eastern and Western religions. The department offers language courses in Hebrew, Arabic, Sanskrit, Tibetan and Chinese, with Greek being taught by Classics. Graduate programme requirements (both MA and PhD) parallel those of the undergraduate programme, except that languages must be in place as an entrance requirement. Breadth requirements in terms of both coursework and comprehensive exams parallel those of McMaster in the 1970s. The Calgary programme, in our minds (Coward, Craigie, McCready) as we developed it, perfected the McMaster vision. It has proven very successful, having today a faculty complement of 15 professors, undergraduate majors numbering 120, 16 MA students and 15 PhD students with graduates employed as religious studies faculty in 12 Canadian universities.

As for the Centre for Studies in Religion and Society at the University of Victoria (a strictly research centre with no teaching), we are now 14 years old and just completed our third external review with flying colours. I was hired as the founding director in 1992; the vision I had in mind was shaped by both my McMaster and Calgary experiences. From McMaster I took the need for openness to the great religious traditions and to the employment of modern methods of interdisciplinary study. My goal was to create a research centre where faculty on sabbatical from anywhere in the world in the writing stage of their research would come together with graduate students also in the writing stages of their MA or PhD theses and form a community of writers all working on various projects. So we have 18 offices for faculty fellows and six research spaces for graduate student fellows. Each are given an office and quiet space to get on with their writing. In the mornings at 10.30 the whole writing community comes together in the Centre's library for coffee and discussion of each other's scholarly work. With various methods being employed and different traditions being studied by scholars from around the world, we have fine academic discussions. It is what I always thought a university should be. To support our scholars we have four administrative staff in addition to the director (an administrator, secretary, assistant secretary and librarian). Our Centre occupies a complete wing of a West Coast-type cedar and glass building with large picture windows. It is such a good place to work that many of our scholars wish to repeat their time with us, but each fellowship (for six months or one year) must be won in a competition run on the same model as SSHRC graduate student or faculty awards. We have about 18 scholars in residence working on their research projects at all times. We have had graduate student fellows from a variety of disciplines, including religious studies, environmental studies, women's studies, geography, political science, anthropology, history, classics, English, French, German and art history. They had in common thesis projects involving religion and society. They also had to be in the writing stage of their MA or PhD thesis project. They found that being in a research community together with faculty members who were also in the writing stages of their research was very helpful. A common mistake made by just about all graduate students is to spend too long in reading before getting down to writing. The motto I would suggest they put over their desk is 'Let writing direct reading', not vice versa. Only as you begin the hard work of actual thesis writing do you discover where you need to read more in order to keep on writing. Reading without writing to direct it can simply be an escape-hatch to avoid the harder work of writing. Like the McMaster vision, in our research centre we always have scholars working on both Eastern and Western religions and using a full range of humanities and social science methods in their analysis. In addition to the individual fellows doing their own projects the Centre puts together team-authored interdisciplinary book projects funded by grants from SSHRC and US foundations like PEW, Ford and Rockefeller. Each team of 10–15 people is made up of leading scholars of the various religious traditions from around the world, the majority often coming from outside Canada. Graduate students are included as full team members and often co-author book chapters. Each of these projects takes three years to complete with the scholars travelling to Victoria for working sessions in a retreat setting. Most of the 16 resulting books have been published by SUNY Press, but some by WLU Press in Canada. Some of these titles I have already mentioned; others include: *Religious Conscience, the State and the Law*; *Visions of a New Earth: Religious Perspectives on Population, Consumption and Ecology*; *The South Asian Religious Diaspora in Britain, Canada and the United States*; and *Just Fish: Ethics and Canadian Marine Fisheries*.[9] Many of these titles are used as textbooks in religious studies, environmental studies, geography, fisheries and other classes in Canada and the US. An influence that I developed in Calgary and brought to Victoria is the application of our academic religious knowledge together with that of our colleagues in science, social science and the humanities to problems facing the world today – thus the titles I just listed dealing with issues like the environmental challenge, and pluralism in civil society, and one we are just now completing on the challenge of GM foods to religious traditions with food prohibitions (e.g. Halal, Kosher, vegetarianism). Thus, some of our book projects are pioneering the application of religious studies knowledge to major public policy issues. Our Centre always has the research and writing of four such team-authored books on the go, making a total of some 60 or 70 faculty and graduate students at work on scholarly research at the Centre at all times. The wide-open scholarly curiosity and valuing of interdisciplinary approaches that was fostered in me as a graduate student at McMaster prepared me for the research work we do in our Centre.

Let me conclude with an example of how McMaster graduate students are making a major contribution to religious studies in Canada at the level of national institutions and contemporary issues. When, in 1995, SSHRC together with the federal department of Heritage Canada launched a new research initiative to study the assimilation of immigrant communities into urban centres called 'The Metropolis Project', the study of ethnic religious diaspora communities such as Hindus, Sikhs, Muslims from different areas, etc. were left out. Although my first research proposal to include them failed, later proposals together with Paul Bowlby and especially Paul Bramadat have succeeded. Today the study of religious ethnic communities is accepted as an important dimension of Metropolis research. Some of this work has been located in our Victoria Centre where it has involved national teams of scholars led by Paul Bramadat and David Seljak. The first volume, which analysed the history and current status of the Hindu, Sikh, Buddhist, Jewish and Muslim immigrant communities in Canada, was published last year under the title *Religion and Ethnicity in Canada*.[10] Research for the second volume, *Christianity and ethnicity in Canada*, also led by Paul and David, was completed in a working retreat at the Centre in February. It will be presented at the CSSR Annual Meeting in May 2006 and will be published in 2007. This volume will add an important dimension to the history of Christianity in Canada by including assessments of immigrant groups such as the Mennonites, Hutterites and Hungarian Catholics along with the mainstream traditions like the Scottish Presbyterians, Dutch Christian Reformed and French Roman Catholics. In many of these team research activities, graduate students have played important roles. This work with scholars from many different disciplines is so exciting and mind-expanding that often the graduate students involved will want to switch their PhD theses to an interdisciplinary problem and method. My advice is usually to complete one's PhD with a disciplinary thesis that demonstrates scholarly rigour and will help one to land a job. Then after one is in a secure faculty position, one can branch off into interdisciplinary work safely.

3 CONCLUSION

Completing my PhD in the McMaster graduate programme from 1970–73 led me to explore approaches to T. S. Eliot's 'still point' that previously were completely unknown to me – for example, Hinduism and Buddhism. It gave me a new language, Sanskrit, and nourished within me a breadth and depth of scholarly curiosity that launched me on a quite wonderful academic career that continues on to this day. Five years into retirement, I am still leading research projects at our Centre, and at home in my study completing the final two chapters on a new book for SUNY Press, my eighteenth authored book. I don't do this for promotion or merit increments, as my pension cheque stays the same even if all I do is sit in the sun. I do it for the sheer joy of discovering more knowledge about the religious traditions and their take on 'the still point of the turning world'. The foundation for this 'joy in scholarly discovery' was evoked within me by my McMaster professors and my fellow students during those three wonderful and challenging years when I was a PhD student here.

The contribution of McMaster's graduate programme to religious studies in Canada was to launch me and many others like me into universities across the land with a new and unique vision of what religious studies should be – a contribution we have passed on to our students. With this vision firmly ingrained within us by the seminars we took, the comprehensive exams we sat, and the theses we wrote, we went out and reformed departments that were too narrow or created new ones as we did at Calgary. We breathed new life into struggling learned societies and created new ones that continue to serve Canada well – all of this when religious studies in Canada was in its formative years. At a time when it was rare in Canada, the McMaster model of requiring rigorous specialization, interdisciplinary approaches to study and knowledge of both Eastern and Western religious traditions gave us a basis to succeed as individual scholars and to create a scholarly approach that has won the support of our academic colleagues and institutions across Canada.

By safeguarding excellent curiosity-driven basic research within the traditional disciplines as well as providing the opportunity for high-quality applied interdisciplinary training, graduate education in religious studies will prove itself to be the place where past and future meet.

6

Events, People and Circumstances: Looking Back at a Largely Unplanned Academic Career in Religious Studies

KLAUS KLOSTERMAIER (EMERITUS, UNIVERSITY OF
MANITOBA)

When Mathieu Courville invited me to contribute an article to this collection of essays for graduate students looking forward to an academic teaching career in religious studies, he suggested personalizing the contribution by adding some autobiographical background. In doing so, I did not intend to give advice on how best to go on to succeed in the profession but to show how real-life events often intervene, crossing our own plans. As a graduate student, I did not envisage a career as a university teacher and certainly had not anticipated spending most of my professional life at the University of Manitoba. Call it karma, fate, providence or chance – life often does not turn out as planned and, looking back, it does not appear a straight line from start to finish, but more like a mountain path that goes up and down, back and forth, around boulders and ice-fields before it ends up on the top of a hill, revealing other mountains near and far. While each life story is different, one can take up certain hints and clues from other people's biographies and put them to work in one's own development or take comfort from the fact that others too had their problems and crises from which one can learn.

1   SOME AUTOBIOGRAPHICAL FRAGMENTS

The year I was born, 1933, was a fateful year for Germany: Hitler had assumed dictatorial powers over Germany and began preparing for war. When I began elementary school, the Second World War began. By summer 1943, when I entered Gymnasium, allied bombing of my hometown, Munich had become so devastating that most schools were closed and we were evacuated to the countryside. By 1944 things became as bad there. And the end in 1945 was terrible. The next three years were years of misery: hunger, cold, ruins. One day my mother remarked: 'You did not have a childhood.'

The only institution that had survived the collapse in 1945 more or less intact was the Catholic Church: it provided protection, comfort and active practical support in those times. It was almost a matter of course for me to opt for service of the Church as a profession. After completing Gymnasium I received a full scholarship for the prestigious Collegio Germanico-Ungarico in Rome.[1] That was in 1952. By then Europe was slowly emerging from the trauma and the devastations of the Second World War, and the world outside our own continent began to enter our consciousness again. Having survived a hateful dictatorship, I deeply sympathized with the efforts of Asian and African countries to become independent from colonial rule. At the same time I noticed the widespread crushing poverty and hunger in the newly independent countries. Having suffered through wartime horror and post-war misery, I acutely felt for the people of the so-called Third World whose plight was increasingly and dramatically brought to my attention, not only through the mass media, but also through individual contacts. I also perceived an acute discrepancy between my lofty ideals and the practices of the bureaucratized institution.

I had been attracted to India for as long as I can remember and I had learned a great deal about its history and culture; all the more, after becoming acquainted with Indian fellow students at the Gregorian University in Rome with its amazingly international student body. I joined a missionary society with the intention of doing what was then called 'development work' in India and began studying Sanskrit and Hindi on my own.

My 'scholarly career' began rather unexpectedly. As part of my training programme, for four years, I attended a seminar in anthropology and comparative religion, conducted by the Africanist Paul Schebesta, famous for his research among the Bambuti of the Ituri Forest. One day Professor Schebesta came to the seminar with a surprising proposition: a Berlin publisher had asked him to write a generally accessible scholarly volume on 'The Origin of Religion', to counter with factual information the then widespread East German communist propaganda on that subject. Professor Schebesta thought I could tackle that with the help of my fellow students. We did the work: in the end I could persuade Professor Schebesta to sign as editor. The book not only saw the light of print in Berlin, but it was also subsequently translated into Dutch, Italian and French.[2] Perhaps not surprisingly all the contributors ended up as academic teachers, some attaining considerable distinction in their fields.

During those years of study I also received numerous requests from journals and newspapers to write articles on issues connected with world religions. I developed contacts with editors and was even offered a permanent position by one of them. When I had completed my preparatory studies, my superiors wanted me to take over the editorship of one of the Society's own magazines. My aim, however, remained to go to India. Professor Schebesta once again proved instrumental. Impressed, among other things, by a minor thesis in comparative religion, entitled 'Salvation in Buddhism and Christianity' that I had written as partial requirement for my Baccalaureate in Theology degree, he persuaded my superiors to let me go in for a doctorate to prepare for work in India.

By that time the Government of India had already imposed severe restrictions on the entry of foreign missionaries. In 1955 an Indian Government appointed commission had come up with a damning assessment of the work of Christian missionaries in India. Following the recommendations of the 'Neogy-Report', the Indian Government clamped down on the entry of foreign missionaries and virtually stopped giving visas, except for purposes of education and technical development. I was advised that I had a better chance to get a visa if I had a PhD – theological degrees did not count. For my thesis I chose the topic 'Modern Hinduism and the social reconstruction of India'. My adviser at the Gregorian University in Rome was the well-known Jesuit sociologist Gustav Gundlach. I was so eager to get to India as quickly as possible that I completed my coursework, my thesis and my defence within one academic year. I had to work hard on my adviser to allow me to finish in such short time. I was proud that I passed with *summa cum laude* with a defence *coram publico*, quite a rare distinction at the Gregorian. I felt ready for my work in India. But would I get a visa?

During my thesis research I had made extensive use of the library maintained by the cultural division of the Indian Embassy in Rome and I had come into contact with some of the embassy staff. One day I was introduced to the ambassador, who expressed his pleasure that I was studying the works of great Indians such as Aurobindo Ghose, Swami Vivekananda, Sarvepalli Radhakrishnan, Mahatma Gandhi and Jawaharlal Nehru. After completing my degree, I applied for a visa and to everybody's surprise I did receive a one-year visa within a few months.

Happy to see my lifelong wish fulfilled, I boarded the *Cambodia*, an ocean liner of the Messageries Maritimes, in Marseilles to sail to Bombay. It was a wonderful and exciting 11-day trip through the Mediterranean, the Suez Canal, the Red Sea and the Arabian Sea. Shortly before landing in Bombay some ominous news reached the boat: Portugal had declared war on India, after Indian troops had forcibly occupied Goa and the other Portuguese possessions in India. The Indian navy had sunk a Portuguese battleship and it looked as if no foreign boat would be allowed to land in Bombay. Somehow or other the conflict ended and our ship docked during an unforgettable sunrise over Bombay.

So I was in India! My first attempts to establish contacts with Church organizations doing development work were not successful: The Jesuit-run Social Institute in Pune, which would later be moved to New Delhi, declared that they only employed collaborators from their own order. Other pertinent institutions reacted in a similar manner. I wrote to a dozen universities for syllabuses and discovered that they mostly contained literature with which

I had already been familiar. Personal contacts suggested by acquaintances brought little encouragement. One day Fr Richard De Smet from the then Papal Seminary in Pune told me about a conference that he had recently attended: a meeting of the Indian branch of the International Association of the History of Religions, organized by Swami Bon Maharaj in his Institute of Oriental Philosophy in Vrindaban, affiliated as a Postgraduate Research Institute with the University of Agra. Vrindaban is a small but famous pilgrimage town near Mathura, in Uttar Pradesh. Swami Bon, inspired by the great theological colleges that he had seen in Europe and America, had planned to establish there a Vaisnava University. In the wake of a reorganization of Indian universities he transformed it into a postgraduate Institute of Oriental Philosophy in order to retain his accreditation with the University Grants Commission. It was to have chairs representing all the major religions in addition to several distinct Hindu traditions, financed by individual Indian State Governments. There also was to be a 'St Peter's Chair of Christian Philosophy', with hoped-for support by the Catholic Church. The proposition sounded interesting to me: it would give me an opportunity to live and work in a genuine Hindu environment and to represent Christianity in an academic setting – quite a unique situation then in India. I contacted the Swami and made arrangements for a visit on an already previously planned tour through Northern India.

This trip became in many unforeseen ways crucial for my future. Not only did I see a great deal of rural central India, visiting a dozen or so mission stations in Madhya Pradesh and thus becoming acquainted with development work among the Bhils, but I also participated in quite a unique Hindu-Christian Dialogue meeting in Rajpur, near Dehra Dun, in the foothills of the Himalayas. The meeting was the second such encounter initiated by Dr Jacques-Albert Cuttat, Ambassador of Switzerland to India from 1960–64.[3] Cuttat, a former Professor of Philosophy at the Sorbonne and a scholar of comparative religion, had invited clergy from several Christian denominations in India who had shown an active interest in Hinduism, in order to talk about Hindu-Christian dialogue, a fairly novel idea at that time. The first meeting had taken place in 1961 in Almora. I had received an invitation to participate in the second meeting in Rajpur. There I had occasion to meet, besides Dr Cuttat, such celebrities as Swami Abhishiktananda, Dom Bede Griffiths, Reverend Murray Rogers and other pioneers of Hindu-Christian encounter. I felt immediately attracted both by the idea of Hindu-Christian dialogue and by the people whom I met. Dr Cuttat suggested that I write a report on it for an influential Austrian-German journal that introduced a wider circle to the then rather novel notion of dialogue between religions.[4] While the meeting itself was only attended by Christians and restricted itself to what Dr Cuttat called 'inner dialogue', it did help to open our minds and eyes to the immense spiritual riches of Hinduism and became instrumental for later meetings with Hindus.

The second major event on this trip that would shape my future was a meeting with Swami Bon Maharaj, who invited me to become the first occupant of the St Peter's Chair of Christian Philosophy in his Institute. Two months later I moved to Vrindaban with a big box of books and a great deal of enthusiasm. The Institute had a small library. One cupboard, with a label 'Christianity', contained the strangest selection of books I had ever seen: almost without exception these were works by members of one Christian church or sect directed against the teachings and practices of other Christian churches or sects, describing in lurid detail their doctrinal and moral shortcomings. One of my priorities then was to build up a basic library in my area, for which I received generous help through the good offices of Dr Anno Quadt, a former fellow student from my Roman days. Although I loved India and everything Indian, I did feel more at home in Vrindaban after I had surrounded myself also with the classics of my own cultural tradition and the great works of Christian theologians and mystics. I have written about my experiences there in a small volume that in its own time became quite popular, especially the chapter 'Theology at 120 degrees Fahrenheit', which was often quoted.[5]

I lived together with staff members and students in the Institute's hostel and established contacts with a number of townspeople, especially with *sadhus* and *swamis*. One particularly memorable local Hindu scholar, with whom I regularly met for discussions, was Dina Sarana Dasa. On parting he presented me with a small Sanskrit text by Visvanatha Cakravartin, a summary of the essence of Gaudiya Vaisnavism, that he asked me to translate.[6] Another unforgettable acquaintance was Swami Yogananda, a young Dasanami *samnyasi*, with whom I felt deeply connected in spirit and aspirations. Swami Bankey Bihari, a highly educated former lawyer, whose ashram devotions I regularly attended, and who was critical of much of the superficial religiosity of the place, wanted me to establish with him a contemplative monastery in the spirit of Teresa of Avila!

The two years that I spent there were probably the most adventurous, the most difficult and the most stimulating in my whole life. As a member of a Hindu institution – Swami Bon Maharaj often took me along on his fundraising and preaching trips or sent me as his representative to public functions – I became an 'insider', participating in the routine not only of a Hindu academic outfit but also in the daily life of one of the most vibrant places of pilgrimage in India, where literally day and night the praises of Krishna and Radha were sung. What better context could I have to complete a volume on living Hinduism, which I had been asked to write by a German publisher at the recommendation of my former doctoral adviser?[7]

I had not forgotten about my original social concerns: I derived some personal satisfaction from the fact that I was living Indian style and on an average Indian budget, earning and spending less than $1 a day, travelling on the railways third class and sharing standing-place in regular, overcrowded buses when going overland. I did not even own a bicycle. I thought that I would express my solidarity with the Indian people also in that way. I felt proud when an elderly disciple of Swami Bon Maharaj described me to visitors as a *pakka sadhu*. Although, as in all pilgrimage centres, there were great numbers of beggars, many of them disfigured by leprosy, sitting before the entrance to the temples, there did not seem to be anybody starving in Vrindaban: a number of *ksetras*, supported by pious business people, distributed free food daily. But there were nevertheless some social problem areas. Swami Bon Maharaj told me about the plight of the thousands of poor widows, mainly from Bengal, who for a pittance chanted in eight-hour shifts, day and night, the names of God for the benefit of the rich merchants that maintained these *bhajana*-ashrams.[8] Apparently, some of these widows, especially the younger ones, were also lured into some kind of prostitution in connection with the pilgrimage business and Swami Bon mentioned a scheme to help these poor women gain independence. When Agnes Kunze, a social worker from Munich, founder of a rehabilitation centre for sufferers of leprosy in Northern India came on a visit, we tried to develop some plans. But we soon ran into such massive opposition from local politicians that it was impossible to continue – they would simply blackmail me to such an extent that I would lose my visa and be expelled from the country. By law all Christian missionary activity was prohibited in the area.

Moving to Bombay after two years brought a good deal of physical and emotional relief, but I also had the feeling of being like a fish out of water – I missed the intensely religious Hindu atmosphere of Vrindaban and the contact and talks with my Hindu friends. I had been invited to apply for a part-time teaching position in Indian anthropology at the Tata Institute of Social Sciences in Bombay-Chembur, an institute that is now a university, and was proud that in a competition with Indian applicants in an interview held in Hindi, I won out and was awarded the contract.

I also had to think of completing the volume on Hinduism that I had been asked to write, side by side with my lecture preparations. My *Hinduismus* came out in late 1965 and generated a number of good reviews in major papers. It later became the basis for my *Survey of Hinduism*.[9] I received an invitation by another German publisher to write a story to be printed in a booklet offered as a Christmas gift to their customers: the editors liked my 'Indian Christmas' and asked for more such stories that eventually led to the publication of *Christ und Hindu in Vrindaban*.[10]

Having established by then good connections to a number of people interested in Hindu-Christian dialogue, I received invitations to both minor and major meetings and conferences. One of the more memorable ones was a meeting organized by Dr Douglas Steere, a Quaker, Professor of Philosophy at the Hartford Foundation, who invited seven Hindus and seven Christians for a week-long reflection on the theme 'Inner Journey' to Ootacamund in the Nilgiris – an unforgettable event in an unforgettable setting.[11] The yearly meetings of the Cuttat group came to a sudden end when Dr Cuttat suffered a serious accident while visiting Colombo. (Sri Lanka was also part of his ambassadorial responsibility.)

Meanwhile, the World Council of Churches under the urging of Stanley Samartha had opened a section for 'Dialogue' and I received an invitation to participate as one of two Roman Catholic observers at the first major meeting in Kandy, Sri Lanka. While still in Vrindaban, I had been appointed, by Pope Paul VI, *Consultor* to the newly created Vatican 'Secretariat for Non-Christians'. While the first WCC meeting was an assembly of Christian theologians and religion experts, later meetings also included representatives of other religions. The most memorable of those in which I participated took place in Ajaltoun/Beirut, Lebanon, in 1970.[12] On that occasion Professor Hassan Askari, an Indian Muslim scholar, famously summed up his evaluation of the week of common search and reflection by saying: 'I have realized in this meeting that my religion is incomplete – that all religions are incomplete without each other.'

The idea of inter-religious dialogue was something that was still very foreign to the Christian communities in Bombay, my new home base. While different religious groups had lived fairly peacefully side by side, there was little contact and even less mutual interest. To awaken some interest in dialogue I contacted a dozen or so young Christian people and invited them on Sunday afternoons to learn something about Hinduism. Some Indian nuns also joined. They had never been inside a Hindu temple. Coming from old Christian families in Kerala, they had been taught by their priests that Hindus worshipped the devil in their temples. Christian boys were encouraged to urinate against Hindu temples to show their contempt for the 'false idols'. They were greatly surprised by the things I told them about Hinduism. Slowly the idea emerged to institutionalize these contacts and I began developing an Institute of Indian Culture, originally housed at the former seminary of the Archdiocese of Bombay in Bombay-Bandra. Cardinal Gracias – the first Indian cardinal – was supportive of the idea, other churchmen less so, and we got embroiled in some controversy. Nevertheless, by 1968 the Institute was established enough to organize conjointly with the Christian Institute for the Study of Religion and Society in Bangalore, which later moved to Delhi, an International Hindu-Christian Dialogue Conference.[13] In the wake of Vatican II, I was also invited to become a member of a committee that prepared an all-India consultation of the Catholic Church, which took place in Bangalore in 1969. When pleading to have a section on spirituality, an Indian priest (he later became bishop) objected, saying that this was 'too nebulous'. The section was established nevertheless, and became one of the best attended of all.[14]

Throughout nine years I had been in the country on a student visa and I had to apply every year for an extension. I had been enrolled first at Agra and then at Bombay University[15] and kept working at my doctoral dissertation in the area of Ancient Indian History and Culture, having realized that one could not understand modern India without being thoroughly acquainted with ancient India, of which so much was still alive! Under the supervision of Professor L. B. Keny, I wrote my second thesis on 'Mythologies and philosophies of salvation in the theistic traditions of India'.[16] With my thesis completed, I could not expect to get another extension of my student visa: nine years were long enough in the opinion of the officials I had to deal with and I had to think about my future outside India and outside the ecclesiastical milieu. Around that time I met Dr Robert Slater, the founder and first director of the Harvard Center for World Religions, who was travelling through India and was interested in the work I was doing. We became good friends, and when I mentioned to him that I was looking for a position, he immediately established contact with the then Sir George Williams University in Montreal (which later became part of Concordia University) where his son Peter had been teaching at that time, whom I had chaperoned through Bombay for a short while earlier.

While waiting for an offer from Montreal I received a letter from Dr Gordon Harland, Head of a newly opened Department of Religion at the University of Manitoba. He mentioned that he had received my dossier from Sir George Williams University and asked me if I was willing to join his department as Assistant Professor for World Religions. First I consulted a world map to locate Winnipeg. Since it would have been prohibitively expensive to invite me for an interview, Dr Harland suggested I meet Dr Edward Moulton, a member of the history department of the University of Manitoba, who just then was spending a year in Delhi as the first director of the recently established Shastri Indo-Canadian Institute. On my way to Beirut, to attend a dialogue meeting of the World Council of Churches, I made a stopover in Delhi and must have impressed Dr Moulton sufficiently that soon after my return to Bombay I found a firm offer from the University of Manitoba in my mail.

Immigration formalities in those days were settled fairly quickly and I arrived in Winnipeg in July 1970 to take up my teaching position. I was asked to teach a first-year course, 'Introduction to World-Religions', a second-year course on 'Religions of Indian Origins', and a third-year seminar of my own choice, for which I chose 'Inter-religious Dialogue'. After a colleague died suddenly about a month into the term, I also took over one of his courses.

I found my students interested in what I had to say and also eager to meet me personally. Some of them I disappointed: they had expected me to tell stories about experimenting with mind-enlarging and consciousness-changing drugs. India then was the destiny of hippies who could freely indulge in narcotics prohibited in the West. Although I had been offered *bhang* from *sadhus* in Vrindaban quite regularly, I had never taken up their offers: even Hindu *samnyasis* consider its use improper. After I had received invitations from some European universities, the University of Manitoba moved quickly to promote me to full professor with tenure within three years of my arrival – an all-time record, as the Dean later told me.

The Department of Religion at the University of Manitoba developed and expanded: new positions were created, graduate programmes for MA and for PhD were established and we were proud both of the quantity and quality of our graduates. For me, life now began to move in a pattern known to all academics: classes, meetings, conferences, publications, etc. I felt honoured when my colleagues elected me Department Head in 1986. When the Dean's office advertised a competition for funds to hold a conference, I applied and won with my proposal to commemorate the twentieth year of the establishment of the Department of Religion at the University of Manitoba with an all-Canadian conference on 'Religious Studies: Past and Future'.[17] The Department re-elected me in 1991 – I declined a third five-year appointment in 1997, convinced that it is not good for anyone with serious academic interests to be more than ten years in an administrative position and that younger colleagues should also be given a chance to lead a department. I had expected to begin a five-year appointment as Academic Director of the new Oxford Centre for Hindu Studies in 1999 but had to decline because of my wife's medical condition and began a new phase of my life as emeritus, continuing to advise some graduate students and teaching occasional courses.

2   RELIGIOUS STUDIES AT PUBLIC UNIVERSITIES

The introduction of religious studies at public universities in North America in the 1960s and 70s did not take place without controversies and the debate is still going on in many quarters. It was not only a question of convincing the opponents to religious studies at supposedly secular institutions of higher learning, but also within the discipline itself sharp controversies arose on questions of content and methodology. While the first generation of teachers in religious studies departments had almost without exception a theological background, the next generation usually did not and this often led to tensions.[18]

After the initial excitement had evaporated – for many students in the 1960s and 70s taking courses in religious studies was part of their counter-culture activities – a number of departments of religious studies were closed down and some others are leading a precarious existence. In the context of a major 'restructuring' effort at the University of Manitoba, the then Dean of Arts also intended to close down our Department of Religion at the end of my tenure of Department Head in 1997. I took the opportunity of an invitation to deliver the 'Distinguished Professor Lecture' at the University of Manitoba 1997 Homecoming Celebration for presenting a case for the continued existence of the department as an independent unit. I summarized what I believed to be the legitimization for the existence of religious studies departments at public universities. I am reproducing below some sections from my lecture with the conviction that my arguments are still valid in spite of the ten years that have passed since then. Let me add that the Department of Religion at the University of Manitoba was not closed down and keeps flourishing.

2.1   *The study of religion at a public university: why–what–how*

Not long after I had begun teaching in the Department of Religion at the University of Manitoba, I received a call from the father of one of my students. One does not get too many calls from students' fathers, and this particular father sounded rather agitated. No, I had not said something outrageous in class, and no, the student did not need a time extension for an essay, and no, the student had not complained about me. It was the father who was upset that his son, a business studies major, had enrolled in my seminar entitled Masters of Spiritual Life. 'What on earth,' the father wanted to know, 'do Masters of Spiritual Life have to do with business?' Being put on the spot I said, 'Nothing.' I tried to explain to him that there were other important interests in life, besides business, and anyhow, it was his son's decision to take the course. I do not know whether I convinced him. His son stayed in my seminar and did rather well. He was genuinely interested in both his business studies and his religious studies. I have not kept in touch with him and if I met him today I would probably ask him what his religious studies course had done for him. If I had a chance to talk to his father, I probably would also give a somewhat different answer.

The larger question, asked by many, inside and outside the university, is of course: WHY? Why religious studies at public universities? Public universities are supposed to have a secular ethos, after having struggled for so long to emancipate themselves from the influence of the Churches. Especially now, when universities are under pressure to demonstrate first and foremost their contribution to the local economy, and when their main function is seen as preparing young people for a job in the real world, the question is raised with new urgency.

Many older universities in Canada – including the University of Manitoba – like most early universities of Europe, grew out of theological colleges or church-run schools. It was a long process of liberalization and of increased reliable public funding that brought about the secular university which we know today, which claims autonomy from all outside interest groups, be they political parties, religious organizations or industry and business. With few exceptions, theology was not recognized as a legitimate course of studies in most of them, and theological degrees were not honoured. 'Religion' was left to the religious bodies, to seminaries and Sunday Schools.

It was a major innovation, and one surrounded by much controversy, when religious studies made their entrance into universities in the 1960s and soon attracted a respectable number of students at all levels. The pioneers of religious studies apparently were able to convince the administrations of public universities that the study of religion was important, and that it could be undertaken in a non-confessional, academic manner. They insisted that it was not Christian theology by another name that was smuggled through the backdoors of public universities, but a genuine component of humanities.

The Department of Religion at the University of Manitoba started to teach in autumn 1968. In his account of the 'Beginnings', Gordon Harland, the founder and first head of the department, refers to the momentous events that characterized the late 1960s – the Cultural Revolution in China, the Vietnam War, the Soviet occupation of Prague, the assassinations of Martin Luther King and Robert Kennedy – and then goes on to say:

> It was a challenging context for the development of departments of religion. There was a diffused sense in the culture of the need for a religious perspective and even a quest for religious experience, but at the same time there was a growing dissatisfaction with the conventional ways of being religious. There was a keenly felt need for the resources embodied in the great religious traditions, but at the same time the very availability of their systems of meaning was radically questioned.[19]

Religion has always been important in the personal lives of many Canadians and also in the public life of the country. That was easily recognized. Within the university, many academic disciplines deal with religion in one way or another: Anthropology and sociology investigate many aspects of religion all over the world; there are numerous works of literature in all known languages that either have religious content or make use of religious symbolism; the history of art is filled with works that represent religious motives; the study of Classics is hardly thinkable without information on Greek and Roman myths, gods and goddesses. The history of any nation also includes its religious history as an important ingredient. This is true of the West and even more so of the East. One simply cannot study arts without including the study of religion.

Whatever one's personal attitude may be, nobody can deny the enormous influence that religion has had on humankind throughout known history (and probably long before that). Its influence, as we all know, was not always for good. '*Tantum malorum potuit suadere religio*' (So much evil religion could persuade people to do!), complained an ancient Roman author – even before Christianity or Islam had arisen. We know well how many more evils have since been caused by religion! It needs the open and critical setting of a public university to study religions and their influence for good and for ill in a detached and objective manner.

The ethos of the secular university with its critical and rational approach to all spheres of life has certainly had a great influence on the development of the discipline of religious studies. In turn, we like to think that the work that we in religious studies have done, often in close conjunction with colleagues in other disciplines, has changed the perception of 'religion' in the minds of many students and faculty. To cite the example of my own department at University of Manitoba: In the numerous master's and doctoral theses completed in the Religion Department, a wide range of issues were dealt with, involving the cooperation of faculty from the Departments of English, French, German, Slavic Studies, History, Native Studies, Asian Studies, Sociology, Classics, Geography, Psychology, Political Studies, Mathematics, Physics, Environmental Studies, Architecture, Linguistics, Genetics and others. The department has profited a great deal from the interaction with colleagues from these departments and we at the Department of Religion like to think that they, in turn, did too. At the very least, as Harold Coward, founding director of the University of Victoria's Centre for the Study of Religion and Society and former Head of the Department of Religious Studies at the University of Calgary pointed out, 'The develop- ment of Religious Studies as a separate department added strength to the Humanities or Arts faculties at a time when there was pressure to move more and more resources into the rapidly expanding professional faculties.'[20]

If we succeeded in persuading our 'secular' colleagues of the relevance of what we are doing in religious studies, on the grounds of its importance in the context of the other humanistic disciplines, we ourselves have a great many additional reasons from within our discipline for advocating religious studies in the framework of public universities. As Raimon Panikkar once said:

> Human beings have a constitutive religious dimension. Every cultural activity contains more or less conspicuous religious elements insofar as it is an activity of the whole human being. Religious Studies has something to say regarding atomic research, nationalism, justice and peace, so that this discipline may often appear to challenge the predominant ideologies. Religious Studies similarly challenges religious institutions, both in their day-to-day operations and in their guiding assumptions and presupposi- tions ... The thoroughgoing critique of religion belongs essentially to Religious Studies, and this often may be sensed – rightly or wrongly – as a threat to more than one religious organization.[21]

We believe that the texts we are studying are not only important landmarks in the cultural history of humankind, but that they are dealing with issues of universal and ultimate human importance that are not discussed in other departments. They are testimonies to the perennial wrestling of humans with the mysteries of life and death, of guilt and grace, of fate and self-determination. They contain myths of profound significance and add reflections with deep meaning. They represent a treasury of long-time human experience with the world and with the transcendent – a living fountain from which we believe we can draw in order to cope with our own lives and our own problems. While refraining from any particular claim with regard to any particular scriptures, we nevertheless tend to believe that they are a special kind of literature, with a peculiar power to move the hearts and the minds of people, addressing a deeper dimension that calls for a personal response. To bring this to bear on contemporary women and men, we feel to be our 'mission' in a Department of Religious Studies: our mission within the overall mission of the public university. We believe that we are raising important questions that are not raised anywhere else in the university and that we are able to open up resources for answering these questions that are not available elsewhere.

By doing so, we are treading on dangerous ground; ground that had been claimed for centuries as their own by the Churches and the professional representatives of established traditional religions. This is probably the reason why religious studies at public universities met with more opposition from fundamentalist theologians than from atheist philosophers. We are not claiming privileged knowledge for ourselves, but we believe that questions of ultimate meaning can be and must be approached from many angles and that these diverse answers given by humans in different parts of the world are meaningful in an intellectual as well as in an existential way. The narrowing down of the Path to a thin line hedged in by often questionable propositions and outdated rules, as has frequently been practised by religious denominations and confessions, does harm not only to people but also to the cause of religion itself. Many souls have been wounded and warped by sectarian teachings that parade as divine revelation, and much damage has been done to young minds by self-centred autocrats that demanded blind obedience in the name of religion, instead of answering legitimate questions. Religious studies, by broadening the perspectives and by allowing critical examination of the issues concerned, has helped many young persons to find their own way intellectually and spiritually and to dispel the paranoia created by narrow-minded bigotry.

One cannot really study great works of art without being stirred in one's depth, if one is a sensitive human being; one cannot explore great music without being shaped in one's tastes and perceptions, if one has any sense for music at all. Similarly, one cannot read great religious classics without a sense of coming in touch with a reality that transcends the humdrum of everyday life, a reality that reassures and challenges at a profound level. Religious studies are not only concerned with the past, but with the present as well: great works of religion are still being written; great people, inspired by religion to perform heroic deeds, are still among us.

The 'WHAT' of religious studies is to some extent determined by the 'WHY': To quote Gordon Harland again, describing the planning of the new Religion Department's curriculum:

> It was thought that whatever else was dealt with in the curriculum, the department should pay particular attention to two things. First courses should be developed which would deal with the classical texts, persons and movements of the great religious traditions of both East and West; second courses should be developed in which these traditions and perspectives could fruitfully engage the intellectual, spiritual, and social issues of the time.[22]

It was one of the concerns of the founders of religious studies that religion be studied not only objectively and critically, but also comprehensively and in a spirit of pluralism. 'Introduction to World Religions' became the basic and the most popular course. A generation that prides itself on being world citizens, of living in the global village and participating in a global economy, should be informed about the lives of other peoples, the cultures of other continents, the ideas of other philosophies and religions. Religious studies from their very beginning had a range and an openness still missing in most other university disciplines: for religious studies it is a matter of course to look at Indian and Chinese traditions alongside Western Christian, Jewish or Islamic notions when dealing with large ideas or important concepts. Knowing how intimately in many cultures religion is intertwined with its entire history, students of world religions learn considerably more than merely about 'religion' in the narrow sense of the word.

The agenda of religious studies evolved over the decades, ever since Religious Studies Departments were founded. While on principle pluralistic, the experts available in the first few years were coming mainly from Christian theological backgrounds. Scripture scholars, church historians and moral theologians formed the bulk of early faculty of Religious Studies Departments, with only a few experts in non-Western traditions available. Within a few years the situation changed and specialists in Asian religions were appointed, often themselves adherents of these. The interaction between Western scholars with a Christian theological background with Asian religions experts brought about a new approach to religious studies that soon became visible both in classroom teaching and in publications. Issues-oriented courses like religious ethics no longer restricted themselves to biblical, Jewish and Christian sources, but included Buddhist, Hindu, Islamic and other materials that became increasingly available. Film and video series were developed, providing visual introductions to the cultures in which non-Western religions play leading roles. They familiarized students not only with new concepts but also with new sights and sounds. By now several thousand academics teaching and writing on religious studies have produced an impressive number of publications that give a good idea of what religious studies are concerned with. Many classical texts, from a great variety of ancient and modern languages have been translated by religious studies scholars, many aspects of historic and contemporary religions have been studied in great detail, and many important issues have been illuminated by reflections from a religious studies perspective. Questions like what makes religious studies different from theology on the one hand and sociology or anthropology of religion on the other are constantly being debated in religious studies journals, and there is no lack of self-criticism in this young and vigorous discipline.

Departments of Religious Studies offer a broad spectrum of introductions into the various great religions as well as problem-oriented courses, usually with a pluralistic agenda. There are many 'Religion and ...' courses that attempt to throw bridges across disciplines and that try to prove the relevance of religion in a variety of areas of general concern. There is 'Religion and Science', an area that has blossomed lately, with hundreds of scientists and religionists engaged in probing common assumptions and possibilities of interaction between these two vast and influential areas of human enterprise. There is 'Religion and Literature', studying not only literary classics that deal with religious themes but also demonstrating the continued pervasive presence of religious motifs in contemporary literature. There is 'Religion and Women', an exciting new dimension of religious studies, redressing not only the gender deficit of traditional patriarchal religions, but also empowering women to take a leading role in shaping religion and religious studies. There is 'Religion and Art', a large field not only in terms of historic materials, but also in terms of contemporary artistic production and exciting theoretical implications. The list goes on ...

As religions themselves are inextricably interwoven with the cultures in which they live, so also religious studies are part and parcel of the intellectual fabric of the university. They give and they receive and thus prove their life and their relevance. And as religions, where they are alive, change and respond to new challenges, religious studies change and respond to the new situations they are facing.

The students taking religious studies have also changed. In the beginning, especially in the United States, students taking religious studies considered this as a counter-culture activity, as protest against a society dominated by the industrial-military complex. Today's students are doing religious studies because it interests them personally, and because it complements other subjects. In my first, rather large class on 'Religions of Indian Origin' in the early 1970s, students eagerly wanted to hear from me, as I noted above, whether my experiences in India had included smoking hash and taking mind-expanding drugs. They were quite disappointed that I had nothing to report along these lines. In my rather small classes on 'Religions of Indian Origin' in the 1990s, students wanted to know which books to read and what papers to write, so that they could gain some insights into issues of personal relevance to them.

The 'HOW' of religious studies is largely determined by the overall mission of a university, as understood today, namely to generate, transmit and preserve worthwhile knowledge and thus to contribute to the development of an educated and well-informed citizenry. I sometimes hear Church people criticize religious studies for its 'lack of commitment'. What they mean, probably, is the absence of a 'faith' stance, the lack of a definite creed, the refusal to ascribe ultimate truth to one particular set of statements. Possibly they also deplore our non-involvement in moral causes sponsored by the Churches. That, however, is necessitated by the nature of academia: we deal with ideas and concepts that people must translate for themselves into actions and decisions in their 'real' lives. In their own way religious studies *are* committed: they are committed to finding truth – truth in religion, truth about religions, a depth dimension in life, and the relevance of spiritual concerns for all human beings.

In Europe, religious studies are often conducted under the name of *Religionswissenschaft*, History of Religion, or Comparative Religion. Theologians used to wisecrack that comparative religion made one 'comparatively religious', implying thereby that theologians were genuinely religious. Religious studies have broadened and deepened the very notion of religion. Where Christian theological works of an earlier period spoke contemptuously of 'heathenism' and 'superstition', of 'false religions' and misguided human efforts at self-redemption, religious studies have created an understanding for traditions past and present that operate on very different presuppositions. The language of religious studies has meanwhile also reached Faculties of Theology, who have come to acknowledge the existence and importance, if not the legitimacy, of other religions, which they formerly did not. Very often, as it turns out, modern young people also in the West find access to the transcendent much more readily and joyously through Buddhist *suttas* or Hindu *upanishads*, through Sufi *ghazals* or Zen *koans* than through traditional Christian Sunday School teaching or dogmatic theology. Many young people belonging to a particular religious community have told us over the years that through religious studies they learned not only to appreciate other religions, but also were led to a better understanding and cherishing of their own.

The notion of academic freedom may not be entirely free from ambiguities, but in the case of religious studies it certainly has proved to be an unambiguous blessing. Most faculty in religious studies, who are members of synagogues or churches, temples or mosques, would have been expelled from their teaching positions in theological schools, had they taught there what they teach here. We can freely critique authorities on the basis of our own insights and we do not have to conform in our expressions of what we hold to be true to what a particular agency has regulated as such. We do not have to pretend to have found *the* Truth but we can be content with publishing what we think to be true. Our students can argue with us and criticize us, and we all have learned and continue to learn a great deal in this way.

Life, as we all know, is a constant give and take. Intellectual life is not different. Religious studies have benefited much by the religious traditions that have guided humankind through the ages: we would not have the Vedas, the Pali Canon, the Bible, the Koran and all the other scriptures which we study, if these had not been cherished and preserved by the communities of Hindus, Buddhists, Jews, Christians and Muslims and all the others. Similarly, the thoughts laid down in the works of religious thinkers whom we read, such as Nagarjuna, Shantideva, Shankara, Ramanuja, Ibn Arabi, Moses Maimonides, Thomas Aquinas, Paul Tillich and countless others, would not have been what they are but for the confessional positions they entertained. While attempting an independent stance, religious studies would be untrue to themselves if they neglected these intellectual giants.

Religious studies have also been given much by the secular public university. Public universities have provided material support and a framework of freedom for teaching and research; they have put at our disposal a vast array of knowledge assembled in many different fields and offered a vital stimulus for the interaction between religious studies and other disciplines.

What are religious studies giving in return? They certainly have given to religious traditions a much-needed widening of horizons, have made informed inter-religious dialogue possible, have provided much spadework for the scholarly study of their sources and, in general, probably have made many people interested in religion, who otherwise would not have been so. Religious studies have also given something in return to the public universities. Apart from establishing viable academic units with programmes that are found attractive by students, religious studies have reintroduced into the modern university issues and concerns that were missing, and by engaging other disciplines they have stimulated these into rethinking their own assumptions. If Theodor Roszak, in the early 1970s, found the 'essential religious impulse exiled from our culture' and deplored the effects this had on the quality of our lives, we believe that religious studies have drawn attention to 'the part the energies of transcendence must play', to use Roszak's own words.[23]

Religious studies must be done in a spirit of dialogue: a dialogue between religion and the other humanities; a dialogue between religion and the social sciences; a dialogue between religion and science; a dialogue between the various religions; a dialogue between different exponents of the same tradition. In its few decades of existence, religious studies have accomplished a great deal in all of these areas. Scholarly associations cultivating Hindu–Christian, Buddhist–Christian, Hindu–Jewish and other dialogues have been founded. A large network of religious studies scholars and scientists has developed, promoting communication between religions and science.

A new type of religious person is developing: shunning traditional pieties and ostentatious religious behaviour, uncomfortable with authoritarian attitudes and the identification of religion with certain formulae or historic regulations, the new religious person is sensitive for the 'religious dimension' of all of life. The new religious person is open to the articulation of spirituality from every source and has a 'vision born of transcendent knowledge'.[24] We would like to think that the by now many thousands of students who took religious studies at public universities do make a difference in their religious communities and in society at large.

Much that was said when arguing for the initial establishment of Religious Studies Departments I believe is still valid, perhaps even more so now: the humanities today are under even greater pressure than in the 1960s; the trend towards seeing the university in terms of professional education and marketability of its 'products' has increased; the overall resources have shrunk; the student population has become smaller; the costs of studying have risen dramatically.

The 1960s were characterized by violent conflict and rebellion against authorities, by liberation movements and the polarization of the world between West and East, Capitalism and Communism. The world today has become conscious of the ecological imperative. Computers and the internet have become part of everybody's life, women-power is recognized, permanent employment has become scarce, and the whole world has become one hugely competitive marketplace for everything. Religious studies in the 1960s addressed the issues of the 1960s: they sympathetically studied liberation movements, they helped to transcend the narrow cultural confines that were responsible for so much misunderstanding between people, they promoted tolerance, they emphasized dialogue as a means to overcome conflicts, and they helped young people to find their identity in their own culture. Religious studies now engage the environment, create awareness for women's roles, participate in the debate about a global ethic, promote peace studies and continue to confront young people with the great and perennial questions that every generation has to face and to answer anew. Religious studies also engage in self-criticism, a necessary and important academic activity as long as it does not turn into self-destruction.

3   REFLECTIONS AND SUGGESTIONS

By the time we reach as students the stage of writing an MA or a PhD dissertation, we have had exposure to a variety of teachers and approaches to the field. We usually select as thesis adviser someone whose philosophy and attitude we perceive as congenial. As teachers and thesis supervisors we are giving personal advice to individual students on specific issues. An ever-changing culture and the varying interests of new generations demand that advising remain flexible and up to date. However, looking back, one notices that one does maintain certain basic positions with regard to the field as a whole as well as on particular issues.[25] I have always taken a religious approach to religious studies and I left it to sociologists, anthropologists, philosophers and psychologist to develop anti-religious positions on the basis of their specific ideologies.

Religion, in Paul Tillich's famous expression, is dealing with questions of 'ultimate concern'. Although a well-known scientist not disingenuously countered that for most people money was the ultimate concern, those who choose religious studies as a career probably would not do so if they were not siding with Tillich rather than with his friendly critic.

Religions everywhere have always dealt with real life-issues: a study of religion has to throw light on these and yield insights that matter to all people and not only to academics. While the expectations of the early repre-sentatives of *Religionswissenschaft* to distil from the teachings of the world's religions a kind of universal religion could not be fulfilled, their study has shown that all of them converge on some central questions of 'ultimate concern'. Robert Zaehner in his *Concordant Discord* used the image of a 'symphony of faiths' – each instrument has its distinct sound and character, but many different instruments can be brought together to play in one and the same orchestral piece. In their eagerness to distance themselves from (confessional) theologians, representatives of the academic study of religion sometimes go so far as to shun all the deeper issues of traditional religious thought and to withdraw to the superficialities of linguistic analysis and anthropological/sociological data-collection.

A misunderstood *'science* of religion' tried to ape what it considered 'the scientific method', in the belief that this constituted the only way to being accepted by the 'secular' academic community.[26] Thoughtful scientists have always cautioned that the so-called scientific method – largely consisting of quantification and mathematical formalization of observations – is neces-sarily limited in its scope and is far from leading to a full understanding even of the natural world, not to speak of cultural phenomena or personal human concerns. 'Science,' Nobel Prize winning physicist Erwin Schroedinger once remarked, 'is maintaining an eerie silence in the face of everything that is really near to our hearts and that is deeply moving us.' Among the things that 'are really near to our hearts', about which science is silent, Schroedinger explicitly mentioned 'God and Eternity'.[27]

In the modern university, largely a creation of the European Enlightenment, 'critical' and 'academic' have become almost synonymous. As part of modern academia, religious studies do not advocate a confessional exposition of religious beliefs in university classrooms, but resort to a critical description of their history and literatures. However, critique by itself cannot be the ultimate aim of academic study. It has to be conscious of its own limits. As Ludwig Feuerbach, certainly considered a critical mind in his own time, remarked: 'You learn to think only by thinking, you recognize truth only through truthfulness, you understand love only if you are loving – you can learn nothing through mere critique.'[28] Using a comparison that may not sound politically correct today, but whose message can still be understood, he added: 'Critique is the housemaid in the realm of knowledge, she is cleaning out. Everything will go to pieces if she wants to be more than a servant.'

The role of a teacher of religious studies at a public university is neither that of a self-destructive critic, nor of a sectarian preacher, but that of an intelligent exponent of what religions in their universality stand for. If the representatives of religious study do not care for religion, who will? It would be unconscionable arrogance to assume that all those who developed the great religious and cultural traditions before us were totally mistaken in their views of reality, and that the ephemeral perspective of a contemporary statistics-based social science or a questionable reductionist psychology should provide the appropriate methodology for religious studies. Religions as human institutions must certainly be subject to scrutiny and critique: but religious studies must judge religions from a religious standpoint to do them justice and to have a worthwhile subject matter.

We must take religions seriously as religions. We do not really understand religions if we only collect objective data connected with their history, their literature and their outward manifestations. To reduce religious studies to a sub-discipline of sociology or anthropology, of literary criticism or psychology, would be tantamount to denying its identity: it would prevent it from making its most important contribution to present-day academia, namely to provide a much needed 'supplement of soul', to quote physicist Erwin Schroedinger again.[29] 'Soul' stands for more than mere analytic intellect and conceptual abstraction. Religions express themselves not only in verbalized doctrines and commandments, but also in song and music, in architecture and sculpture, in poetry and painting, at the level of folk culture as well as on the level of high art. It is not by chance that much of what religions consider their 'Holy Scriptures' is in the form of poetry, often recited to musical tunes and that images play such a great role in most of them. Religions always had and have a component of feeling in addition to the intellectual quest, and they always tried to shape the mores of their adherents. If philosophers today rediscover the importance of emotions in human life, they simply restate what religions had always known. The fact that religious emotions have often been overstressed and artificially blown up does not speak against their importance. Similarly, the fact that political leaders have misused religion for political aims and that religions have often been unable to impress their moral standards on their adherents, does not invalidate the principle of a religious foundation for ethical norms. Religious studies cannot bracket out these vital areas and restrict itself to a linguistic analysis of doctrinal statements and creeds.

Historically, religions have not only produced systems of thought about God and the world, but they have also engaged in transforming people: the difference between a member and a non-member lies not only in a different set of beliefs, but more so in a different set of practices: a Buddhist has to practise meditation; a Christian has to say regular prayers; a Muslim must observe the daily times of *salat*; a Vaisnava has to worship a sacred image – these few references will be enough to make the point. Meditation, prayer and worship are not only external identification marks; they transform the personality. When I lived for two years among Hindus in Vrindaban, I was never questioned: 'What do you believe?' but I was often asked: 'What is your *sadhana*?' i.e. the practice I had chosen to reach the ultimate aim.

Unmusical persons do not make convincing musicologists. Reducing all of music to the physics of sound may be all right for a sound-technician but it would not do justice to a genuine musician's understanding of music. A certain 'musicality' is required also for the study of religion. Also genuine empathy is needed with the particular tradition that one makes the main focus of one's study.[30] Someone who hates musical instruments should not become a musician, however justified the personal dislike of a particular kind of noise produced by a particular instrument may be. Similarly, an anti-religious attitude is not a good starting point for understanding religion, however bad an experience someone may have had with persons or institutions associated with a particular religion. While wine can be made into vinegar, the opposite is not the case. One can critically deconstruct religion, but one cannot reconstruct religion from mere negative critique. It cannot be the purpose of religious studies to turn the precious old wine of religious insight into the vinegar of contemporary cynicism.

Moreover, it is not good enough for religious studies to focus on scurrilities associated with certain local manifestations of religion. No doubt religious people have been very fertile in producing oddities and strange behaviour; just as the study of physics cannot be reduced to stories about quirks and foibles of great physicists – which they undoubtedly possessed – so also, religious studies cannot be exhausted with narratives about ridiculous customs developed in a particular religious tradition. It would be more profitable to focus on the essentials that the religions themselves consider crucial in reaching their goals.

We have to take the great traditions seriously as the repositories of the experiences and reflections also of many generations of intellectuals and as guides to understanding religion in its naturally grown historic context. They do contain much that reflects the limited knowledge of earlier generations in some areas where a more recent science has provided better information and they do maintain positions in some other areas that we reject today. But they did keep the great human questions alive and they provided answers that are still worth pondering. They also demonstrate the long and painful process of articulating profound insights and applying their ramifications in day-to-day life. Our present understanding of the processes of nature as well as our laws and social conventions will appear to some future generations as outdated and as scurrile as those of earlier ages appear to us.[31] We could be proud if the rest of our thinking would remain as relevant as that of the great ancient and medieval exponents of traditional Buddhism and Hinduism, Taoism and Confucianism, Judaism, Christianity and Islam, whose writings we study!

One of the graduate seminars that my students enjoyed most and remembered best was entitled 'Masters of Spiritual Life', in which we read and discussed classics of spirituality from different traditions, ancient and modern. Often students remarked how relevant and pertinent they found many of these texts! Textual studies seem to have receded into the background of religious studies parallel to the diminishing of interest in literature in the humanities as such. They should regain a central place again. Paying attention to ancient texts implies the need to study the original languages in which they were written. While in principle every language should be translatable into every other language, as a matter of fact many important and profound texts written in a certain language cannot be translated into another language without great loss of meaning and significance. Quite a few religious traditions insist that only the original language be used in ritual settings and that the original has a power of its own that is lost in translations. A sacred text is more than a source of information about matters of general interest. Those who have studied any of the sacred languages and have become familiar with the associations that the original words evoke – associations not connected with even the best scholarly translations – will understand the indispensability of language studies.

Religious studies also should have something to say to today's problems: they should be 'relevant'! Relevance does not consist of playing to the galleries, but in the judicious addressing of real issues. For anybody who has followed world affairs in the past few years, it should be obvious that religion in many parts of the world is of great relevance to people and of great importance in far-reaching political decisions.

Some issues will always remain relevant – humankind has been asking certain questions since its beginning – whereas others do change: therefore one should avoid overspecializing too soon. It may be attractive to carve out one's own little niche and to become a specialist in an area that no one else knows anything about. Unless one finds an institution that pays one for just cultivating that hobbyhorse, one should keep one's interests wide open and flexible. We must beware of academic fashions: they are shortlived and usually of little intrinsic merit. Someone may impress some people for some time by following every academic fad – ten years later one cannot stand reading that once fashionable writing!

We also must acquire first-hand experience in our areas of competence. All religions have their historic, linguistic and geographic bases and are practised by people living in particular places that shape their inhabitants in many ways: unless one has lived with them and has come to know the specifics, one should not talk or write about them! Nothing can replace first-hand and personal experience: it will also help to interpret other people's writings.

Having experienced a religion first hand provides a feel for the real issues and makes one go for these, rather than force upon religious studies a set of problems derived from literary criticism, psychology or sociology. To mention one important example of 'applied religious studies': inter-religious dialogue. Living religions are concerned with real humans and their destiny; they express their concerns through a variety of means.

'No (wo)man is an island' – as scholars we are not lone stars shining on a heaven of our own making but we are always members of a community of teachers and researchers in a variety of different disciplines. While there is competitive pressure to individually get established in a specialism, in the end we thrive or perish as a community. For me, a major scholarly stimulus was provided by colleagues in the natural sciences and in fine arts. Besides my professional interests in India and religion, I always kept reading in the natural sciences. I noticed also in my contacts with Hindus in India that they often supported their scriptural expositions with references to modern sciences. One of the important contacts I made in India was with Carl Friedrich von Weizsaecker, a physicist turned philosopher, who also was interested in Indian thought. I met him when he visited India in his capacity as delegate of a development agency – Professor Steere of Ootacamund had told him about me and he contacted me in Bombay to talk to me. He invited me in subsequent summers as scholar-in-residence to the Max Planck Institute that he had founded and directed and we kept in touch over many years, exchanging ideas on India, development, science and religion. When beginning to teach at the University of Manitoba, I was happy to discover in Robin Connor, then Dean of Science, a physicist with complementary interests in religion. Our team-taught graduate seminars in Science and Religion not only yielded a coveted Templeton Course Award but also gave me immense intellectual stimulation and satisfaction.[32]

Universities expect their faculty to be active in research, to become recognized through their publications by their peers worldwide and effectively to contribute to the advancement of knowledge in their fields.[33] Star quality in research has often been emphasized to the detriment of teaching. While research of the highest calibre is often going on also outside universities in industry-related centres, teaching is the central social mission of the university. Universities have to provide comprehensive advanced education to the citizens of their locality and all those who choose to live there. Teaching, as we all know – actively as teachers, passively as students – is more than textbook-drill. Teaching – especially in the humanities – is the means to communicate insights, to stimulate independent thinking, to educate.

Most of our students will not become professional religious studies scholars, but many will be holding responsible positions in administration, will become doctors, dentists, lawyers or teachers, in elementary schools and in high schools. A course in religious studies is often the entry to a world of ideas and values absent in the rest of their university studies, leading to a lifelong interest in things other than professional matters. I always consider it a compliment when former students tell me that they have kept reading lists of my courses, sometimes for decades, to choose their leisure-time serious reading from it.

While engaged in religious studies we should not be satisfied with 'counting other people's cows', but we should also feel personally challenged by the writings of great religious teachers and understand the implications for our own lives.[34] Although not preachers of a religious sect or teachers of a particular orthodoxy, we certainly must have a feel for that dimension of reality that religions are concerned with. The thoughts and practices through which untold generations expected to reach inner peace and personal fulfilment should not simply be relegated to footnotes in a 'critical' article. People today are as much in need of establishing contact with the unseen Presence, and they can derive as much comfort from it as did former generations.

We have chosen to teach at a university and do research in a particular field because we love to do it: we enjoy our work! This is a privilege, shared by only few others. I once heard someone say: We are being paid for our hobbies! A large proportion of the joy and satisfaction we find in our work derives from contact with our students and our colleagues. Eager students and supportive colleagues are a real blessing and we should not only be grateful for this gift, but also actively reciprocate. While competition is a fact of academic life, it should be tempered by a sense of collegiality. Egomaniac lone-star scholars may win honours and promotions, but they usually are not very happy people.

Scholarship takes time, a lot of time, and often we enjoy it so much that we forget to devote enough of our time and attention to our nearest and dearest. This is a shortcoming few of us will be able to completely absolve ourselves from. But we have to work at it: we owe so much also as scholars to our families that we must repay the debt to them as generously as possible. Expressions of gratitude to marriage partners in the prefaces to learned tomes are not empty gestures, but recognition of genuine and essential support.

To end my reflections and connect with where I began: I did not realize my original ambitions, but in retrospect I believe that by accepting the chances and challenges that the circumstances offered, I could not do more for my beloved India than what I have done, had I been able to follow my original plans. Not that India does not need socio-economic development, but it also needs understanding and appreciation of its people and its culture, genuine sympathy for its spiritual and religious aspirations. Having been assured by Hindus that they recognized their traditions in what I described as 'Hinduism',[35] I hope that I made a modest contribution to the mutual understanding between East and West. Seeking Truth and fostering Peace seem to me the two great missions of religious studies – and the two might well be one and the same.[36]

7

Studying Religion in South Africa

DAVID CHIDESTER (UNIVERSITY OF CAPE TOWN)

For over 20 years, I have been studying religion and politics in South Africa. When I was a graduate student, happy to be a graduate student in Santa Barbara, California, this was certainly not my intention. I wanted to study religion and poetry. Having been formed, for better or worse, within the intense politics and poetics of the 1960s, I was more poeticized than politicized. For me, moving out of the United States, moving to South Africa, changed everything. Even my poetics became politicized.

In Santa Barbara, I had written a doctoral dissertation, which had been about the poetics of seeing and hearing in religious discourse, but it suffered in this relocation. Revising it for publication, as an experiment, testing the academic waters, I sent the manuscript out to 12 university presses, with a preface that began: 'I have lost interest in this topic.' Understandably, I received 12 rejection letters. Why would any press publish a book that did not even interest the author? But I was struggling with my relocation to South Africa. Seeing and hearing, I thought, are obviously still important. However, as I said in a revised preface, 'I find myself more recently compelled to pay attention to a different range of perceptual metaphors frequently drawn upon in the formation of religious discourse within my present working environment. In fact, my research interests have moved in entirely different directions as the result of such things as the accidents of geography, the force of events, and the pressures of working in a highly charged, politicized, and even violent place ... the perceptual metaphors of more immediate (and, I should say, more pressing) concern are tactile – the powerful metaphors of oppression and resistance.'[1] So, there I was, finding myself in South Africa.

Today, as any tourist brochure might tell you, South Africa is a multireligious country. Although over 70 per cent of South Africans claim allegiance to Christianity, South Africa is home for a variety of religious traditions – indigenous African, Muslim, Jewish, Hindu, Buddhist and others – that have established strong, vital constituencies. With a deep and enduring African religious heritage, South Africa is a country that embraces all the major world religions. Each of these religions, including Christianity, is a diverse category, encompassing many different understandings of religious life. At the same time, many South Africans draw their under-standing of the world, ethical principles and human values from sources independent of religious institutions. In the most profound matters of life orientation, diversity is a fact of South African national life.

Given the diversity of language, culture and religion in South Africa, the post-apartheid government of South Africa, which came to office after the first democratic elections of 1994, has sought ways to turn diversity from a potential obstacle to nationalism into a national resource, seeking not uniformity but unity, as the new Coat of Arms urges: 'Diverse people unite.' Endeavouring to come to terms with the legacy of apartheid, the South African government has worked to find new ways of transforming the vicious divisions of the past into the vital diversity of a free, open and democratic society.

But I had arrived in apartheid South Africa, living in a political system based on exclusion and incorporation, the exclusion of the black majority from citizenship and the incorporation of the black majority as exploitable labour. That was apartheid politics. In recent accounts of the South African transition from apartheid to democracy, analysts have been divided between those framing the process as an 'anatomy of a miracle'[2] or 'a miracle mis-understood'.[3] The South African 'miracle', however, still bears traces, deep traces, of a long history of slavery, colonialism and apartheid. The political struggle continues, but the poetic struggle also continues; an ongoing struggle to make sense in which the study of religion can play a part.

Over the past 20 years, I have found South Africa to be a particularly fruitful place to study religion. I have learned a lot just by being here. Very briefly, let me identify five things this place has taught me about defining, theorizing, humanizing, nationalizing and globalizing religion.

1   DEFINING RELIGION

First, South Africa has taught me about the politics of defining religion. Here I learned that *religion* has always been an inherently oppositional term. The ancient Latin, *religio*, whatever it might have meant – and there is so much dispute about what it might have meant that we can almost conclude that nobody has ever known what it meant – was inevitably defined in opposition to *superstitio*. In whatever way *religio* might have been under-stood in Latin antiquity, whether as pious repetition, as paying attention, or as binding relations, it was always understood in contrast to its opposite, *superstitio*. I like to say that the great linguist, Emile Benveniste, taught us about the oppositional definition of *religio*, because he observed that in ancient Roman usage the piety of *religio* was defined as the contrary of the ignorance, fear and fraud of *superstitio*. As Benveniste wrote, 'the notion of "religion" requires, so to speak, by opposition, that of "superstition".'[4] I have cited this insight many times,[5] but I would not have recognized it as an insight at all if I had not found that this oppositional definition of religion had been definitive in South African history.

From a South African perspective, our keyword, 'religion', did not come from Greco-Roman antiquity or the European Enlightenment. It came from the sea in ships. It was carried by European travellers, traders, missionaries and colonial administrators, who first deployed it as an instrument of denial, as a weapon, by reporting that Africans had no religion. Sometimes, European sailors just looked over the side of the boat and found that people on the land had no religion. Eventually, they entered contested frontiers and found that people on the battlefield had no religion and therefore had no right to the land.

This colonial dynamic of discovering vacant land, which was vacant because of religious defects or absences among the people inhabiting the land, was a constant and recurring theme, repeated all over the world, as a supplement to European overseas expansion. People who allegedly lacked such an important human faculty as religion were also alleged to be less than fully human and therefore to have no human rights to their land, their live-stock, or control over their own labour. Defining religion, therefore, meant something.

Against a backdrop of worrying about diverse laws and sects,[6] Europeans were prepared to recognize a diversity of religions, beyond the two religions, Protestant and Catholic, which were included when the word 'religions' first appeared in English in the 1590s,[7] to incorporate Christians, Jews, Muslims and the extremely vague but potentially expansive category of Pagans under the generic designation, 'religion'.[8] Therefore, finding that people had 'no religion' was not the same as finding people who were not Christians. Peformatively, it was a denial of their humanity.

Although this denial of religion can be interpreted as a strategic interven-tion in contested territory, the 'discovery' of indigenous African religions in nineteenth-century southern Africa was also situated in the management and control of local populations. On the Eastern Cape frontier, for example, every European intruder, whether traveller, trader, missionary or colonial agent, consistently found that indigenous Xhosa-speaking people lacked any trace of religion, allegedly living, by contrast, in a world of superstition, until their political independence was destroyed and they were placed under the authority of a colonial administrative system. In 1858, the colonial magis-trate, J. C. Warner, reported on the 'religious system' of the Xhosa who had been shattered by colonial warfare and contained within the colonial 'village system'. With the imposition of this colonial administrative system for native control, surveillance and tax collection, Warner discovered that the Xhosa actually had a religion, even a religious system, that counted as a religion because it fulfilled the two basic functions of any religious system by providing a sense of psychological security and reinforcing social stability.

According to this proto-functionalist in the Eastern Cape, therefore, the Xhosa had a religious system that could be reduced to these psychological and social functions – security and stability – that oddly duplicated the aims of the colonial administrative system in keeping people in place.[9]

Rather than representing an advance in human recognition, this discovery of an indigenous religious system was a strategy of colonial containment that mirrored the structure of the magisterial system, location system or reserve system.[10] With the destruction of the last independent African polity in the 1890s, when every African was in principle contained within an urban location system or a rural reserve system, European observers found that every African man, woman and child shared the same religious system, which was designated as 'Bantu religion' that fulfilled psychological and social functions that kept people in their place.

Finding our keyword, 'religion', situated within this history of denial and containment, we might want to abandon the word entirely. But I do not think we can shake off this colonial legacy so easily. I think we are stuck with the word, for better or worse, so we are faced with the ongoing challenge of engaging 'religion' as an occasion for critical reflection and creative analysis.

2   THEORIZING RELIGION

Second, South Africa has taught me about the history of theorizing religion, the cultural, social and political history of theorizing religion. In graduate school, I learned that my academic discipline had a founder, F. Max Müller, whose 1870 lectures in London on the science of religion inaugurated an academic study of religion. Of course, I also learned that everything he said was wrong, but at least I had a founding ancestor in an ancestral lineage that included other late-Victorian British intellectuals, such as E. B. Tylor, Andrew Lang and James Frazer. Rereading their work in South Africa, I realized they were not just talking about religion; they were talking about us. Their theorizing about the original, 'primitive', religion was directly related to British imperial ambitions and colonial adventures in South Africa.

In the case of F. Max Müller, I found that his theorizing about religion was informed not only by the library of the 'Sacred Books of the East', but also by the scope of the British Empire, especially by its imperial anchors in India and South Africa. As an expert in Sanskrit, translator of the Vedas and commentator on the religious traditions of India, Max Müller might be expected to have a professional and perhaps even political interest in India. His ongoing, lifelong interest in South Africa might be surprising. But he corresponded with early researchers in South Africa from the mid-1850s – the Anglican Bishop J. W. Colenso, the philologist W. H. I. Bleek and the missionary ethnographer Henry Callaway – and he incorporated their 'findings' into his theorizing about religion. In their reports about the Zulu of South Africa, Müller found primary data he could incorporate into his generic reflections on language, mythology and religion.

This exchange between Oxford and South Africa drew Max Müller into some significant contradictions in theorizing religion. On the one hand, his correspondents in South Africa could also theorize. W. H. I. Bleek, a theorist in his own right, had been mentored, like Max Müller, by Christian von Bunsen to look to language as the key to religion. Although Müller frequently invoked Bleek in support of his own theory of myth as a disease of language, in which poetic metaphors are reified as transcendent beings, in which *nomina* become *numina*, Bleek's dedicated investigations of language and religion among the Khoisan and Zulu in South Africa contradicted Müller. Basically, where Müller placed the 'disease of language' at the beginning of religious evolution, Bleek found in South Africa that the ancestor-worshipping Zulu, with a language that did not classify nouns by gender, were more original and more primitive than the sky-worshipping Khoisan whose gendered language reflected a later evolutionary stage that had 'filled the sky with gods'.[11]

On the other hand, Max Müller's correspondents in South Africa produced extremely unstable data. The missionary, medical doctor and ethnographer Henry Callaway was also a theorist in his own right. In 1871 he presented a paper to the Royal Anthropological Society in London on his research among the Zulu, advancing a kind of cognitive theory of 'brain-sensation' to explain Zulu religion, but not all members of the society were happy with the results, since Walter Cooper Dendy complained that Callaway had produced 'the most prolix and monotonous paper read before the Institute during this session; indeed it was a real infliction ... if we hear nothing from southern-eastern Africa more rational, the sooner the district is tabooed the better.'[12] Although he might not have been recognized in London as a theorist, Callaway's book, *The Religious System of the Amazulu*,[13] collected primary data, providing British theorists of religion with what E. B. Tylor called 'the best knowledge of the lower phases of religious belief'.[14] Callaway's data, however, was unstable because he had recorded not a religious system, but a vital argument about religion. Africans living within a shifting, unstable political environment, which extended from Swazi territory to the north to Xhosa territory in the Eastern Cape, which included African traditionalists, Christian converts and Christian apostates around Callaway's mission station, in all their diversity, were recorded in this text. Nevertheless, British theorists consistently referenced Callaway as if he had provided primary data, directly, in the voice of the natives, of primitive religion. Max Müller worried about all this, especially when he read contrary claims about Zulu religion in the 1890s. 'If we can no longer quote Callaway on Zulus,' he complained, 'whom shall we quote?'[15] But we have to ask: Why were these British theorists quoting Callaway, appropriating his 'data', in the first place?

Clearly, they were theorizing religion. They were just trying to figure out religion. But they were also engaged in a complex process of mediating between the past and the present, the centre and the periphery, in underwriting an imperial world. South African data was instrumental in these mediations. Henry Callaway's Zulus, the colonized Zulu 'savages', who continued to oppose British colonial rule throughout the nineteenth century, were transposed into the 'best knowledge' about the most archaic primitives – the earliest, the lowest – and relegated to the deepest recesses of time immemorial at the beginning of the religious evolution of humanity.

From the imperial centre, having adopted a British imperial position in the world, F. Max Müller amplified this imperial worldview in his last publication that appeared before his death, a vigorous and polemical defence of British sovereignty over South Africa.[16] Having relegated the Zulu outside historical time, sending them back to the primitive origin of humanity, this gesture erased them from the political geography of empire.

What difference does any of this make? Setting politics aside, British imperial theorists could still have insights – Max Müller on language and religion, E. B. Tylor on cognition and religion, Andrew Lang on culture and religion, and so on – that might still be valid. After all, we are talking about the early stages of an emerging science of religion. Yes, I agree. I am not interested in vilifying my own ancestors in the academic study of religion. I am not telling a simple story about 'good guys' and 'bad guys' in the study of religion. Again, trying to come to terms with my location in South Africa, I have been working to understand how theorizing about religion has been related – historically and geographically – to the people of this place.

I have found what I call a triple mediation – imperial theorists mediating their understanding of the human between 'primitive' ancestors of humanity and 'savages' on the periphery of empire; colonial settlers, including those 'men on the spot' such as Colenso, Bleek and Callaway, mediating between the metropolitan centre and the contested and shifting colonial terrain; and indigenous Africans, increasingly dispossessed and dislocated, mediating between ancestral traditions and new religious, social and economic forces in a colonial situation. All of these mediations, I think, can be brought together in gaining a rich, multifaceted understanding of the cultural history of theorizing religion.

3   HUMANIZING RELIGION

Third, South Africa has taught me about the human dynamics of the inherent ambivalence of religion. However we might define or theorize the term, religion is a truly ambivalent human enterprise – legitimating oppression, mobilizing liberation. As both the best and the worst, as both humanizing and dehumanizing, religion is truly a human problem.

During the 1980s in South Africa, I learned about this ambivalence as much from Oliver Tambo, the President of the African National Congress in exile, as from Desmond Tutu, Archbishop of Cape Town. While the archbishop, in the name of God, was opposing apartheid by urging for the human recognition of *ubuntu*, an indigenous term for a relational understanding of humanity,[17] Oliver Tambo was critically analysing the religiopolitical terrain within apartheid South Africa in which the human was poised between the superhuman claims of the apartheid state and the dehumanization suffered by the majority of the people in South Africa within a capitalist economy.

Under apartheid, the human was at stake. Religion, although it might very well refer to the more than human, is at least a human thing. It is something that human beings do. Studying religion in apartheid South Africa, I found, meant studying something human beings do under dehumanizing conditions, either as something done to legitimate, reinforce and entrench the dehumanization of subject people, which, as both Tutu and Tambo agreed, substantially dehumanized the dehumanizers, or as something done by people undergoing a dehumanizing regime, strategically and tactically, drawing upon resources at hand, in struggles for recovering humanity under dehumanizing conditions. Under apartheid, what it meant to be human was urgently at stake for everyone.

During the late 1980s, under the weight of this oppression, with the smell of teargas in our offices, I tried to write about religion in this regard, rendering religion as a repertoire of strategies and tactics for negotiating the meaning and power of being human. But I could not write about South Africa directly, since I had taken a personal vow not to become an 'instant expert', as so many academic visitors, including prominent international scholars, had claimed to be. I had promised myself not to say a word about South Africa for three years. So, instead of writing about South Africa, I wrote about America, but I wrote about an America that looked like apartheid South Africa from the perspective of people dehumanized by racism, sexism and capitalist exploitation. I wrote a book about Jim Jones, the People's Temple and Jonestown, trying to get that story straight, which involved spending many days attending to archives and tape recording at the J. Edgar Hoover Building in Washington DC, but also trying to surface possibilities for analysing religion that would resonate in America and South Africa.

In South Africa, between 1984 and 1990, transatlantic relations were extremely difficult. The United States was widely perceived within South Africa as complicit with apartheid, with religious legitimization for the apartheid regime readily forthcoming from the New Christian Right. In a graduate seminar in 1985, I showed a videotape of Jerry Falwell defending the apartheid regime, praising apartheid South Africa as a Christian country, on the front lines against godless communism, upholding human rights – the human rights of the unborn, because abortion was illegal. In response, a graduate student in the classroom pulled out a knife, waved it around, and declared, 'I'm going to kill every American in this room.' Unfortunately, I was the only American present. Fortunately, he was only kidding, only making a point, so I survived, and fortunately he is now a Professor of Religious Studies at a South African university.

In this context, working out an interpretation of the religious worldview of Jim Jones' People's Temple, I was trying to be true to my academic discipline, or my own academic formation, by balancing the phenomenological epoché I had learned from Ninian Smart with the critical, historical structuralism I had learned from Jonathan Z. Smith. But I was also trying to be true to my location in apartheid South Africa. The result was a book, *Salvation and Suicide*.[18] The theoretical underpinning of the book was tested over and over again during the process of writing in graduate seminars and undergraduate classrooms. Setting aside, for the moment, our personal investments, I asked students to imagine a worldview that was negotiated along two axes: classification of persons and orientation in space and time. Although I had adapted these theoretical manoeuvres from Smart and Smith, I found that my South African students immediately recognized the salience of theory because it was illustrated and animated by vivid claims on the world – that God was God, Almighty, Socialism; that religion could address dehumanization under conditions like apartheid; and that religion could mobilize people with the apocalyptic hope of transforming such an oppressive space in time – and these claims resonated profoundly with the South African situation. So, I do not know that epoché actually worked, in this process, because my South African students during this time overwhelmingly thought that Jim Jones was right.

During this same period, I was teaching a graduate seminar on comparative religion and politics, United States and South Africa. Our library, I felt, did not have the relevant literature on American religious history. But even the relevant literature would not have spoken to the South African situation. So, while I was writing a book on Jonestown, for this graduate seminar I wrote an essay every other week on American religion and politics that we could discuss in relation to the South African situation. Those essays ended up as a book, *Patterns of Power: Religion and Politics in American Culture*.[19] Published the same year as *Salvation and Suicide*, this book was about America, but it was also about South Africa. *Patterns of Power*, I thought, was a 'responsible' book about America to balance my 'irresponsible' book about racist, oppressive America.

After my vow of silence expired, and I felt I could write about South Africa directly, I was inspired by a British academic who had thrown a tomato at the apartheid State President, P. W. Botha. Although she had only hit his feet, she was immediately deported. So, I planned my first book about South Africa as a completely irresponsible book, as if it were a tomato, drawing upon current events and informed by the theory and practice of liberation movements, underground and in exile, with extensive citations of banned literature. Imagining I would be deported, I wrote, at the same time, a responsible book, the first history of religions of South Africa, hoping to leave something behind.[20]

In February 1990, we were all surprised when the banned became unbanned, when P. W. Botha's successor, the apartheid State President, F. W. de Klerk, lifted legal restrictions on free political activity and communication. As the exiles returned and the underground surfaced, I found myself with a manuscript for a book that was now a tomato defused. Starting over, rewriting everything, I still ended up with the same theoretical position that I had developed in writing about Jim Jones, the People's Temple and Jonestown – religion is about classification and orientation, an open set of resources and strategies for negotiating what it is to be a human person in a human place. But this theoretical position was situated in South Africa and informed by South African insights.

During the long struggle against apartheid, President of the African National Congress, Oliver Reginald Tambo, had profound insights into these dynamics of being human in a human place.[21] O. R. Tambo knew, very well, that religion was about classifying persons – superhuman, subhuman – and struggling to be human within those classifications. As Tambo observed, the racists of the apartheid regime, claiming superhuman superiority, 'enrobe racist ideas and practices with the cloak of religion'. They draw superhuman legitimization from 'the God they dragoon to serve their interests and whom they claim to worship'. Claiming a special relationship with this superhuman power, the racists of the apartheid regime operated on the assumption that 'the European was a higher being deposited on this planet to play God over "the Natives".' In these terms, as outlined by O. R. Tambo, religion in South Africa was poised between the superhuman claims of the apartheid state, acting as God, and the dehumanization of the indigenous African majority.

However, within this imposed, oppressive classification of persons, the apartheid God was in for a surprise. Human beings, dehumanized, can recover their humanity through superhuman acts of opposition, resistance and rebellion, all in the face of death. 'The arrogantly racist architects of the apartheid system,' Tambo observed, 'thought the oppressed [were] not sufficiently human to rebel against the inhuman system they have imposed in our country.' Humans, dehumanized within an inhuman system, affirm their humanity by rising up against this system. 'By rising up in favour of justice,' as Tambo promised, 'we have turned these maniacal dreams into a nightmare.'[22]

This struggle to recover humanity in and through rising against oppression, although echoing Fanon's idea of recovering humanity through

redemptive violence against colonialism, bore traces of a history of theoretical reflection on human rights within the African National Congress.²³
But these rights are not merely abstract principles. They must be realized, in
practice, in the midst of their denial, by people being 'sufficiently human to
rebel against the inhuman system', reinforced by the 'God they dragoon' so
they can 'play God'. This religious classification of persons – superhuman,
subhuman and human – is thought out, worked out and fought out on a
battlefield.

Always, under difficult conditions, these classifications of the human
involve orienting the human in time and space, negotiating what it is to be
a human being in a human place. Here also O. R. Tambo was insightful.
In its struggle to reclaim humanity against a dehumanizing regime, the
armed wing of the African National Congress, Umkhonto we Sizwe (MK),
engaged in acts of sabotage, 'armed propaganda' against the apartheid
regime. During the mid-1980s, the strategic leadership of MK had devised
a plan to blow up the Voortrekker Monument in Pretoria. As a colossal
shrine to the birth of white, Afrikaner nationalism, which was unveiled in
1950, the Voortrekker Monument celebrated in stone the mythic creation
of a nation on 16 December 1838, a nation that could be traced back to
the European immigrants into the southern Africa interior who entered
into a covenant with God for the purpose of killing Africans and pre-
serving a white race in Africa. As the sun came through the aperture in the
ceiling every 16 December to fall directly upon the central altar stone, this
monument stood for a particularly violent religious nationalism that was
a sacred site in struggles over religious and political legitimacy during the
1980s. While the ruling National Party of the apartheid regime controlled
official observances within the monument, right-wing Afrikaner national-
ists tried to assert competing claims on its heritage.²⁴ Understandably, the
armed wing of the ANC thought it might very well be a good idea to blow
it up.

As in all operations that the ANC called 'armed propaganda', those acts
of sabotage that were designed to send a forceful message against the regime
on behalf of the oppressed masses, MK submitted the proposal to blow up
the Voortrekker Monument to careful strategic analysis. By identifying the
monument as a target, they had to decide if its destruction would advance
strategic objectives of maximum symbolic impact – addressing the apartheid
state, mobilizing the oppressed masses – while at the same time maintaining
the morality governing MK operations that were in principle committed
to ensuring the minimum loss of human life. Having passed this strategic
analysis, the proposal to blow up the Voortrekker Monument was next
subjected to logistical analysis. Realistic estimates were produced for the
quantity of explosives, the number of cadres, the routes of access and retreat
and the time it would take to accomplish the operation. As a result of this
analysis, MK commanders determined that blowing up the Voortrekker

Monument was both strategically desirable and logistically possible, so they took the proposal to ANC President in exile, O. R. Tambo.

Tambo rejected the proposal to blow up the Voortrekker Monument. Although I have to confess that I initially experienced a certain disappointment when I learned that we had come so close to blowing it up, upon sober reflection I must defer to O. R. Tambo's insight as an analyst of what I regard as the political economy of the sacred. Reportedly, President Tambo gave two reasons for refusing to allow any attack on the monument, both of which suggest that he was adept at supplementing conventional military analysis – strategic and logistical – with a mode of analysis that might be called applied religious studies, an acute sense of the dynamics of the sacred.

First, Tambo recalled that the ANC was engaged in a struggle against a state that had consistently and systematically destroyed the sanctity of the land, the lives and the humanity of the people of South Africa. In opposing the desecrating apartheid state, Tambo argued, the ANC had to maintain a political, moral and religious economy in which it would never descend to destroying something that anyone held to be sacred. Even the monumental shrine of this inherently violent, triumphalist and oppressive Afrikaner nationalism, therefore, could not be a legitimate target because it would implicate the ANC in such an act of desecration. In thinking through this dilemma, Tambo relied on an intimate knowledge of the contested dynamics of the political economy of the sacred in South Africa, in which refusal to destroy a sacred site was not a concession to religious interests but an active promotion of a human commitment. In that human commitment, the ANC was struggling not to sacralize South Africa by replacing the Christian legitimization of apartheid with a different regime of religious legitimacy but to protect all South Africans from violation by any act of desecration. Even such a horrible sacred edifice as the Voortrekker Monument, therefore, could not be a legitimate target for destruction.

Second, showing remarkable foresight, O. R. Tambo advised that the ANC might one day be involved in a process of national reconciliation. Certainly, during the 1980s, any kind of negotiated resolution seemed impossible. Nevertheless, Tambo refused to sanction the destruction of the Voortrekker Monument because he looked forward to the possibility that in the future South Africans might be faced with the challenges of reconciliation that would only be made more difficult if the ANC had destroyed a nationalist monument that was held sacred by a segment of the South African population. Although competing interest groups within that segment of the population might continue to contend over the legitimate ownership of the heritage represented by the monument, the ANC should not intervene. The ANC would be in a stronger negotiating position if it adhered to a principled respect for the sacredness of a site that it did not own, since it had no particular investment in claiming the contested heritage it represented, but nevertheless did not destroy.[25]

As events developed and a negotiated transition to democratic governance actually transpired, O. R. Tambo's refusal to destroy the Voortrekker Monument might be regarded as an important, although unknown and unacknowledged contribution to the South African transition. Based on a careful analysis of the political economy of the sacred, Tambo insisted that strategic and logistical considerations had to be reviewed according to an analysis of the dynamics of the sacred – assessing the risks of desecration, projecting the possibilities of reconciliation – within the shifting terrain of political struggle.

4   NATIONALIZING RELIGION

Fourth, since the transition to democracy in 1994, South Africa has taught me about the potential (and limitations) of religion in nation-building. Adopting a 'cooperative model' for relations between religion and state, the new constitutional order did not create a 'wall of separation' that cordoned off a privatized religion from the public sphere.[26] Rather, in keeping with the national motto, 'unity in diversity', the post-apartheid state has tried to draw upon the resources of the many religions of the country in the national interest. For example, during a busy weekend visiting religious communities in September 2003, including the Jewish Board of Deputies, a new Hindu organization and the Zion Christian Church, President Thabo Mbeki observed: 'Given our divided history, religious organizations have an important role to play in the reconstruction and development of our country, especially in the welfare and civil society sectors.'[27]

While seeking to mobilize all the religious constituencies of the country, the post-apartheid state has also implemented a new policy for teaching and learning about religion, religions and religious diversity, which Minister of Education Naledi Pandor recently called 'an exciting and distinctively South African response to an educational challenge faced by our society'.

> Our educational policy recognises the difference between religious, theological, or confessional interests, and the educational objectives of Religion Education. While respecting religious interests and valuing religious contributions to our country, the policy charts a course for our schools to make their own, distinctive contribution to teaching and learning about religion in ways that will celebrate our diversity and affirm our national unity.[28]

Certainly, these national projects – harnessing the potential of religion, limiting discrimination on the basis of religion, expanding the scope of mutual human recognition and understanding in the midst of religious difference

– are difficult (and problematic), but they grow out of an admirable willingness to take religion seriously as a significant feature of public life.

Of course, the apartheid regime had taken religion seriously, establishing South Africa, constitutionally, as a 'Christian country', and developing a civil religion[29] or political mythology[30] that invested white Afrikaner nationalism with a sacred aura. Over the first decade of democracy, the new democratic state engaged in nation-building projects that suggested an emerging civil religion. For example, South Africa's Truth and Reconciliation Commission was launched in 1995 by its Chair, Archbishop Desmond Tutu, who proclaimed the commission as not merely a legal mechanism, mandated by the Constitution, for adjudicating amnesty, but also as public ritual: a 'corporate nationwide process of healing through contrition, confession and forgiveness'.[31] Renegotiating national sacred time, the post-apartheid government redefined the annual progression of public holidays, in the process reclaiming the contested sacred day of 16 December – Day of the Covenant in the sacred calendar of Afrikaner nationalism, Heroes Day in the sacred calendar of the African National Congress – as a new South African holiday, the Day of Reconciliation. Renegotiating national sacred space, the post-apartheid government identified new sacred sites, such as the island prison of Robben Island, for pilgrimage and tourism.

Being present at the birth of a new nation, ironically, when nations were supposedly going out of style under globalizing conditions, I have learned a lot about the religious character of nationalism. Although recent research on nationalism has tended to assume the contingent, imagined, invented, manufactured or produced character of a nation, the question remains: Out of what is a nation produced? Linking the production of nations to characteristic patterns and processes in the history of religions, the French Marxist Régis Debray argued that a nation is made out of sacred stuff. As Debray proposed:

> We should not become obsessed by the determinate historical form of the nation-state but try to see what that form is made out of. It is created from a natural organization proper to *homo sapiens*, through which life itself is rendered untouchable or sacred. This sacred character constitutes the real national question.

In specifying the sacred substance of the national question, Debray pointed explicitly to two 'anti-death processes', the production of sacred time and sacred space. In the first case, the national question depends upon 'a delimitation of time, or the assignation of origins'. Like Mircea Eliade, who documented the 'myth of the eternal return' in the history of religions, Debray observed that the mythic temporal origin, the 'zero point or starting point is what allows ritual repetition, the ritualization of memory', with ritual re-enactment 'signifying defeat of the irreversibility of time'. In the second instance, the national question depends upon the 'delimitation of an enclosed space'. Within the highly charged confines of that delimited sacred space, whether a sacred site, environment or territory, national interests intersect with 'an encounter with the sacred'. The national question, according to Debray, raises over and over again the problem of the precise location of 'a sacred space within which divination could be undertaken'.[32] In the production of sacred space and places, meaning and power coalesce; the national question is answered in the ritualization of memory and the divination of a shared future.

In South Africa, this link between memory and future has been anchored in a new sacred site for public ritual, Freedom Park. As a Presidential Legacy Project, with a mandate to memorialize the struggle for liberation, Freedom Park is situated on Salvokop, an Anglo-Boer War battlefield, and adjacent to the Voortrekker Monument, that monumental shrine to white Afrikaner nationalism. This new national shrine, therefore, represents a ritualized bridge from the cultural nationalism of the old regime to the cultural nationalism of the new. As a ceremonial complex, Freedom Park revolves around a shrine, *Isivivane*, for the spirits of all the heroes and heroines who have sacrificed their lives for freedom. Other design features of Freedom Park – a Wall of Remembrance, a Museum of 3.6 billion years of South African history and a Pan-African archive – were being positioned to do significant symbolic, cultural and religious work. Although the site was planned for completion in 2009, by 2005 it was already actively involved in public ritual. As a heritage site for pilgrimage, drawing visitors into its architecture of memory, which was explicitly defined as a 'sacred place', Freedom Park was also a missionary project, going out to perform new purification rituals, 'Cleansing, Healing and Symbolic Reparations Ceremonies', in every province within South Africa and even in some neighbouring countries that had been frontline states in the struggle against apartheid.[33]

5   GLOBALIZING RELIGION

Fifth, South Africa has taught me about globalization, both as a description of a changing culture[34] and a changing culture of description,[35] which has altered the terrain for thinking about religion. In my recent research, I have been interested in two problems:

a) What happens when the 'indigenous', intimately grounded in a specific place, goes global? The Zulu witchdoctor, sangoma, sanusi and now shaman Credo Mutwa, for example, who has been described in our popular press as a 'fake, fraud and charlatan', has emerged in the global circuit of neo-shamanism as the bedrock of African indigenous authenticity to underwrite a variety of projects, including New Age spirituality, alternative healing, crime prevention, business management, environmentalism and encounters with aliens from outer space, not to mention the work of conspiracy theorist David Icke.[36]

b) What happens when the 'global', crossing boundaries, makes claims on our place? Afrika Bambaataa, for example, the African-American god-father of Hip Hop, whose group, Zulu Nation, was not African, Zulu or a nation, nevertheless moved into our space to identify two kinds of religion: On the one side, Afrika Bambaataa identified the 'go to sleep slavery type of religion'; the religion of the dream, the religion of the oppressed that sealed their oppression. On the other side, there was the 'spiritual wake up, revo-lutionary' religion of conscious, positive action, 'like the prophets', in which 'knowledge, wisdom, [and] understanding of self and others' inform a 'do for self and others type of religion'.[37]

These examples raise the question of authenticity. Which is more true to our experience: the commoditized religious export or the revolutionary religious expert? Now that Oprah Winfrey, through DNA testing, has discovered her Zulu roots, this question of authenticity – locally, globally – will perhaps be clarified.[38] In the meantime, we dwell in the dilemma of authenticity.

Although I am an American (or Californian), I long ago found myself in South Africa saying, 'us' – 'us' South Africans, 'us' Africans – in ways that certainly embody this transatlantic dilemma. Born in America, I have also been made in South Africa. The question of how any 'I' becomes an 'us', how the first person singular transforms into the first person plural, how personal subjectivity intersects with a social collectiveness,[39] is an important question for the academic study of religion. If we follow Durkheim in attending to the sacred as that which is 'set apart', we must also notice that the sacred is set apart at the centre of social relations, forming what Durkheim called a 'single moral community',[40] perhaps, but also animating contests and con-flicts over resources, including the symbolic resources of the sacred.

Hoping, one day, to return to studying religion and poetry, I still find myself at the moment trying to understand the factors and forces of the political economy of the sacred, in South Africa, but also in the globalizing relations and exchanges of our world.

8

Caution! Prospective Graduate Students of Religion in Judaism and Islam

MARC H. ELLIS (BAYLOR UNIVERSITY)

What would I say to graduate students in religion? Don't enter the pro-gramme, or stop immediately, unless there is something inside of you that has no choice; something that says to you that you will never be fulfilled if you choose to go elsewhere, to do something else with your life. There are certainly other possibilities in life, easier jobs to be had and better pay as well. And don't sign on simply to study the religiosity of others. The religiosity of others is not nearly as interesting as your own. And please don't study a religion that is not your own; you will always be a voyeur teaching students who are also voyeurs.

Yes, of course, the aforementioned is too dogmatic, too limiting and most of all too demanding. But think it over: if you choose religion after contem-plating these negatives, then your choice will be amply rewarding.

All disciplines have their risks, and religion is no exception. Studying any religion from a sociological and critical vantage point can be exciting and important – but only if you are engaged as well. The point is not for a teacher to have a simple affirmation of faith – what kind of faith could that be anyway? Rather the challenge is to be self-critical and involved. Otherwise the journey that is religion and spirituality will be lost. How can you inspire students if you are not yourself inspired?

On the Jewish side, the study of Judaism is fraught with dissonance that is unique to the history of Jews in the West. For years neglected or demeaned in the study of religion, Judaism now has a special place in academia. Unfortunately, too often this entails an affirmative teaching of the Jewish experience. Romanticizing Judaism and Jews is the order of the day. Strangely, this romanticization leads to what many see as the culmina-tion of the Jewish experience, the Holocaust.

How can the Holocaust be romanticized? I do not mean here the celebra-tion of death by the millions; far from it. Instead the grisly recounting of death assumes, in a curious juxtaposition, the place of safety, looking out at the suffering and at those who caused it. How popular Holocaust courses are today and how well paid the Jewish scholars who teach them!

Recounting the death of millions causes a tremendous respect for living Jews, as it should. But it also frees Jews from anything untoward in Jewish history or what we are involved in today. Years ago the Holocaust was a time to celebrate Israel as the natural evolution of Jewish life after. Now, even mention of Israel is usually declared off limits; there are too many accusing images of what has and is happening to Palestinians.

Some say Israel and the Palestinians should never have been in the Holocaust curriculum, a different era, unrelated, messing with the political. Then should the Holocaust be taught as if there were no lessons to be drawn from this most horrible event? Without the 'lessons' there would be few students attending the ever-growing number of Holocaust classes taught in universities across Canada and America. Who would read the proliferating number of textbooks published each year that seek to corner the Holocaust course market?

There is little of the critical edge left to the study of the Holocaust such as I experienced in the early 1970s when I encountered Richard Rubenstein, author of the now classic *After Auschwitz*.[1] I studied with him as often as I could, taking course after course – but even with him, then, he did not teach a course devoted specifically to the Holocaust. I read *After Auschwitz* in his course on the sociology of religion. This was before Holocaust was a designated subject; it was also before the mass production of materials related to this subject that grows ever larger over time.

Neither let the era of specialization fool you or lure you into a job that only makes sense as a vocation. If you take *After Auschwitz* and his subsequent study, *The Cunning of History*, it is all there.[2] The rest is commentary.

Indeed. For most that come into the study of religion, and Jewish studies in particular, the knowledge lies before you like a bountiful cafeteria. But what do you bring to the facts other than an assumed knowledge of many of them? The point is only what you have to bring to them, a sense of journey but also a critical inquiry about the facts before you.

In Jewish studies, however, there is more than meets the eye and a critical sense of the Jewish world, even one you are in solidarity with, is often frowned upon. This may represent a limitation of intellectual ability among the scholars in the field. More likely it is a fear of stepping out of the mainstream and not accepting the canon as given. It may also represent a fear that the world is not ready for a critical understanding of Jews and Judaism. Honesty may encourage the revival of anti-Semitism. Let sleeping dogs lie.

Yet here represents another danger. Is your study and teaching of Judaism only for your students and fellow academics? Or is there a fashioning of understandings that need to be communicated to the world? The former sense of task limits the knowledge learned and disseminated. The latter opens up the windows for all, including your students, to engage the world.

Beware of the censorship that others, including Jewish donors and local Jewish communities, feel they have over the study of Jews and Judaism. Independence is essential, but don't assume that you will have the support of the university in this regard. There is a definite double standard regarding the hiring and survival of those who teach in Jewish studies.[3]

The double standard declares off-limits what is expected of other scholarly endeavours of religion. Try teaching a romanticized version of Christianity as the path toward tenure. Try teaching a critical sense of the new religion of Holocaust and Israel as a path toward tenure. Good luck!

Islam is the next romanticized religion to be taught and critical scholars of Islam, especially if they are Muslim in background, also beware; your life in the university may indeed be short, especially if the position is funded by a Muslim of wealth or the local community or a person of wealth from Saudi Arabia.

Of course the same arguments that are given regarding Judaism can be made with reference to Islam. Minorities are struggling for respect and acceptance; violence surrounds them in the popular media and a riotous reaction is only an event away. September 11 is an example. On the other hand, as the Danish cartoon controversy demonstrates, an Islamic community demanding respect on its own terms may see critical thought as anti-Islamic.

So why teach Judaism and Islam? If not presented as a form of religious apologetics, the downside is remarkable. Downward mobility is the coin of the realm.

Only do it if your own fidelity is at stake.

In an era of academic specialization emphasizing vocation and fidelity, rather than disinterested scholarship, this might seem like blasphemy.

1 PROFESSIONALIZATION AND ITS DISCONTENTS

Of course we know that 'disinterested scholarship' is always interested, and especially when the claim of disinterest is made, or the claim of objectivity. One's beware-quotient should increase proportionally to the claims; disinterest is interest disguised. Does that mean that those who make no such claims are therefore transparent, without disguise and therefore more disinterested than the disinterested? Not at all. The point here is that fields of study, the boundaries that mark the fields as well as the agreed-upon subject matter, have been in their formation and remain in their developed stages highly contested. Only a sophisticated and normative disguise can shield the student from this contested nature.

The question remains: if one accepts this disguise, accepting that more or less everything is settled, why join this static enterprise? This is one of the reasons that many academics are mediocre in their energy and self-discovery, the acceptance of the parameters laid out in advance. The field, in general, being stuck in malaise, attracts those who are also stuck, or wish to be. How then is thought to move forward, since thought is restless, always crossing boundaries, looking for the points of contrast and conflict, seeking light where mystification is in place? Thought seeks new territory, or the rediscovery of territory that has become buried under tried and true truisms. Can thought flourish within the parameters of acceptable discourse?

Think fields of study: all of them more or less recent inventions, constructs that upended the parameters of acceptable thought, nineteenth- and twentieth-century inventions that structured knowledge in new and creative ways. Sociology, political science, anthropology and the like, almost every university major and graduate focus, is relatively new. But old enough that the structures they originally challenged are now structured so that little new thought can enter. It is the classic case of the subversive gone orthodox and the orthodox, like the previous orthodox, now battling against the newly subversive, without naming the subversive as such and assuming that each new wave of thinking can be absorbed within the present structures.

Religious studies – the general study of religion – is surely a case in point. When it broke onto the scene with fresh eyes in the 1960s, the idea of studying religion as an observer was criticized, by those who thought that religion shouldn't be studied because religion is a belief structure rather than an analytical tool to investigate what people believe and why, and by those who thought religion was archaic, unworthy of adherence or study. Who needed religion when a sophisticated and scientific modernity had arrived? Perhaps the study of primitive peoples and their belief structures was in order, as this could shed light on human origins and the linear progression that ultimately would make religion obsolete, but the field here would be anthropology rather than religion. Religious studies, if it belonged anywhere, should be taught in the seminary.

Of course, religious folk, especially clerics, looked askance at the teaching of religion in universities. Too much knowledge might result, critical thought would probably diminish belief, and who would approve the people who taught religion? Surely not other academics whose religious affiliations might be suspect. In universities controlled and funded by the state, the reach of religious authorities would be limited. And – a big one – other religions would be taught beside Christianity. As equals?

No religion wants a level playing field unless another dominant religion is denying it one. Then the level creation is undercut.

As a minority religion in America, one with a chequered history with Christianity, Judaism had ambivalent thoughts about the development of the field of religious studies. On the negative side, Judaism would be taught within an academic setting; freeing the study of Judaism and Jewishness from the rabbinic setting playing field is an upgrade, a chance, sometime in the future, to become dominant. Or, if that doesn't look promising, a level playing field at least denies the dominant religion the privileges it demands almost as a birthright. The danger is – and here the dominant religion is quite right – that other religions will be used to bring the dominant religion down a peg or two, and worse, equalizing religion at least in their academic study, ultimately the dominant religion's claim to truth superiority. If another religion is plausible to its believers, that plausibility can be ascribed to the dominant religion as well. But plausibility being what it is, something that makes sense within a certain framework, the claim is beyond frame-work and human.

How authentic could such a study be and who would teach Judaism as an authentic religion, in and of itself, as legitimate and with its own struc-tures and independent from Christianity? On the positive side, the study of Judaism, independent of the synagogue and its rivalry with Christianity, allowed new openings for Judaism in public life. Seen as a world religion and as the progenitor of Christianity and Islam, Judaism became much bigger in the study of religion than either its population of adherents could justify, and allowed it an independent voice to voice itself, which emphasized the particularity of Judaism as well as its universal quality.

From there the Jewish community took on the study of Judaism as a tool of cultural and political empowerment. That, combined with the emergence of the Holocaust and the new wave of Jewish pride accompanying Israel's victory in the 1967 Arab–Israeli war, made Jews quite comfortable with the public articulation of Jewishness, especially since the study of Judaism and Jewish history stopped at the water's edge of critical thought. In those early years the study of Judaism emphasized the beauty and innocence of Jewish life against the horrors it had experienced from Christianity and Christian history. This was the time when Holocaust theology was developing; a theology that championed Jewish innocence in the Holocaust and in the creation of the state of Israel. It was also a time when Jews were finding their own public voice, a voice that had previously been denied Jews, and one that Jews cultivated as a now uncontested field; a lone voice through which all religions could be viewed and judged.[4]

Holocaust theology was deep, wide-ranging and eclectic. It took from the world the ingredients it needed to ask the question of what it meant to be Jewish after. This understanding of the Holocaust as a watershed event, there being a before and after the Holocaust, was pioneered by Richard Rubenstein in his book appropriately and provocatively titled *After Auschwitz*. Published in 1966, but gaining momentum in the wake of Israel's lightning victory in the 1967 Arab–Israeli war, Rubenstein pushed the limits of an engaged theology, one responsive to the history of a people in light of its historic foundations. In sum, Rubenstein found those foundations wanting; he thus issued a clarion call to thinking Jews as to the inability of affirming the Jewish covenant after Auschwitz. The question was simple and devastating: where was God in Auschwitz?[5]

Coming across Rubenstein as a student in 1970 just as this theology was emerging allowed me a window into the contested nature of religious studies. Hearing Rubenstein, I also heard much of the religious studies movement in America at the time. A former clergy person with a doctorate, the religious community was too confining for him. Indeed, to follow his innovative theological understandings, he had to bolt the synagogue and anything directly affiliated with Jewish life. He was able to chart his theological path in the university and it is clear to me now that the university functioned as a parallel religious community for Jews and professors with other religious affiliations.

The study of religion has always functioned as a parallel synagogue and church. In the coming years it will also function in the same way for Muslims. And it will be contested by the Islamic community as Rubenstein was by the Jewish community and as some Christians have been opposed by the Christian community. The question here is one of authority and who is authorized to speak of a religion or even a religious worldview. As a case in point, Rubenstein was the primary teacher of Judaism at my university. His competence was without doubt; his distance from mainstream Judaism was also not in doubt. Seeing no future in Jewish belief, except one that accepted the Holocaust as part of God's plan, many in the Jewish community doubted Rubenstein's ability to 'objectively' convey the fundamentals of Jewish life. Of course, Rubenstein thought through the Holocaust and its meaning for Jews before the advent of Jewish studies as a discipline, so that, technically speaking, Rubenstein didn't teach courses on Judaism. However, the person hired to teach more mainstream Jewish courses in the curriculum had difficulty competing with the power of Rubenstein's thought and soon disappeared from the department. The department had made a choice in relation to how Judaism, with a future or not, would be presented at the university.

Christianity was also being presented in the department and, again, former clergy held the majority of teaching posts. The Christianity presented was for the most part Protestant; the Catholic post was held by an ex-priest. The Christianity I learned was far from a church-oriented, faith-based Christianity that was typical fare in the surrounding community or almost anywhere else in America. In classes we learned the history of Christianity according to the critical scholarship of the day and also studied the Bible using form criticism. In the evenings we had speakers like Rosemary Ruether and James Cone, in the early 1970s becoming known for their pioneering work in feminist and Black liberation theologies.

Again, like the origins of Holocaust theology, insurgent forces, free of congregants and church hierarchies, reshaped the theological map. The study of religion was on the move and responsive to various events within history, now including the struggle of women and African-Americans in society. What kind of theology did the struggling need? Who would articulate these struggles, and how?

The professionalization of religious studies came later and to the discipline's detriment. Certainly aspects of the next generation of teacher training bolstered the ability to decipher languages and aspects of religiosity; by and large the quest for meaning was gone and with it the larger religious questions facing us as human beings in the world. Ex-clergy were a thing of the past, as was the engagement with the world. Most of the next generation of religious studies teachers went straight from classroom to classroom, undergraduate, master's and doctorate, without missing a beat.

In the meantime, religions on the outside, with their authority and congregations, made a comeback in society and in their influence on the classroom. One can see this clearly in the emerging field of Jewish studies, originating with the idea of presenting a dignified and innocent Judaism to non-Jewish and Jewish students, then becoming caught up in the presentation of the Holocaust and the state of Israel as the sum total of Jewish life. To do this, with authority and money, the rough edges of Rubenstein's understandings had to be rounded off, if not buried altogether. Instead we began to hear a steady drumbeat of the tried and true, the Holocaust in need of commemoration by everyone everywhere, and Israel to be embraced with enthusiasm and hope as the only response to the Holocaust and as the litmus test of anti-Semitism. Any narrative that challenged the centrality of the Holocaust and Israel was banished.

2   THE WAR AGAINST JEWS OF CONSCIENCE

Today there is an all-out war on Jews who dissent. The few who are in the academy are on the run. Often they or their presidents are 'visited' by local Jews to discuss what is being taught about Jews and Judaism in the classroom. These Jews, often accepted by the president as people of status and knowledge, assume the mantle of authentic Jews. They are the proper arbiters of what is Jewish and therefore per force can judge whether the professor is indeed the one to properly communicate the subject to the 'uninformed' students. Often they bring studies by Jewish academics who also judge the character and fitness of what is being taught. Such diverse studies such as David Horowitz's, *The Professors: The 101 Most Dangerous Professors in America*, and a recent study by Alvin Rosenfeld '"Progressive" Jews and the new anti-Semitism' – a study commissioned by the American Jewish Committee – are often read and offered as proof of the unfitness of the professor.[6]

The visits are clearly motivated to censure thought about Israel and the Holocaust, especially thoughts that are critical of Israeli policy toward the Palestinians and investigations of the formation of the state itself. Often the local Jews come in armed with books and studies of these kinds, insisting that what is being taught is dangerous and anti-Semitic. If the administration is not open to working with the self-appointed leaders of the Jewish community then threats of withholding funding and even publicizing the university as anti-Semitic are made. The threat is clear: limit free thinking on these issues or else suffer the consequences.

On the one hand, Horowitz is a political right-wing campaigner against most any critical thought, though a high percentage of his dangerous professors deal with Middle East issues. Rosenfeld is the more academic type, laying out the groundwork for calling Jewish progressives anti-Semitic and then listing their crimes. But it is also accompanied by articles in Jewish periodicals listing his main ideas and then naming the names associated with this Jewish anti-Semitism. This includes a recent opinion piece by the wife of the president of Brandeis University.[7]

Jimmy Carter's book, *Palestine: Peace Not Apartheid*,[8] has also provided a forum for the accusations of anti-Semitism relating to critical thinking about Israel and the Palestinians. The assault on the former president has been extreme and ongoing; again Jewish academics, like Deborah Lipstadt, have weighed in with public pronouncements. Again rather than analysing the actual content of the book or the real situation of Israeli expansion and Palestinian displacement, Lipstadt questions Carter's commitment to Israel, his Christianity perhaps leading him toward anti-Semitism, and his wonderings about why the story of Palestinians is not known in the United States. Lipstadt also cautions that Carter is predisposed toward Jewish conspiracy theory. How else would Carter take such an ill-formed stance on Israel, especially when Israel is such a friend of the United States? Especially after 9/11.[9]

Lipstadt's language is telling; it is also typical: 'It is hard to criticize an icon. Jimmy Carter's humanitarian work has saved countless lives. Yet his life has also been shaped by the Bible, where the Hebrew prophets taught us to speak truth to power. So I write.' So she writes, pointing the prophetic finger outward rather than inward. As if the prophetic couldn't possibly apply to her, our community, Israel, the people or the state. Then the second part of the setup: 'Carter's book *Palestine: Peace Not Apartheid*, while exceptionally sensitive to Palestinian suffering, ignores a legacy of mistreatment, expulsion and murder committed against Jews. It trivializes the murder of Israelis. Now, facing a storm of criticism, he has relied on anti-Semitic stereotypes in defense.' The crime: only two 'fleeting' references to the Holocaust. Doesn't the Holocaust have to pervade Carter's thinking, everyone's thinking, determining their outlook toward everything, not being able to get out of bed without thinking about the Holocaust as the centre of the world? The world, itself, must revolve around the Holocaust. And the Holocaust interpreted in a certain way; as silencing any dissent on Israel.

'Carter never discusses the Jewish refugees who were prevented from entering Palestine before and after the war. One of Israel's first acts upon declaring statehood was to send ships to take those people "home",' Lipstadt writes, again glossing the historical relating to Israel's and America's Jewry's response to the Holocaust and the survivors: as the record goes, a decidedly mixed response indeed. But Carter's book is not about Israel, its formation or internal workings. Carter writes about Palestine defined as the West Bank, Gaza and East Jerusalem. What if Carter had dwelled on the formation of Israel itself, the ethnic cleansing involved, if he or others have permission to call it such when Jews do it? Perhaps the complement to Carter's book on the Palestinian territories is Ilan Pappe's *The Ethnic Cleansing of Palestine*.[10] Here the Jewish-Israeli historian recounts the origins of the state of Israel in gruesome detail.

Lipstadt is in deep water; much deeper than she would care to admit or even seems to understand, avoiding questions as she encourages a pile on. But again, while ignoring the topic that Carter is writing on she strikes back with her own rhetorical Holocaust sensibility and its connection to Israel's right to exist: 'In contrast, by almost ignoring the Holocaust, Carter gives inadvertent comfort to those who deny its importance or even its historical reality, in part because it helps them deny Israel's right to exist. This from the president who signed the legislation creating the US Holocaust Memorial Museum.' Yes, the Holocaust Museum. And Camp David, which by freeing Israel from military threats from Egypt allowed Israel a free hand in other matters, including a sustained and relatively uncontested settlement policy in Jerusalem and the West Bank. Where is the credit due for a single-term president who helped permanently enshrine Holocaust remembrance in the American national consciousness – and thus its political culture – and also gained Israel recognition by Egypt and freedom from the threat of invasion by the one country that could threaten Israel?

Still the real charge is coming: 'Carter has repeatedly fallen back – possibly unconsciously – on traditional anti-Semitic canards,' Lipstadt writes. 'In the Los Angeles Times last month, he declared it "politically suicide" for a politician to advocate a "balanced position" on the crisis. On Al-Jazeera TV, he dismissed the critique of his book by declaring that "most of the condemnations of my book came from Jewish-American organizations."' Jeffrey Goldberg, who lambasted the book in *The Post* last month, writes for the *New Yorker*.[11] Ethan Bronner, who in the *New York Times* called the book 'a distortion', is the *Times*' deputy foreign editor.[12] *Slate*'s Michael Kinsley declared it 'moronic'.[13] Dennis Ross, who was chief negotiator on the conflict in the administrations of George H. W. Bush and Bill Clinton, described the book as a rewriting and misrepresentation of history. Alan Dershowitz teaches at Harvard and Ken Stein at Emory.[14] Both have criticized the book. Because of the book's inaccuracies and imbalance and Carter's subsequent behaviour, 14 members of the Carter Center's Board of Councilors have resigned – many in anguish because they so respect Carter's other work. All are Jews. Does that invalidate their criticism – and mine – or render us representatives of Jewish organizations? No, clearly it doesn't invalidate Lipstadt's criticisms. However, it does reinforce Carter's point that the placement of Israel supporters in the American establishment – which includes, as Carter points out, many Christians – does make it difficult, if not impossible, to discuss Israeli policy rather than be accused of anti-Semitic, Holocaust-denying attitudes. All of this has led to the ratcheting up of the discussion of the Holocaust as an event likely to happen again in the near future.

So then Benny Morris, the first Israeli historian who documented what Pappe labels ethnic cleansing, but who has now turned to the right politically, published a doomsday scenario in Israel, just a few days after the Lipstadt op-ed appeared in America. While Lipstadt meditated on Carter's anti-Semitism, Morris foresees the next Holocaust: 'The second Holocaust will not be like the first', Morris writes:

> The Nazis, of course, industrialized mass murder. But still, the perpetrators had one-on-one contact with the victims. They may have dehumanized them over months and years of appalling debasement and in their minds, before the actual killing. But, still, they were in eye and ear contact, some-times in tactile contact, with their victim. The second Holocaust will be quite different. One bright morning, in five or ten years, perhaps during a regional crisis, perhaps out of the blue, a day or a year or five years after Iran's acquisition of the Bomb, the mullahs in Qom will convene in secret session, under a portrait of the steely-eyed Ayatollah Khomeini, and give President Mahmoud Ahmadinejad, by then in his second or third term, the go-ahead. With a country the size and shape of Israel (an elongated 20,000 square kilometers), probably four or five hits will suffice: No more Israel. A million or more Israelis in the greater Tel Aviv, Haifa and Jerusalem areas will die immediately. Millions will be seriously irradiated. Israel has about seven million inhabitants. No Iranian will see or touch an Israeli. It will be quite impersonal.[15]

What about Jerusalem?

After all, the city contains Islam's third holiest shrines (after Mecca and Medina), Al Aksa Mosque and the Mosque of Omar. But Ali Khamenei, the supreme spiritual leader, and Ahmadinejad most likely would reply much as they would to the wider question regarding the destruction and radioactive pollution of Palestine as a whole: The city, like the land, by God's grace, in 20 or 50 years' time, will recover. And it will be restored to Islam (and the Arabs). And the deeper pollution will have been eradi-cated. To judge from Ahmadinejad's continuous reference to Palestine and the need to destroy Israel, and his denial of the first Holocaust, he is a man obsessed. He shares this with the mullahs: All were brought up on the teachings of Khomeini, a prolific anti-Semite who often fulminated against 'the Little Satan'. To judge from Ahmadinejad's organization of the Holocaust cartoon competition and the Holocaust denial conference, the Iranian president's hatreds are deep (and, of course, shameless).[16]

3   TEACHING UNDER THREAT

Teaching Jewish studies, while clearly a challenge, is also an opportunity. In the previous generation, the challenge was to introduce, mostly for the first time, students to a positive view of Jews and Judaism. This was done primarily through teaching introductory courses on Judaism, Jewish life and through the Holocaust. Today the challenge is to teach a critical understanding of Judaism, Jews and the Holocaust in the context of contemporary Jewish life. This cannot be done without analysing the Holocaust as it has come to function in Jewish life and the political dynamics of Holocaust theology in the twenty-first century.

To do this with integrity, the state of Israel must be analysed in the same way: its history and the way it functions in the politics of the Jewish community and beyond. To do this – again with integrity – the Palestinian question must be included as integral to the discussion. In Jewish studies, the Palestinians are, for the most part, faceless as they are in the discussion of Jewish life, Judaism, the Holocaust and Israel. This cannot continue. The Palestinians must be allowed to be interlocutors, as Jews have been interlocutors of Christian history in the academic scene for decades. The history of Palestine, the ethnic cleansing of Palestinians in 1948 and the continuing displacement of Palestinians in the expansion of Israel must assume its rightful place in Jewish studies. Of course, this is more than allowing Palestinians to speak; it is bringing to the fore Jewish voices of dissent and conscience, a surprisingly strong contingent once their voices are recognized as legitimate.

Clearly, a lone teaching voice cannot survive the onslaught of the community pressure when it is applied to the university structure. So that administrations within and overseeing the university must also see this as their mission, that is the promotion and protection of academic freedom in the teaching of Jewish studies.

Can graduate students bank on this protection? And where will they get the knowledge to make the Jewish studies curriculum more inclusive? If this other side of contemporary Jewish history is not being taught – just the opposite, Jewish studies is being taught over against this inclusion – where can it be found by the students, supported in research and then its expression? Where will the students find the place and safety to take the next step in Jewish studies so that their voice will not be stifled and so that the next step of Jewish studies will be taken?

Islamic studies is in its infancy and, of course, has its own dynamic. At the same time, the trajectory of Jewish studies provides a warning. How is critical thought about Islam, the Muslim community and Islamic history to be researched and promulgated? In their attempt to communicate a positive view of Islam, especially in the post-September 11 period, will Islamic scholars follow Jewish scholars in their willingness to communicate a false image of Islam as only and everywhere innocent? Will it use its difficult situation in the West and in different parts of the world to be present as a defence of Islam so that anyone critical of that defence will be found wanting, denied research and teaching opportunities? Graduate students need to take the next step in the study of Islam. Will there be mentors and funding opportunities for such study? As within the Jewish community, it is doubtful that community funding of Islamic centres will provide this opportunity. Again, it will be up to university administrations to fund programmes in Islam, hire and protect Islamic scholars who have a critical sensibility, while fending off the community critics who only want the good face of Islam to be presented in public.

Are the universities that have failed so miserably in this endeavour related to Jewish studies up for the next battle regarding critical studies with Islam? Again, a caution is necessary. Whatever their rhetoric, universities, and their departments with them, most often take the easy way out. Their rhetoric regarding the role of the university as supplying critical thought to society is, for the most part, lip service. Most are willing to sacrifice academic integrity for peace at home and the possibility of large donations.

In the final analysis this reticence is telling. It means that most Jews and Muslims, as well as university administrators and faculty, don't care enough about the future of Jews and Muslims to venture out, take criticism and even fight for the right of free and critical inquiry. Should graduate students care that much for the future when their elders in the universities don't?

It is unlikely that this situation will change in the near future. In fact, the situation is becoming worse. As word gets out that the image of Judaism and Islam is not what the reality is, the powers that be become even more anxious to consolidate their power. Thought, even under assault, can help move the question forward. If this doesn't happen immediately, it may happen over time if enough people dedicate their lives to the critical evaluation of Judaism and Islam. The question remains of how many scholars – or would-be scholars – will be sacrificed in the mean time. Be aware. It is doubtful you will escape.

9

Teachings of Blessing as Elements of Reconciliation: Intra- and Inter-Religious Hermeneutical Challenges and Opportunities in the Face of Violent Deep-Rooted Conflict[1]

VERN NEUFELD REDEKOP (ST PAUL UNIVERSITY, OTTAWA)

Thomas Mooren has argued that the Abrahamic faiths are vulnerable to being co-opted in the interests of violence because their sacred texts contain texts of violence which lend themselves to be used as the ideological basis for violent practices.[2] Mark Juergensmeyer has demonstrated how religious teachings have been used to support violent destructive actions associated with terrorism in five cases in different parts of the world.[3] The interpretations of cartoons of Mohammed (PBUH) as being a violent affront to the faith of millions and the violent reactions illustrate ties between religions and violence. Deep-rooted conflict is based on a threat to identity need satisfiers that occur at the interface between the emotional, cognitive and spiritual dimensions of life out of which and through which ideas, actions and events are interpreted.[4] As such, religious concepts and metaphors often play a key role in conceptualizing and framing threats to identity.

In the face of the potential for religious-based violence, some scholars have highlighted a role for Religion in the making of peace.[5] I would like to build on their contribution by showing how a focus on hermeneutics generally, and within an ethical vision of blessing specifically, will enable religious scholars and leaders to generate teachings of blessing that can be used in the interest of reconciliation within a context of potential or real violent deep-rooted conflict. My claims are meant to apply to Religion generally; however, my argument will be grounded within the Hebrew Bible. In order to make the claim that what I am proposing is not specific to a particular religious tradition and at the same time make constructive use of heuristic insights from particular texts, I will subject the key concepts, *teachings* and *blessing*, to a hermeneutical circle form of inquiry whereby there will be a conceptual transformation from the specific to the general.

The hermeneutical circle will have a four-step process associated with it. First, it will take as a starting point the Hebrew concepts of ברכה (*berikah*) and תורה (*torah*) respectively, as developed in the Hebrew Bible. Each will then be, second, subjected to the *challenges*[6] that come from the field of deep-rooted conflict, and third, developed in terms of the conceptual *opportunities* embedded within the concept. Fourth, a new synthesis will be presented which will take the form of a technical redefinition of each term such that it can be appropriated within the field of deep-rooted conflict and reconciliation and applied to Religion generally in a manner that does not limit them to the original concepts.

With these new terms in hand, I will develop the concept of an ethical vision of blessing, which will contribute to an understanding of reconciliation as both a process and a goal. Next I will present a framework for reconciliation within which teachings of blessing play an essential role in relation to other elements of reconciliation. This raises the question, then, of how such teachings are to be derived, leading to the hermeneutical challenges and opportunities. The final argument will be that a hermeneutics of blessing could be used by leaders and scholars within all religious traditions to harness their own sacred writings in the interest of reconciliations within local relational systems (inter- and intra-religious) but also mimetically on a global scale (inter-religious). In other words, I will present a vision for religious-based (and Religion-based) mimetic structures of blessing.

1   CONCEPTUAL HERMENEUTIC CIRCLE ONE: BLESSING

I will present the concept of *berikah* as it is used within the Hebrew Bible; then I will show what is needed conceptually within the field of identity-based conflict (challenge). These first steps will provide a basis for the creative heuristic move in which new conceptual possibilities will be opened up, leading finally to a conceptual paring back of the concept of blessing such that it will have a manageable definition.

1.1   Berikah *in the Hebrew Bible*

ברכה *berikah* is the noun form of the Hebrew verb ברך *barak*, to bless, the root metaphor of which is to kneel; it was customary to kneel when receiving a blessing. This root metaphor suggests both receptivity on the part of the one receiving a blessing and generosity on the part of one giving it. The usage of *barak* within the Hebrew Bible suggests an association with empowerment.[7] *Barak* and its Arabic counterpart, *barakat*, denote a context in which there is creative enhancement of wellbeing. There is a concrete dimension to blessing in its association with a gift of land – source of abundance and rest.[8]

In the context of the Hebrew Bible, if someone is blessed, it means that in some way they are going to thrive. This thriving means that they may be in a position to enjoy that which gives them meaning, comfort, security and delight and that they are empowered to act. The action of blessing is verbal; there is in the Hebrew Bible an understanding that words carry with them a power to make a difference. Hence, a word of blessing will make a difference to the wellbeing of the person blessed. Sometimes it is a general blessing, as in Genesis 1 where God blessed humankind – be fruitful and multiply and fill the earth – and sometimes it is specific to the person involved. For example, in Genesis 17 God blesses Sarah, the childless wife of Abraham, saying that she will have a son; she eventually does and his name is Isaac. Isaac becomes the father of Jacob. Later, in Genesis 48, elderly Jacob, whose name was changed to Israel, wants to give a special blessing to his son Joseph. Jacob is now in Egypt where his family had to move to escape drought. He is about to die. Joseph, his favourite son, comes to him and Jacob says:

> El Shaddai [God] appeared to me at Luz, in the land of Canaan, and He blessed me, and said to me, 'I will make you fertile and numerous, making of you a community of peoples; and I will assign this land to your offspring to come for an everlasting possession.'[9]

Jacob then states that Joseph's two sons, Ephraim and Manasseh, will count as sons of Jacob, meaning that Joseph gets a double standing within the family. He will be the generator of two tribes. Jacob notices the two sons standing there and asks that they be brought to him for a blessing. Joseph carefully positions the two boys such that Manasseh, the older of the two, lines up with Jacob's right hand, implying that he will get the better blessing. Jacob deliberately crosses his hands so his right hand is on the head of Ephraim.

And he blessed Joseph, saying:

> The God in whose ways my father Abraham and Isaac walked,
> The God who has been my shepherd from my birth to this day—
> The Angel who has redeemed me from all harm—
> Bless the lads,
> In them may my name be recalled,
> And the names of my fathers Abraham and Isaac,
> And may they be teeming multitudes upon the earth.[10]

He went on to say that Ephraim would be greater than his older brother.

What is interesting in the telling of the story is that eventually the tribe of Ephraim became the dominant tribe of the people of Israel and when the original kingdom of Israel was split, the northern portion which contained Ephraim retained the name Israel and its capital, Samaria, was in the tribal territory of Ephraim. In prophetic literature, Ephraim is used synecdochically for all of Israel (Northern Kingdom) indicating its overwhelming dominance.

The point of all this is to see how the word ברכה *berikah* is used and understood. We note that Jacob, who was blessed in his youth, passes on a blessing to others. The association with land and offspring show an association with primary values – both of these are a source of power, understood as a capacity to look after oneself and one's interests. Both of these are sources of long-term empowerment. The effect of the blessing is to grant satisfiers to identity needs for meaning, security, recognition, agency, connectedness and continuity.[11] There is a synchronic dimension to the blessing in that the status of the person receiving the blessing is immediately changed; and there is a diachronic dimension in that the blessing is meant to continue into distant future time.

There is also an instrumental notion of blessing in the Hebrew Bible. When Abraham receives his initial blessing, he is told that through him and his offspring, all the peoples of the earth will be blessed.

An interesting twist on the use of the word 'to bless' is apparent in the words of one of the ancient poets of Israel in a poem that only serves to strengthen the link between 'blessing' and Religion:

Bless the LORD, O my soul
All my being, His holy Name.[12]

This raises many questions: Who is the LORD? And what could it possibly mean to bless the LORD's name? The Hebrew word translated LORD is יהוה. No one knows exactly what it means but it appears to be etymologically related to the answer God gave to Moses when Moses asked who he was – אהיה שאר אהיה.[13] 'I am who I am' is the traditional translation, but the future-oriented diachronic form of the verb היה 'to be' suggests 'I will be who I will be', or even 'I will become who I will become'. This word, יהוה, was regarded as the name of God. Given the commandment not to use the name of God in an empty way, within Judaism it was never uttered. When it appeared in the text of the Hebrew Bible the word *Adonai*, Hebrew for 'lord', was spoken. Hence, in modern translations LORD is used to respect this tradition. The fact that the LORD, who is the one blessing people, should be blessed by people raises two interesting points. The first is that the conception of God in the Hebrew Bible is that God needs something of humans; the relationship is important to the Divine. Second, blessing turns out to be a two-way street. It is mutual. For the second question about what it means to 'bless the LORD' we look to the rest of the psalm which continues:

Bless the LORD, O my soul
And do not forget all His bounties.[14]

What follows is a list of things that God does for people, emphasizing God's compassion, graciousness and mercy, and demonstrating a capacity to get over anger aroused at being wronged. Given the importance of parallel structures it would appear that the manner in which one blesses the LORD is through remembering and enumerating the LORD's positive actions and characteristics. Second, near the end of the psalm, it is suggested that blessing the LORD implies doing the will of the LORD.

The intention of the blessing is unambiguously to enhance the wellbeing of those involved. Thus it signifies a particular orientation. This orientation is contrasted to that of a curse which places limits on the capacity of the other and corresponds to the verbal field of violence. Included in the concept of blessing are creativity, beauty and a celebration of life.[15]

1.2   *The challenges of deep-rooted conflict*

Deep-rooted conflict introduces mimetic structures of violence into relational systems such that the parties involved are caught in patterns of thinking that increase mutual antipathy.[16] Hatred, the impulse to seek revenge and acquisitive mimetic desire grow and can explode in paroxysms of violence – rockets, bombs, shells, rape, suicide bombs, and the list goes on.

It is a discursive challenge to introduce the word 'blessing' within this context for a number of reasons. First, it is seen as a specifically religious word; for those who are in a post-religious frame of mind, or those who have framed religion as basically a negative force among people, the association of a word with a religious tradition discredits it. Second, the fact that Christianity, one of the religions in question, has played a role in colonizing indigenous peoples around the world, discrediting and wiping out traditional religious practice, makes it particularly suspect. By association, words that play a prominent role in Christian religious discourse generally and liturgy in particular are held suspect. Third, the very association of 'blessing' with the land of Israel is problematic for some. The use of blessings, which gave land to ancient patriarchs, to legitimize Jewish people re-inhabiting the land of Israel, occupying and settling Palestinian territory contributes to further conflicts in the use of this word. For all these reasons, the use of the word 'blessing' has the potential of igniting emotional reactions and potentially stoking deep-rooted conflict.

Furthermore, the fact that blessing seems tied to a locutionary event – pronouncing a blessing – would make it seem anachronistic. Similarly the preoccupation with blessing the name of someone as a way of achieving continuity of memory seems out of place in a post-enlightenment context.

For some people, using such a word is scandalous; it is a stumbling block. To draw on the work of René Girard, scandal and stumbling block are associated with the scapegoat.[17] Hence, the very use of the word blessing risks making a scapegoat out of the word and possibly an academic scapegoat out of those who use it.

However, at another level, the challenge within the field of deep-rooted conflict is to develop a discursive field and conceptual framework that can enable the human imagination to find a way to transcend intractable, violent conflict and envisage a new way for peoples to be in relationship to one another. It may be that 'blessing' could play a helpful role.

1.3   Opportunities for 'blessing' in the discursive field of violence

One step in my sustained effort to discover a hermeneutical framework to understand why humans commit atrocities to one another was to apply a set of theoretical concepts to a particular violent conflict.[18] As I did so, I was struck by the phenomenon whereby well-meaning people seemed to be pushed by a force greater than each of them into the field of violence. In an attempt to name this phenomenon, I coined the phrase mimetic structure of violence, drawing conceptually on the work of René Girard.[19] The various components of these structures are described in *From Violence to Blessing*. For our purposes I wish to draw on observations I made about the mimetic structure of violence as a whole.

These structures tend to be closed, confining, having an acquisitive character, they are death-oriented and tend to reduce options as to how people can live together. They take on a life of their own as thought patterns that tend to reproduce themselves mimetically within a relational system and from one relational system to another. They may be compared to a thought virus that infects relational systems and the people implicated in those systems.

By introducing mimetic structures of violence as an overarching concept to describe the meta-dynamics of violent deep-rooted conflict, I introduced a new paradigm to the field. One of the key features of this is that it allows people to think strategically about addressing violence in terms of changing structures. The alternatives are to fight violence with violence or to describe violent people as evil and hence in need of destruction or at least immobilization.

Suppose the paradigm of mimetic structure of violence is accepted as a way of viewing intractable violent conflicts, it then begs the question: What other mimetic structures are there? More to the point, given the phenomenon of people, individually and collectively, building positive life-enhancing relationships, can we not talk about mimetic structures that enhance human wellbeing? In my own quest to come up with an appropriate designation for such structures my mind repeatedly returned to 'blessing'.

The obvious alternative was 'peace'. Mimetic structures of peace – why not? Peace for many is defined in terms of war. Negative peace is the absence of war.[20] Janine Chanteur goes so far as to suggest that even philosophers of peace accept war as normative.[21] There is much to be said for reducing war and enhancing peace. 'Peace' is even given additional meaning by some in the field who associate positive peace with 'the capacity to deal with conflict non-violently and creatively'[22] or with 'human rights, development, solidarity and world order'.[23] The phrase 'culture of peace' speaks of the values and orientations that enable people to live together without lethal conflict. However, there is an ongoing verbal association of peace with passivity.

Given the characteristics of mimetic structures of violence as described above, there is a need for a term that expresses a mimetic structure characterized by dynamic, creative, life-oriented generation of options and possibilities whereby the lives of those in the relational system are mutually enhanced. It is a structure of generosity, as opposed to acquisitiveness; a structure of abundance, as opposed to scarcity. It opens the relational system to make it more inclusive as opposed to the exclusive and excluding dimensions of mimetic structures of violence. It is dynamic, conflict is inevitable but within this structure it is transformed to creativity; hence dissent is embraced. 'Blessing' comes to the fore as a word that expresses what is needed. It definitely speaks of wellbeing. The orientation is one in which those involved in blessing seek the wellbeing of the other. It has the connotation of sustainability and conceptually it can include creativity. Even the phrase 'blessing in disguise' opens up the possibility for dynamic, almost playful possibilities within the structure.

1.4   Back to 'blessing'

Searching for the opposite to the concept of mimetic structure of violence functioned heuristically to draw out a set of qualifiers to describe a new concept that would designate a situation in which people contribute mutually to each other's wellbeing. The word 'blessing' was chosen as the word to designate such a structure, in part because of the resonance of many of these qualifiers with the Hebrew word *berikah* translated as blessing. Given some of the concerns with this word in contemporary society, where does that leave us?

There are some concepts that can be drawn from the Hebrew roots that provided added value and meaning to mimetic structure of blessing. From the root metaphor of *barak*, as to kneel, we can make a connection between blessing and receptivity, a key concept in Taoism. Receptivity stands in contrast to power, which is an overwhelming value within mimetic structures of violence. But, insofar as mimetic structures of blessing are to provide a context and base for empowerment, it suggests both the receptivity to receive from others as well as the action-oriented dimension of working to provide to others what they might need. Generosity must be balanced by receptivity for mutuality to work. The Hebrew association of blessing and land speaks to the need to include the environment in the equation. If land/environment is a necessary condition to living well, it becomes a partner in sustaining mimetic structures of blessing. Even though the literal significance of a locutionary act of pronouncing a blessing seems out of place today, that very concept can function heuristically by raising the question of the link between speech and intentionality and hence between speech and the orientation of the locutionary actor. Even the fact that blessings often were intended to extend for generations can play the heuristic role of suggesting that mimetic structures of blessing should be constructed in such a way that they are sustainable through the generations. It links to the First Nations teaching that decisions are to take into account the history of the past seven generations and are to be made in such a way that the benefits will be felt seven generations into the future.

Furthermore, within a relational system marked by mimetic structures of blessing, there will be conflict, understood as a clash of identity need satisfiers, interests or desires that can result in mutual hurt. Within such a structure, however, conflict is transformed into an occasion for creativity so that there can be mutual contributions to the wellbeing of all parties. There is also a discursive field that includes compassion, patience, mercy and forgiveness that can contribute to the ongoing restoration of relationships when they get off the rails.[24]

Blessing is used to connote a life-oriented, creative impulse, oriented toward the mutual wellbeing of Self and Other.[25] Within a mimetic structure of blessing, Self and Other feed one another at many different levels of reality. If blessing becomes mimetic, both parties are at the same time receptive and generous. Symptoms of blessing are joy, confidence, self-esteem, peace, dignity and respect.

If deep-rooted conflict generates mimetic structures of violence, reconciliation can be seen as the generator of mimetic structures of blessing. This raises the question of how is it that people will come to the understandings needed to proceed in a process of reconciliation, particularly when the emotional trauma resulting from victimization calls for a violent justice of retribution. The answer may lie in part in the teachings that they have received.

2   CONCEPTUAL HERMENEUTIC CIRCLE TWO: TEACHINGS

In this section we will start with the concept of *torah* in the Hebrew Bible and then subject it to a hermeneutic of suspicion as we examine the challenges to using this word. We will then look at opportunities for its use and come up with a new synthesis.

2.1 Torah *in the Hebrew Bible*

The emphasis on 'teaching' is derived from *torah*, understood as a polyvalent concept functioning at different levels. Etymologically, *torah* is derived from *yarah*, meaning to teach. It, in turn, is derived from the word for light;[26] hence teaching is concerned with shedding light on the situation. Torah also designates the first five books of the Hebrew Bible – the central core of Judaic faith. There is another link between verb and noun in that traditionally these books are associated with the era in which Moses taught the liberated slaves a new way to live as they wandered in the desert. At another level, one can see that ancient Jewish scholars, probably in the time of the Exile in the sixth century BCE, assembled this compilation of teachings as the finest expression of what defines a people in a covenant relationship with a unitary Creator of the universe. Torah was portrayed as the means of shaping an oppressed people so as to exemplify a non-oppressive way of being.[27] For Jews, a distinction is made between the written Torah as described above and the oral Torah, which includes the Mishnah and Talmud. Together they define the 'ethnos, ethics and ethos' of Judaism.[28]

There is another valence to my deliberate emphasis on *torah* as teaching. This comes from the fact that when the Hebrew Bible was translated into Greek, *torah* was rendered as *nomos*, which was then translated into English and other European languages as 'law' or its equivalents. The shift in understanding from 'teaching' to 'law' in Greek set up in Christian theology a false dichotomy between law and grace; whereas within the Jewish tradition Torah was seen as a life-giving gift to be celebrated, not a law to oppress. The association with *nomos* was deadly in that *nomos* also can be used to mean legalism. Within the New Testament this same word was used both for attacking an empty legalism in a negative way and for celebrating the ongoing significance of Torah. Unfortunately, within the Christian consciousness, an essential link was made between the two concepts – *nomos* as *torah* and *nomos* as legalism – leading to a negative stereotype of Judaism. However, the Jewish understanding of Torah places it in the verbal field of grace – a gift with no strings attached, but which is to be accepted respectfully and lived by.[29] *Teachings* come in the form of stories, customs, wisdom sayings and deontological imperatives.[30] They are meant to be unequivocally life-oriented.[31]

2.2 *Challenges to teaching in the field of violence*

While the word 'teaching' does not have as direct an association with religion as does the word 'blessing', given the way it has been presented with links to Torah, it still does have a clear religious connotation. For many Christians with a supersessionist bent, there is an understanding that Torah has been replaced by something new and better in Christianity. Torah is absolutely central to the life and worship of Judaism. To those who see no place for the role of Religion in addressing conflict or even shedding significant light on violence, this concept is also scandalous.

Even if we disregard the religious derivation of the concept, the word 'teaching' scarcely seems appropriate. What are teachings? Isn't this a little prosaic? Who can be presumptuous enough to think that they can teach? Isn't this a little much in a postmodern world?

2.3   Opportunities for teaching in mimetic structures of blessing

Teachings can be considered as value-laden content that drives processes, routine actions, heuristic endeavours, change and continuity. They may be collected into a text or they can be passed on orally. Note the following paragraph from a 1989 justice proposal prepared by the Sandy Lake First Nation quoted by Rupert Ross:

> Probably one of the most serious gaps in the system is the different perception of wrongdoing and how to best treat it. In the non-Indian community, committing a crime seems to mean that the individual is a bad person and therefore must be punished ... The Indian communities view a wrongdoing *as a misbehaviour which requires teaching or an illness which requires healing.*[32]

Culture, Science and Religion are given shape by teachings.[33] Political and economic systems function on the basis of teachings.[34] Civilizations and societies run on teachings. Some teachings are presented formally through education systems and some are informally woven into daily discourse. Children are subject to teachings before they can talk.[35] Teachings lie behind routines and rituals. They form the network of unwritten rules that you need to know to function in various cultural environments. Some teachings are rooted in traditions that go back millennia and others are the result of recent insights. Teachings are operative at any level of consciousness.[36]

Michael Polanyi's epistemology emphasizes tacit knowledge, a vast body of knowledge that cannot be put into words – knowledge that is built up through teachings.[37] It includes skills, values and experiential learnings. It is out of the tacit dimension that we make our judgements and set a course for the practices that give shape to our lives. Teachings that we receive from childhood make their way into this tacit dimension, shaping our individual *Weltanschauungen.*

Teachings are lived out; in fact, it is in the living out of teachings that they are passed on with the greatest cogency.[38] People living out certain teachings become models subject to mimesis. The mimetic effect of articulated teachings that are demonstrated in real life can be truly contagious within a group of people.[39]

Those who have taken strong leadership roles in the development of mimetic structures of blessing in the face of violence and gross injustice have been profoundly influenced by teachings that informed their action. For Gandhi it was teachings about *Satya* (truth), *Satyagraha* (truth force) and *Ahimsa* (action based on refusal to harm).[40] Archbishop Desmond Tutu drew strength and inspiration from teachings about *Ubuntu*.[41] John Paul Lederach was guided by 'the intermixing of three tributaries of ideas: the Mennonite theological discourse on pacifism, the social-change orientation of active non-violence, and the practical perspectives proposed by the conflict resolution field.'[42]

Teachings of blessing help come to terms with mimetic structures of violence, reducing their hold on relational systems, and generate, nurture, support and maintain mimetic structures of blessing. Discourse around teachings of blessing makes sense within a theoretical framework based on a distinction between mimetic structures of violence and mimetic structures of blessing.[43]

2.4   A new synthesis

The processes of reconciliation rely on teachings and the very articulation of reconciliation as a goal goes back to teachings. This assertion follows from the sense of teachings as being value-laden information that drives processes. It can be affirmed in the abstract without acknowledging which particular teachings might be involved. However, once potential teachings are identified, they can be held up to critical scrutiny, refined or perhaps combined with other teachings to create new insights which can be the basis for even better processes, but we are getting ahead of ourselves.

Getting back to the link with Torah, it can be shown that there are specific teachings in the Torah that have a germ of insight in relation to reconciliation that could prove to be heuristically potent. For example, the commandments about the Sabbath, understood within the context of the Ancient Near East, have a strong social justice component to them. In the Exodus version it is significant that slaves, immigrants and animals are to have a day of rest – oppression cannot be complete.[44] The Deuteronomic version of the Shabbat commandment emphasizes a hermeneutic of remembrance: remember each Shabbat that you were slaves in Egypt.[45] The weekly remembering would tend to make the treatment of slaves more humane.

Similarly the teachings concerning the Sabbath year and Jubilee – forgiveness of debts, release of slaves, a return of land to the original families – suggest that it is important to build into the functioning of society a time for a radical readjustment of power configurations.[46] This insight is structurally akin to having periodic elections that in principle are to give the power to the people to determine who their leaders should be. They also suggest that the temporal dimension of justice-making is extremely important.

The concept of teaching assumes that there is something deliberate about the generation of appropriate value-laden insights and the passing on of these insights to others.

If there are 'teachings', there must be teachers. The Torah was linked with the person of Moses, who received teachings but who also taught the people. Insofar as the teachings helped to restore both order and mutual wellbeing in the face of harmful activity, he functioned as a judge to arbitrate; but at the same time, with the arbitration he established precedents and demonstrated how to navigate the complexities of applying principles to ambiguous contexts. Furthermore, he literally taught other judges.[47] All this is to say that in the Hebrew Bible it is impossible to isolate the teachings from the teacher. That is, the teachings take on the value needed to impact how people live in large measure on the basis of them coming from particular teachers. The same point could be made in Islam in relation to the Prophet Mohammed being the teacher both as recipient of the Koran as well as the one who brought the teachings of the Koran to life in Mecca and Medina.

What this suggests is that if we take the conceptual development out of specific religions and as we pursue the idea of teachings, we must be mindful about who might be potential teachers. Given the basic mimetic nature of humankind, effective teachers are those who bring a certain presence to the teaching process. They also model what the teachings are all about. Among Canada's First Nations and Inuit peoples, elders play the role of teachers. In academia, professors not only teach, they model academic life and the value of a pursuit of truth through their research. This concept starts to connect with the insight regarding mediation: that the presence and modelling action of a particular mediator can be determinative of positive outcomes.

The initial statements indicated that religious teachings can be used as the basis of violence. The impact of particular teachings is largely a function of how they are interpreted. The question then becomes: How can we hold interpreters accountable such that the teachings they reconfigure for particular situations will actually contribute to human wellbeing? Or in terms of my colleague, Ken Bush, who has developed a Peace and Conflict Impact Assessment (PCIA) tool, can we in effect do a PCIA on teachings?[48]

The same challenge that faces the religious interpreter also faces the interpreter of any texts that are thought to play a normative function. For example, Lenin and Stalin's interpretation of Marx certainly produced violent results that were contrary to what many interpreters of Marx understood him to mean. In the section that follows, I will address the issue of the place of teachings of blessing in reconciliation and argue for a hermeneutics of blessing that can guide the development and evolution of such teachings. First, though, I will develop an ethical vision of blessing as a meta-framework for reconciliation and interpretation.

3   TEACHINGS OF BLESSING IN THE CONTEXT OF RECONCILIATION

The development will move from the role of teachings of blessing in establishing an overall ethical vision to guide action, to the presentation of a framework for reconciliation in which teachings of blessing are a vital element, to the necessity of a hermeneutics of blessing by which teachings of blessing can be derived from a number of sources.

3.1   *An ethical vision of blessing*

The ethical is that aspect of the practical, understood in the philosophical sense of having to do with action, thus concerned with values and standards of rightness. It normally includes a deontological dimension expressed as moral principles or codes and a teleological component that includes the consequences of the action and the intentional dimension. By introducing the concept of an ethical vision, I am introducing a meta-ethical concept that can give overall direction to the sorting out of moral principles and evaluating the teleological dimensions of the ethical dimension.

What this means in terms of practice is that the moral principles we bring to bear in evaluating a potential or realized action should be chosen on the basis of whether or not these principles will contribute to the mutual creative empowerment of the parties involved. Likewise, when we evaluate outcomes or consequences of action, we should do so on the basis of whether or not they contribute to mimetic structures of blessing. Regarding intentionality, it too should be constructed around the concept of blessing. Put another way, the creation and nurturing of mimetic structures of blessing is itself an individual and collective transcendent 'good' in that it goes beyond individual self-interest, acknowledging that ultimately the wellbeing of self and other are inextricably tied together.

3.2   *A framework for reconciliation*

Reconciliation is defined in terms of freedom *from* mimetic structures of violence and freedom *to* generate mimetic structures of blessing. As such it is both a process and a goal.[49] In the wake of significant victimization there is a human emotionally charged urge to correct a perceived relational imbalance that is expressed in a cry for 'justice'. Justice in the first instance is often understood as a desire to make the perpetrator suffer. In other words, the one who caused violence is thought to deserve, mimetically, to be made a victim of violence. The equalizing of the balance in retributive justice (as in revenge) is a balance of violence. The emotional make-up of individuals prompts them to desire the suffering of perpetrators as a form of justice. This is given evidence in the cries of victims again and again and again. This is not the only concept of justice that may be operative.

To move in the direction of reconciliation is in some way to clear the way to mutually empowering relationships. This means that, from the perspective of a victim, the perpetrator in some way should, at the end of the process, at the very least be put in a position of not having to suffer, but should be empowered to empower. From the perspective of the perpetrator, this means that every ounce of personal energy should be devoted to 'making things right' – to empowering the victim. This notion of reconciliation goes against the intuitive grain of many people, contravening their sense of justice. However, it is an inclination that underlies another concept of justice which has become known as restorative justice. It includes within it concepts of mercy and forgiveness, and carries forth the teleological potential for healing. Teachings in many indigenous cultures emphasize justice as healing and are not punishment-based.[50] This concept is further developed as a justice of blessing.

The theoretical question arising from this conceptualization is: Where does the impulse and motivation for reconciliation come from? One response is that it comes from teachings of blessing. That is, people have been given a combination of moral teaching and archetypal stories that function as mimetic models that enable them to embrace reconciliation as a goal and as a process.

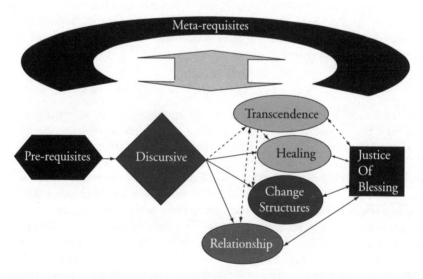

Figure 9.1: Reconciliation

Teachings of blessing are not all that is needed for reconciliation to occur. A secure environment, a mimetic dance called GRIT (Gradual, Reciprocal Initiative in Tension-reduction), expressions of remorse and acts of reparation, healing rituals and changes of structure are all part of the overall process which is presented in Figure 9.1.

Within this framework, at the heart of the overall process are the discursive and symbolic processes, where initial transformation takes place. The result areas of healing, structural change, new relationships and transcendence are managed within a justice of blessing process. Justice of blessing has an informal and a formal component. Informally, victims and perpetrators contribute to each other's development through ongoing acts of gratitude on the part of the perpetrator for any mercy shown and of openness on the part of victims. Mutually empowering expressions lead to healing and a new relationship. On the formal side, there is a periodic assessment of what has happened in the key result areas and appropriate adjustments are made to the pattern of interaction to make certain that optimum progress is made.

One of the prerequisites is an initial vision and mandate for reconciliation. Another is the creation of a safe space – physically and emotionally – within which reconciliation processes can take place.

The meta-requisites are required to guide all stages of the process. Foremost among the meta-requisites are teachings of blessing that can provide the initial impulse to reconcile; they can guide and strengthen the discursive processes and they can provide values, mimetic models and heuristic guides for the key result areas. The other side of the teaching coin is learning, which is vital for peaceful change.[51] Other meta-requisites include the GRIT process that may need to happen again and again in all of the phases of reconciliation, and the building of institutions.

Our final question becomes, then: How can teachings of blessing be discovered within religious traditions? This involves a hermeneutics of blessing, a concept developed in the next section.

3.3   Hermeneutic challenges and opportunities

Within most religious traditions is a vision for a more peaceful world. Within many sacred texts, however, are texts of violence; texts that could be used to inspire violence if interpreted in a certain way. Where there is an oral tradition, there is the potential for interpreting teaching for the sake of violence or blessing.[52] A hermeneutics of blessing interprets religious texts in such a way as to harness the energy and insights of these texts for the sake of blessing. There are a number of methodological emphases that underpin this hermeneutical approach.

First is a heuristic impulse oriented toward blessing. Michael Polanyi argues effectively that scientists are motivated by an 'intellectual passion'.[53]

Often there is something that they have a hunch exists and they are determined to find it. With the discovery of mimetic structures of blessing
comes an intellectual passion to discover more about these structures –
what are their roots? How are they initiated? How are they maintained?
What makes them vulnerable? One has a hunch that particular teachings
have played a role. Biologist Mary Clark makes the point that human development has been made possible through bonds of connectedness that allow
for sustained human communities.[54] These exist through time such that
one generation can build on the insights of previous generations. Insofar as
these communities contribute to the mutual wellbeing of their members,
we could say that they exemplify mimetic structures of blessing. This begs
the question, 'How is this possible?' which then leads to the question,
'What might be the role of teachings of blessing?' This impetus within the
context of Religion is strengthened as we reflect on what is at stake. With
the potential that texts of violence can be taken out of context and used to
motivate people to harm one another, the urgency to find a methodology
of blessing is brought to the fore.

Second, it is important to look at the various dimensions of texts and
orally transmitted teachings. One way of differentiating these dimensions
is through Paul Ricoeur's distinction between the *idem* and *ipse* dimensions
of the human person.[55] The *idem* dimension represents key characteristics
that are atemporal and can be compared with others. The *ipse* dimension
is temporal, always changing, and includes a sense of history as conveyed
through narrative and a horizon of the future with a promissory dimension. *Mutatis mutandis*, relating this to teachings we can say that teachings
have an *idem* dimension which is not limited to time; there is, for example,
something about the Golden Rule that is not limited to time or place. In
fact, 13 different religious traditions have some form of this teaching.[56] The
ipse dimension pays attention to the historical context of a teaching; not only
that, it attends to the historical dynamics by which that teaching has survived to the present time. In the case of texts, attention to the history of the
development of the text becomes important. If a text has survived intact for
a period of time, one can attend to the interpretations of the text at various
times and places. Insights about the nature and functions of teachings of
blessing come about through a methodological path using all of the tools of
historical, textual and redaction criticism.

With this same heuristic impulse one can find additional layers of meaning
by using literary and theoretical methods to examine the inner dynamics of
teachings – be they in the form of apodictic law, wisdom sayings or stories.
René Girard, for instance, placed prohibitions generated to maintain peace
within a community in the framework of scapegoat and sacrificial cycles.[57]
The taboos, taken as teachings of blessing, would be framed as preventive
measures to avoid the outbreak of violent crises that could destroy a community. By attending to their intended effect, the deconstruction of these

texts can uncover principles that can be reshaped in new contexts. For example, Walter Harrelson has deconstructed the Ten Commandments, and reconstructed from them essential principles that have shaped current understandings of human rights.[58] Rhetorical and form-critical methods provide clues to the various manners of giving emphasis to key points.

Another factor in the search for a hermeneutics of blessing is to look for teachings about teachings. This search for meta-teachings of blessing includes looking for explicit and implicit clues that highlight what might be seen as a hermeneutical key for understanding the whole. Thomas Mooren, a scholar of Islam, has suggested, for instance, that the opening words of the Koran could function as such a key within Islam. *Besmillah Alracham Alracheem* – in the name of Allah most merciful and compassionate – signals that the book as a whole is meant to convey teachings that strengthen the impulse toward mercy and compassion.[59] Biblical scholars have noted that the teaching to love one's neighbour as oneself is found at the middle of the book of Leviticus which is the middle book of the five books of the Torah. This literary centrality was given ideational centrality by both Hillel and Jesus.

A hermeneutics of blessing also asks how teachings have been used and modified for blessing at different times and places. One can see in the *Sanhedrin* of the Talmud how teachings about the death penalty have been interpreted by the Jewish community to virtually eliminate the use of capital punishment. While this exemplifies the 'toning down' of a text of violence, it also makes possible the discernment of underlying principles of justice that help in the constitution of a mimetic structure of blessing.[60]

Discovering, generating and validating teachings of blessing involves groups of people engaged together in a heuristic endeavour. Sometimes the engagement of the hermeneutical community in focusing on teachings of blessing can itself create a mimetic structure of blessing.[61] Sometimes the results help to identify teachings from one tradition that can apply to another. The very endeavour can mimetically inspire other communities to adopt a similar methodology.

One important aspect of the dynamics of a hermeneutical community is to develop a dialogical space – a discursive structural environment conducive to the free flowing of ideas, an openness on the part of participants to question their own previously held 'mental models' and a commitment to principles of dignity and respect. A dialogical space is one in which there is a free flow of thoughts and ideas including the presuppositions and intellectual passions driving the search for truth. This dialogical space can be seen as both derivative of and contributing to teachings of blessing.

4   CONCLUSION

I have argued that, despite cogent objectives to the contrary, the concept of teachings of blessing describes a necessary element of reconciliation even though it has not been named as such in many past instances of people bridging the rift between them to construct a new relationship. I have demonstrated that conceptual depth comes from indwelling meaning within a particular religious text with its own context, and that conceptual breadth comes from a hermeneutical circle that includes a hermeneutic of suspicion and a hermeneutic of possibility. The conceptual synthesis enables a broad application both within the domain of conflict and reconciliation studies as well as the domain of Religion. Teachings of blessing contribute to a meta-ethical framework wherein they give guidance to a hermeneutical enterprise aimed at identifying teachings of blessing that might offer particular guidance in specific contexts that involve deep-rooted conflict. One example comes from Abdi Hersi, who used sloganeering for irenic purposes in his native Somalia. Peace-oriented proverbs were put on placards to remind people of teachings of blessing in their own tradition.

Religious scholars, understood both as scholars who are religious and as scholars who study religions, are challenged to do research that (a) discovers teachings of blessing in religious texts, (b) advances hermeneutical principles whereby the potential for the use of religious texts to foment violence is reduced, and (c) deconstructs texts in order to uncover principles that help to understand the roots of evil and the impulse toward reconciliation. At another level, there is an intellectual challenge to bridge the differences among social and physical sciences on the one hand and theology, with its openness to transcendence, on the other. This challenge opens the possibility for higher level teachings of blessing that function at the level of epistemology and methodology. In this regard, the writings of such thinkers as Paul Ricoeur, Bernard Lonergan and Michael Polanyi could be reframed as teachings of blessing.

10

Speak White *or* Parler Femme:
Conversing in Contested Territories

CAROLYN SHARP (ST PAUL UNIVERSITY, OTTAWA)

When the Catholic Theology Society of America met in San Antonio, Texas in 2006, the Women's Constructive Theology Seminar chose to meet around the theme 'Undomestic Conversations: Women Talking Around Borders'. Theologically and politically grounded in the Québec women's movement, I was invited to participate in this conversation. I used the opportunity to explore the notion of borders as they impact upon our lives as scholars, but especially as a metaphor for the challenges that we face as feminist theologians if we truly embrace a politics of anti-subordination.

1   BORDER CROSSINGS

Returning to North America from fieldwork in West Africa, a doctoral student is detained when she changes planes in Paris. Although her papers are in order and she holds a substantial fellowship, her African passport as well as the presence of a family member living legally in France marks her as a suspicious person; she is held overnight in a cell. Following the political assassination of a colleague, a scholar is granted refugee status in Canada. Two years later, he faces difficulty travelling to an international conference at which he is to give the keynote; the Canadian government has yet to provide him with the necessary travel documents. At a recent international gathering of Catholic moral theologians in Italy, in addition to the burdensome cost of air tickets, visa applications require massive expenditure of time, energy and resources by scholars from the global South. At an international conference on violence against girl-children, a major researcher from a war-torn country cannot attend because she is denied a visa. En route to an annual scholarly meeting, I drive across the Canada–US border. In three minutes, having responded to four questions and displayed six inches of laminated paper, I pass through the checkpoint. The ease with which I regularly cross borders is an expression of privilege: the privilege of my whiteness, the privilege of class, the privilege of nationality. Indeed, the contrast between my experience and that of scholars from the South suggest an operational definition of privilege – the ability to cross through checkpoints rapidly, easily and smoothly.

Borders are places where two or more worlds meet, at times overlapping, at times turning their backs on each other. Living in Québec and teaching in Ontario, I cross the Outaouais/Ottawa River daily, moving between a society where French is the common language, although not dominant, to one where it is clearly subordinate, and often inaudible. The borders which surround Québec allow it to shape its collective identity and destiny. Fragile and porous, they are necessary to its ongoing existence and flourishing. They are places of fertile contact with other worlds and places where the dynamics of domination express their threat. For Ontarians, the same border functions as a rampart over which few throw more than the occasional glance. With few exceptions, publishing in French guarantees that one's work will not be widely read in either the Canadian or the North American academy.[1] Another constitutive element of privilege is the freedom to ignore what lies outside of one's own borders.

As it happens, I often cross from Canada to the United States at Akwesasne. As I drive across the bridge that spans the Saint Lawrence River, I enter Mohawk territory, its geography criss-crossed by multiple claims of jurisdiction. The governments of Canada and the United States, the provinces of Ontario and Québec and the State of New York all claim to legitimately govern a piece of this territory.[2] Exercised through a Canadian Band Council, through a US Tribal Council as well as through the Longhouses, Mohawk self-government is similarly divided, even when there is cooperation among these instances. As various signs and flags along my route recall, my border crossings at Akwesasne thus take me through contested territory. To cross such a border is to enter a place of resistance and affirmation, discomfort and rupture. An important aspect of privilege is that it allows one to disregard the conflicts that transform land into contested territory.

These concrete experiences of crossing borders highlight the challenge of conversing at borders and in contested territories. I want to examine the difficulties privilege creates for us as feminist scholars, both those who are doubly and triply privileged and those who are not. I also want to explore how we can subvert the borders that are imposed on us in order to engage in a theological production of knowledge that can contribute to the destruction of the structures of oppression. In order to do this I want to borrow two expressions from the Québec context, *speak white* and *parler femme*.

2   *SPEAK WHITE*: POLICING THE BOUNDARIES

On the Canadian Prairies, the expression *speak white* was an insult first directed toward Métis people, descendants of French Canadian voyagers, British merchants and native women, who spoke Cree, Objiway, French. To *speak white* was to speak English. The insult was quickly extended to encompass all French-Canadians, Québécois and Acadians, those who stubbornly refused to give up their language and have struggled to maintain and nourish French as the everyday language of home, church, school, government, in their economic, cultural and political worlds. To *speak white* is to speak the language of the Empire. *White* is the language of domination, ruling and policing. As a member of a subordinate culture, the constant injunction to *speak white* is a summons to take up one's place within the imperial relations of dominance; it involves acceptance of one's subordination and the loss of one's culture and identity. Ultimately, it is to become inaudible.

I want to borrow the expression *speak white* to understand the challenge we face as feminist theologians. In my understanding, feminist theology involves a transformative praxis of doing theology that requires a twofold commitment of faithfulness to the experience of women, most of whom are excluded from the academy, and groundedness in the emancipatory struggle of the women's movement. Such an understanding has methodological consequences. Feminist theology cannot make it alone in the academy. On the one hand, it requires feminist theory, the ongoing dialogue with feminists scholars outside of theology which holds us accountable to the greater effort to think about feminist ways of seeing, understanding and doing.[3] On the other hand, like all feminist scholarship, it requires feminist praxis, both within but especially without the academy. Beyond our own individual concrete praxis, it must sustain ways of listening to feminist communities of struggle, both within the Church and in society, and value speaking in terms accountable to these communities.

In spite of this feminist commitment, as theologians we are constantly enjoined to *speak white*. The Canadian feminist sociologist Dorothy Smith has written extensively on how the various disciplines function to establish and police the boundaries between that which counts as knowledge and that which is discounted.[4] To speak as a theologian, as a sociologist, as a psychologist, is to *speak white*. Disciplinary language is the language of ruling. Its use plunges us into a set of relations wherein the authorization to speak depends upon conformity to the required grammatical and lexicographical practices that set the speaker apart from those whose speech is not authorized and does not conform. Scholarly societies, writes Elisabeth Schüssler Fiorenza, are authoritative communities. 'They possess the power to ostracize or to embrace, to foster or restrict membership, to recognize or to define what "true scholarship" entails.'[5] Disciplinary language is thus an effective tool for policing boundaries. *Speaking white*, feminist theologians are able to move within and across disciplinary boundaries. But as we do so, we find ourselves crossing through contested territories. Crossing these boundaries, we exercise privilege and risk leaving parts of ourselves behind.

In her classic article, 'A Sociology for Women', Smith explores this dilemma.[6] She argues that when, under the impulse of the women's

movement, women moved into the academy, they experienced a discon-
nection between their actual lives and the language of the disciplines. 'The
circle of speakers and hearers among men was a closed circle of significance
into which women did not enter as such.'[7] From within this line of fault,
a feminist critical scholarship emerged that moved beyond a critique of
content, one which sought to add women as objects of study, and toward a
critique of the methods that produce knowledge and the power structures
that controlled its production.

For women in theology (and especially for women in Catholic theology),
the fault line was, and remains, double.[8] First, as women in the academy,
they experience the chilly climate of malestream collegiality.[9] In a discipline governed by historical mindedness, decades of feminist scholarship
competes with difficulty against centuries of androcentric scholarship. The
desire to reduce women's voices to a single line of (always optional) grace
notes and to define the feminist project in the singular, as if women did
not disagree among ourselves or as if feminist controversies were not worth
attending to, gives rise to a search for the authentic voice of women, as if
only one was possible. Second, feminist theology and the communities of
struggle in which it is grounded find themselves at the heart of the conflicts
between patriarchal church hierarchies and women's affirmation of their
person, rights and value. The substantive and methodological contributions
of feminist theology have been marginalized and misrepresented, as clerical
elites largely ignore women as theologians and shun their contribution.
Catholic theologians are advised to speak gingerly, if at all, on the closed
questions of ordination, reproductive rights and sexuality. Well-meaning
mentors encourage young theologians to shy away from these debates. Too
often, the example of sanctions imposed on those who have spoken freely as
women, rarely able to call upon institutional counterweights, makes these
questions into matters for whispering among ourselves.

Feminist women moved into the academy because they became aware
of themselves and other women as knowers and of the emancipatory need
for knowledge to empower women to analyse the worlds they inhabited
and to uncover the possibilities for the transformation of these worlds.
Feminist theologians shared this impulse. Early feminist voices undertook
to critique theology's service of male dominance and to invest in ways of
reading, praying, speaking, doing, loving that opened up spaces for women
to do theology differently. 'Feminist theology is communal theology,' wrote
Sheila Collins.[10] 'The method is an action/reflection process from which
theological insights arise rather than to which they are applied ... it is of the
essence of women's theology that form must mirror content.'[11]

The praxis of women in theology straddles Church and society. The
exclusion of women from ministry, the exploration of women's absence
in theological discourses, the naming of the divine, issues of sexuality
and spirituality have fuelled a collective quest for women in the Church

and have given rise to fruitful conversations and radical disputes among feminists. The political, social and cultural transformation of women's lives through the women's movement, the perduring violence faced by women, the ongoing impoverishment of women, the destruction of the earth and the construction of a global women's movement open corridors onto the broader women's movement. As the Québec feminist collective *l'Autre Parole* stresses, feminist theologians' self-understanding as feminists means that no boundary ghettoizes them within church circles nor isolates from solidarity with all women. In my experience teaching feminist theology, women often express a great enthusiasm for the exploration of the theology that arises from this double praxis and a desire to participate in what they perceive to be a collective and open process. For many, it allows the pursuit of questions that are not heard elsewhere.

3   DISCIPLINARY DISCOURSE: RE/DRAWING THE BOUNDARIES

Women have entered the disciplinary circles. In developing feminist scholarship, they have worked to redraw these circles, in order to create a porous surface between the everyday world of women and the world of knowledge. Feminist scholars have sought to reconnect the lived world and the world of knowledge because they have continued to believe that an emancipatory practice of knowing is not only possible but necessary. In many ways, this work has been successful, bearing fruit in a substantial body of scholarship supporting women in their ongoing struggle to transform their worlds.

Not only women, however, are excluded from the circle of disciplinary knowledge. Working-class people, people of colour, gays and lesbians and two-thirds world peoples are also strangers in the halls of knowledge and their presence there invites suspicion lest they overstep the bounds of propriety. Their emancipatory need of knowledge as tool in their struggle against oppression suffers from the line of fault that separates the actualities of their lives from the practices of scholarly knowing. In her book, *Looking White People in the Eye*, Sherene Razack argues that feminist scholarship itself *speaks white* and disciplines women of colour when they speak in the wrong language. '[Women of colour] who speak out of their own experience and talk about their differences are likely to be heard as essentialists while [white women who listen] to the talk about how race structures lives and relationships get to sit back in judgement. In such a scenario, those who judge have a better chance of appearing calm, confident, all knowing, and in control, while natives, pleading their case, can only be described as restless.'[12] The Botswanan biblical scholar Musa Dube echoes this insight: 'In short the logic of radical democracy invites international women to the *ekklesia* as long as they speak the language of the "civilized" and the "cultured" and not necessarily to bring traditions that were devalued by Western *kyriarchal* logic and to seek out liberating ways of coexistence – a move that would truly destabilize the exclusionary and subversive centre.'[13]

Razack argues that feminist scholarship needs to move beyond an inclusive politics of diversity and towards a politics of anti-subordination that contests the interlocking and mutually sustaining systems of domination. It is not enough to speak of women's experience in a general manner and then add a sentence or a paragraph or even a chapter on sexuality or race or class. Rather feminist scholars need to engage in difficult conversations at the places where male dominance, white supremacy, heterosexism and capitalism and other structures of dominance merge. The shadows of race and class have long floated over feminist theology. In the 1970s, Collins wrote 'Racism, sexism, class exploitation and ecological destruction are four interlocking pillars upon which the structure of patriarchy rests ... The feminist experience has enabled us to penetrate the superficial differences to see the systemic and psychic links.'[14] Elisabeth Schüssler Fiorenza's recent proposal of 'kyriarchy' in the place of 'patriarchy' displays a similar intention.[15] However, collectively, feminist theology has yet to find the means to adequately address the inter-relationship of systems of dominance. The collapsing of all oppressions into patriarchy (or kyriarchy) blurs the specific actualities of the various systems, including the concrete experiences of subordination, exploitation and humiliation as well as the actual histories of struggle, resistance and production of knowledge. It also obscures how the failure to address privilege fashions feminist theology as a disciplinary discourse that *speaks white*.

Privilege is the fruit of subordination.[16] Privilege and subordination are not separate worlds, but are joined in an interlocking dynamic in which the latter sustains and enriches the former. Whether it is the ease of a straight woman in the Church or the assurance of a white North American travelling to Europe, the privilege enjoyed is made possible through the subordination of the other. Because of its dependence upon subordination, the world of privilege cannot furnish the normative alternative to subordination, but needs itself to be grasped as contested territory. Feminists engaged in a transformative and emancipatory praxis of knowing need to stand at the boundaries that criss-cross the contested territories of privilege and subordination as places of discomfort and resistance, rupture and creation. At these boundaries, we need to undertake the conversations that challenge the disciplinary policing of the borders of power and privilege and in which *not speaking white* is possible.

In seeking to explore the contours of this conversation in contested territory, I would like to turn to the expression *parler femme*: literally, to speak woman.

4   *PARLER FEMME*: CONTESTING THE BOUNDARIES

The expression *parler femme* came into being in the French-speaking women's movement in the 1970s as a call for women to embrace their feminine status in opposition to an earlier egalitarian feminism that urged women to think and write like men.[17] In my experience, the expression was widely used in the women's movement in Québec in the late 1970s and 1980s. *Parler femme* represents a subversive embracing of women's grammatical particularity. In French, when 1,000 women and a tomcat cross a border, the proper pronoun is the third person masculine plural.[18] Because neither I nor God is ever neutral, but always feminine or masculine, feminist linguistic politics turn around the feminization of language more than inclusive language. Women's mother tongue, *parler femme,* is a language learned in the kitchen and silenced in the parlour. In the bedroom, punctuated by ecstasy and anguish, *parler femme* explodes in a morphological disordering of syntax. Suffocated even there by a phallocentric discourse that reduces even women's pleasure to a self-same logic,[19] *parler femme* finds voice again in women's presence to themselves.

Writers as diverse as Nicole Brossard, Luce Irigiray and Annie Leclerc understood *parler femme* as the politicized language of the women's movement. *To speak as a woman speaking as a woman* is to reveal the maleness of the normative voice; *to speak among ourselves as women speaking as women* is to embrace the disruptive and creative power of otherness speaking otherwise. Out of this practice of women speaking among ourselves arose not only new words and contents, but also new cultural and representational frameworks, new methods and new visions. 'The emergence of a culture *au féminin* depends upon the energy that we possess/will possess. At the present moment, we generate acts, words and thought that can still make room for the patriarchal linear-binary mentality. I say energy, because the spiralling emergence of a culture *au féminin* is tightly connected to the mental image that we hold and will hold of ourselves as a source of energy for other women and the form which our exchanges of energy will take in the social, the intimate and the political.'[20] The conversation is open-ended, the creative potential unleashed moves forward in an ongoing action.

Speaking among ourselves as women, women have come to know that the personal is political and that women's rights are human rights. Feminist activists and theorists speaking together have contested the division of the world into a public world in which the male subject exercises the rights of man[21] and a private sphere in which the logic of rights is not operable. Listening to women and listening to ourselves as women, we have politicized sexuality and reproduction, women's health and integrity, women's ability to choose and control our destinies. More importantly, we have proclaimed that the person, and not the family, is the basic unit of society, that women's lives belong to them and that no person, family, group, institution, religion or state may legitimately deprive women of their life or liberty. Feminist theologians understood the political language of spirituality also required an inventiveness that could not find expression within the inherited norms.[22] The *parler femme* of *l'Autre Parole* says *Dieue*:[23] God with a feminine 'e'. To speak of *Dieue* or *Christa* or *Sophia* accords the female subject and God; it thus disrupts and resists the constant re-inscription of the divine masculine into thought, proclamation and prayer. *Dieue* opens onto the ecstasy and anguish of *women speaking among women as women* of their own experience of the divine, but also onto the healing transformative power of *women journeying together as women*, even as patriarchal hierarchies ordain their incapacity to bear the divine. Women's blessedness is human blessedness, the glory of *Dieue* is woman fully alive and if woman is not assumed as woman then the crucified, resurrected and glorified Christ/a is not saviour.

5   CONVERSING IN CONTESTED TERRITORIES: RESISTING PRIVILEGE

This proposed turn to the *parler femme* may elicit surprise. The attention to the interplay between the morphology of women's bodies and their apprehension of the world in the work of Irigiray and others has led to a concern about essentialism and reductionism. Given the patriarchal idealization of women in the late Pope John Paul II's theology of the body and in the magisterial justification of women's subordination, this is a concern that feminist theologians must take seriously.[24] Moreover, concerns are rightfully raised about how the re-inscription of a hegemonic eurocentrism (as evidenced by orientalism that colours Irigiray's recent writings in spirituality[25]) furthers a politics of othering that transforms women outside the metropolis into the Other's Other. However, these considerations neither invalidate the purposeful and politically self-conscious embrace of linguistic delinquency of the *parler femme* nor undercut its strategic cultivation of ways of thinking and speaking that shatter the categories and strictures of androcentric language; because its creative utterance invites correction, such speech makes audible the continued silencing of women in scholarship and in culture. However, these critical perspectives do require moving beyond the original project in order to appropriate *parler femme* for an anti-subordinationist feminist theory and practice that does not *speak white*.

Speaking among ourselves as women speaking not white has been and remains difficult. In speaking this politicized language of struggle, we have encountered difference and diversity, disagreement and conflict. For even as we have listened each other into existence, we have known uncomfortable conversations, punctuated by hurt and anger, isolation and silencing.[26] Caught at the intersection of the structures of dominance, too often, we have hidden behind privilege and power to stave off the risks inherent in inhabiting contested territories. The challenge is to invent and value ways of listening and speaking, reading and writing that break down the practices of knowing that at once protect and obscure the privilege that informs our disciplinary discourses as feminist scholars and as theologians. The task is epistemological. In thus problematizing our own scholarship, we can delineate the dynamics of privilege and subordination and take up the uncomfortable and necessary position that makes possible, if not easy, undomestic conversations.

Sunday Mornin' Comin' Down: Waking Up in Women's Studies

DARLENE JUSCHKA (UNIVERSITY OF REGINA)

In this chapter I want to think about working the ground of religious studies. To do this I will first locate myself as a religious studies scholar. From here I will then discuss the identity of religious studies and developing one's theoretical lens in relation to one's area of expertise. Finally, I will focus on interdisciplinarity in the study of religion and with this in mind speak to the future of our discipline.

The ultimate intention of this chapter is to encourage graduate students to embrace and develop their individual, and sometimes idiosyncratic, academic interests in order to bring these to religious studies. Although the job market might suggest otherwise, there is room for a variety of theories and methods in religious studies, and multiplicity such as this, I believe, ultimately makes for a strong and vibrant area of study. Multiplicity has been viewed with suspicion and even eschewed at times, but this is due in large part to an inherent conservativeness in religious studies that can act as a powerful force to limit the field. For example, gender continues to be an under-analysed category in work done in the field. The tendency is to allow the feminists and lesbians and gay men to take up gender, sex and sexuality as if these categories have little to do with systems of belief and practice. In religious studies these categories, along with race, geopolitical location and class have been separated off from religious studies as if they are secondary categories that are of some interest, as opposed to primary categories that shape systems of belief and practice. I continue to argue against this conceptualization of 'religion' and the categories mentioned above.

1   SITUATING THE AUTHOR

But before I speak about what I deem to be the identity of religious studies, I will speak about my own identity. I do this in order that readers understand where I situate myself in relation to the topic I am pursuing.

My first degree was in classical studies and it is a field of study that continues to shape my knowledge and teaching. My master's degree was in religion and culture generally, but more specifically in ritual studies. It was my work with ritual and myth during my master's that further fashioned, and continues to fashion, how I do my work. In my PhD, I again shifted, never being happy to stay in one place too long, and began a project of examining the play of symbol, myth and ritual in the work of three significant feminist theo(a)logians; Mary Daly, Elisabeth Schüssler Fiorenza and Rosemary Rather Ruether. It was at this juncture that I established the three fields of study that would take me into feminism: feminist literary criticism, feminist philosophy and epistemology, and feminist theorizing.

During my work at the University of Toronto, I worked with a number of extraordinary women and men: professors and students alike. It was at this time that I developed an interest in method and theory in religious studies and worked for a number of years as one of the editors of the journal *Method and Theory in the Study of Religion*, founded in 1989 by doctoral students at the Centre for the Study of Religion, University of Toronto. It was during my tenure as editor that I was introduced to the fractures and fissures that represented, and continue to represent, the stresses in the field. I was intrigued by method and theory considerations, and it became apparent to me that developing a project focused on feminist interventions in religious studies could be nicely linked to methodological and theoretical concerns in the field.

What does this mean, then, in terms of situating myself for the purposes of this chapter? It means that I tend to look at structures and points of stress. It means that I work to make apparent the implications of these stresses, and to speak about the ways that stresses can be useful and hindering.[1] One such stress that I think is important in religious studies is its inherent interdisciplinarity, while another is the issue of a theological orientation versus a religious studies orientation. There are of course other stresses, such as the illicit affair between religious studies and postmodernism or the fracture between what are called Eastern and Western 'religions' (and of course indigenous 'religions', which simply don't make the east–west cut). But these latter two fissures, although very important, will not be taken up here in any significant way.

2   IDENTITY OF RELIGIOUS STUDIES

Many of these stresses in religious studies, I believed and continue to believe, have to do with issues of definition or identity: just what is religion, and subsequently the study of religion? One text, among a number, that has engaged this issue in a significant way is the *Guide to the Study of Religion*.[2]

In the *Guide*, as it is affectionately referred to, both the prologue, 'Religion' and 'Definition' consider religion as a category of analysis and religious studies as the disciplinary base wherein analyses take place.[3] Willi Braun, ever a pragmatic and analytical thinker, argues that religion is a 'spectre' and 'a free floating Something' commenting that '[a]s a spectre, "religion" presents us with the dual problem of being flamboyantly real, meeting us in all forms of speech and in material representations, on the one hand, and frustratingly apt to turn coy or disintegrate altogether when put under inquisition, on the other.'[4] As a free-floating signifier, religion is impossibly difficult to nail down simply because it is 'capable of attaching itself to a dizzying range of objects – many of them remarkably obscure – to countless blurry ideas and a host of often imprecise definitional propositions.'[5]

At the outset of William Arnal's 'Definition' piece in the *Guide*, he comments on the 'artificiality' of the concept of religion and its 'synthetic' constructions. Religion as a concept is a theoretical model that is subsequently mapped onto, as Russell McCutcheon argues following Jonathan Z. Smith, 'what might otherwise simply be termed observable human behaviour'.[6] The entire first section of Arnal's chapter examines the various thinkers who have sought to define religion, and who have in many ways been used to determine the boundaries of religious studies. All of these thinkers, except for Mircea Eliade, are outside of religious studies and so it should come as no surprise that religion has multiple definitions while religious studies is largely a combination of a variety of perspectives, theories and methods.

In both chapters of the *Guide*, the vacuity of something called religion is emphasized. Although old-school religious studies scholars and self-proclaimed theologians would argue that there is a concrete something called religion, both Braun and Arnal argue that there is not: religion is concept. As Arnal argues '[t]he concept of religion is a way of demarcating a certain socio-political reality that is only problematized with the advent of modernity in which the state at least claims to eschew culture *per se*.'[7]

In the effort, then, to grapple with a 'something' that is a nothing, we might have better success letting the 'it' of religion go and instead think of religion as a MacGuffin.[8] Why a MacGuffin? Well, the MacGuffin is ultimately immaterial as object since it is simply a mechanism that propels the plot forward. In other words, the MacGuffin has no real value in and of itself, as evident in the Hitchcock film *Psycho* wherein the stolen money has no value as such, but simply is the means to get the protagonist to the Bates Motel. The MacGuffin is also accepted by the characters of the story with little or no justification and in the end it is of no real consequence to the story. A classic instance of a MacGuffin is the Maltese falcon in the 1941 Sam Spade mystery *The Maltese Falcon* directed by John Huston, or a more recent example is the mysterious briefcase of Marsellus Wallace in the 1994 film *Pulp Fiction*. The MacGuffin is the spectre that drives the story forward, and yet, in the end, has no real significance to the characters or the story. Although real in some sense, an object such as a falcon or briefcase, the MacGuffin remains unrealized and because of this lacks materiality. Instead of being literal or material, the elusive MacGuffin is about human desire and it is this desire that gives it a sense of materiality.

If one thinks about 'religion' as a MacGuffin it becomes apparent there are similarities between the two. As a concept, like the MacGuffin, religion registers human desire. As particular instances of 'religion', Islams, Hinduisms, Santorias, Christianities, Buddhisms and so forth equally have no materiality. Rather, each is a sign whereby particular desires are gathered up and placed under, and then are related to the concept of religion. Like the MacGuffin, then, the materiality they (as 'religions') have is not directly realized, but must be derived through a secondary materialization such as a designated building (e.g. synagogue), a signified object (e.g. a sand painting), a style of dress (e.g. vestments), or a gesture (the evil eye), among many secondary materializations. Much like the MacGuffin, then, religion cannot be found as a real object in the world and is, as Braun has argued, a spectre. And so, like the MacGuffin, religion is about desire and, of course, in large measure is accepted with little justification by the players within the system of belief and practice.

Accepting for the moment that the 'object' of our study is a MacGuffin, what does this suggested about the identity of religious studies and the work we do therein? Working with religion as MacGuffin requires, it seems to me, an awareness that there is no object per se; rather there is desire directed toward an non-existent object, or spectre as Braun has argued. Therefore, from the outset it means that seeking the origin of religion carries little to no credence.[9] It means that determining the veracity of divinity and/or accompanying phenomena is pointless as determining the 'truth' can only be a circular activity. It means that questions related to faith are outside the area's concern. It means that searching for 'authentic' or original Buddhism, Islam, Christianity, Hinduism, or any system of belief and practice, is misguided. It means that seeking to determine any one system of belief and practice as better, more sophisticated or more rational is completely wrong-headed. These questions are theologically driven and therefore could be seen as legitimate inquiries in theological studies, but certainly not in religious studies. Taking this position does not mean that I am unsympathetic to feminist theologians seeking to redefine women and women's place within systems of belief and practice. My dissertation was primarily an examination of this kind of endeavour. However, what I examined was how systems of belief and practice (via symbol, myth and ritual) were reread, reconceived and reconstructed in light of a feminist agenda.[10] In my dissertation my investigations tended toward examining the 'how' rather than the 'why'.[11]

One of the most sagacious thinkers on the issue of theology versus religious studies is Donald Wiebe, a professor I first came to know during my time at the Centre for the Study of Religion at the University of Toronto. Wiebe has written books and articles on the subject and although we disagree on what 'religion' is, Wiebe insisting on the scientific study of religion and therefore taking the position that there is something called religion, while my approach is to understand religion as a discursive construct, we do agree on the necessity to approach the study of religion in a non-religious fashion. Situating Wiebe, he comments:

> It may be appropriate, however, to summarize my understanding of what a scientific study of religion appropriate to the academic context (repeatedly referred to in this article as a search for neutral and objective knowledge about religion and religions) involves. By 'scientific' I mean essentially that the study of religion in the context of the modern research university aims at achieving what we might call 'public knowledge of public facts', mediated through intersubjectively testable sets of statements, whether at the descriptive level of history, ethnography, and phenomenology, or at the explanatory level of law-like generalizations and theory. This, basically, is what scientific students of religion consider objective knowledge claims to be, because for them, the intersubjective procedures of assessing and testing claims ensures that the student avoids idiosyncratic subjective bias in the claims she or he makes.[12]

Again, although I do not take Wiebe's position on religion as object or advocate for objectivity, I am sympathetic to critical analysis and in this amenable to aspects of Wiebe's position. In my academic endeavours, then, I tend to follow Russell McCutcheon's dictum that religious studies scholars are 'critics and not caretakers'.[13] McCutcheon and Wiebe have their theoretical differences, but it is very clear that Wiebe has had a significant effect on McCutcheon's theoretical position.

In the end what is the identity of religious studies? I would argue that it is what scholars make it. Disciplines are built upon generations of scholars who shape and make the field, and it is this long disciplinary history that provides an identity for a field of study. Several hundred years of development assist toward a discipline constructing a firm identity much as is the case for English, philosophy, history or theology. There have not been, however, generations of scholars in religious studies, as the discipline is still young. Possibly we are currently coming up on three generations of scholars in religious studies, so a particular academic identity remains undetermined.

However, this does not mean that there are not generations of thinkers who have thought about 'religion'. Since the European Enlightenment, theologians, philosophers, linguists, anthropologists, sociologists, psychoanalysts, historians and the like have thought and written about 'religion', the elusive 'object' of religious studies. These, then, are the generations of thinkers, David Hume, G. W. F. Hegel, Emmanuel Kant, Jane Harrison, Sigmund Freud, Karl Marx, Emile Durkheim and so forth, who have been appropriated to act as the epistemological foundation of religious studies, and procure for it an impressive pedigree. Their work on 'religion' represents the multitude of theoretical and methodological strands that are woven together to signify religious studies.

3   RELIGIOUS STUDIES: THE THEORY IN ME

This may seem a rather odd section in light of the fact that I am currently an associate professor of women's studies. However, I do continue to teach courses in religious studies, and publish primarily in the area and so feel comfortable to comment on the theory in religious studies. I raise theory because it affects significantly the work that we do in religious studies: I would argue unequivocally that it is one of the most significant factors that shapes the labour in the field. However, all too often it operates implicitly so that many in the field do not pay attention to their and others' theoretical orientations. Let me provide a couple of examples.

First, throughout my tenure as a graduate student, I was introduced to a plethora of thinkers in the field, but often with little in-depth attention to the theoretical orientation of the thinker. Instead I was presented with the name, work and their basic idea, but the theoretical developments that supported their ideas tended to be largely unexamined.[14] Often, then, I would adopt those scholars I found most appealing without fully understanding why they appealed to me.

My second example comes from when I was seeking a position in the field. There were at least two job interviews that went horribly wrong simply because I did not have a clear enough understanding of my own theoretical orientation (although I would argue at this point I had a better understanding than many, largely because I worked as an editor on the journal *Method and Theory in the Study of Religion*) and nor did my interviewers. In the worst of these two interviews, I ended up in a very public conflict with the chair of the department (I was giving my paper). His general orientation was ecumenical, seeking to find common ground and responsibility, whether this be about antagonisms between religions, rich and poor, white and black and so forth. I, on the other hand, operated from a deconstructive position, one that engaged ideology critique. Added to this very basic difference in general orientation, he worked from an essentialist position understanding religion or race, for example, to be concrete things, whereas I worked, and continue to do so, from a constructionist position and understand religion and race to be concepts that have concrete effects. Had we been able to recognize that our basic positions were at odds, we might not have ended up in conflict; a conflict which surely lost me any chance at the position and certainly caused him some serious ire.

Knowing one's theoretical self allows the scholar more freedom and in the end more autonomy. I am better able to ascertain projects that I can make a contribution to, and which will also contribute to my own work, by knowing the theory in me.

4 THEORIES IN CONFLICT WITH AREAS

Bringing together one's area of expertise with her/his theoretical orientation can be difficult. This is due, in some measure, to rigid boundaries between areas of study that can hamper transference of knowledge, and to critiques generated by feminist, antiracist, postmodern and postcolonial studies. In the instance of rigid boundaries, boundaries generated by epistemological compartmentalization, e.g. sociology, English, history, and university structures, e.g. departments, constrict knowledge transference, although some movement toward interdisciplinarity is currently under way, something I will say more about in the next section of this chapter. In the instance of the challenge of feminist et al. studies, objectivity and universality were problematized. Scholars in these areas argued that knowledge and its generation were contextually bound and subject to all the vagaries of such a binding. For example, feminist analyses challenged the proposition that 'man' and the knowledge he generated represented the sum total of all human life and evolution. In their view, a view I agree with, knowledge, its production and those who produce it are socially and historically bound and therefore subject to the all the conditions, e.g. history, politics, power, environment, etc. of this contextualization.

I fully agree, then, that there is no meta-position, or a place where one can stand outside of human existence to speak objectively about that existence. But this does not mean I must reject theory as if theory is the realm of white, elite men of the Eurowest. Instead I would argue that theorizing, which entails describing, categorizing, assessing, interpreting and explaining, is engaged by all social bodies, and humans therein, across time and space.[15] The act of theorizing is not the variable; rather, motivation, content, outcomes, understanding and process are variables. Indeed in each of the areas mentioned, feminist, antiracist, postmodern and postcolonial studies, theorizing is central to the work done.

Still, in the postmodern era theorizing has been vilified and instead experience[16] has become the privileged category of knowledge production; particularly in the four areas mentioned above, but also in a number of disciplinary areas such as women's studies, anthropology, sociology and very markedly in religious studies. I find it rather odd that experience and theory are often seen as antithetical. Experience would mean nothing if it was not theorized; it is the act of thinking, reflecting and assessing that allows random events and actions to become something called experience, while theory itself is derived from experience. They are, rather, two sides of the same coin.[17]

If theorizing is vilified and experience given primacy within disciplines, then sharing theories across disciplinary boundaries becomes even more problematic. Already divided into knowledge regimes with university structures concretely reinforcing these divisions, the vilification of theory further hampers the free exchange of ideas.[18] Therefore when one seeks to develop their 'know-how' in an area of interest, such as systems of belief and practice in India or the Middle East, or in different historical periods, emphatic boundaries are already in place. First, one learns that datum is unique to the location and/or time period and second, as unique it requires a unique theory. I fully agree data are particular to context, but particular does not mean unique. Unique assumes that there has been, is and will be nothing else like it. Therefore, theory developed in one time or place cannot be applied to datum from another time or place.[19] Such an understanding has generated a rejection of theory as it is impossible to develop a theory for each instance of datum.

Interpreting the correctives from feminist, postmodern, antiracist and postcolonial studies as requiring unique theory (or no theory at all) is I think to misunderstand their critique. Rather, it is a call to do good theorizing, and good theorizing requires awareness of the social and historical ground of both theory and data. It further requires attention to complexity and detail. So in my work I combine feminist post-structural analysis, nuanced by semiotics (women's studies), with structuralist and performative approaches to symbol, myth and ritual (religious studies). I am equally mindful of the social and historical dimensions of data and that data have already been constructed (cultural, performative and academic).

Responding to this anchoring of theory and data by requiring a unique theory for a unique datum leads to solipsism, while eschewing theory altogether leads to obfuscation. In the first, solipsism does not allow for understanding and indeed resists it: it cannot be understood, as it is unlike anything else. But rejecting the idea of uniqueness does not mean a call for meta-theory. Instead if data are understood as particular, rather than unique, then ways to view the data can be multiple. There are multiple theories, theories that are malleable and adaptable, and they can tell us different things when applied to the same datum.

5   SLIPPING THROUGH THE CRACKS: THE POTENTIAL FOR INTERDISCIPLINARITY IN RELIGIOUS STUDIES

Religious studies is a variegate discipline and, as I have commented elsewhere,[20] religious studies and women's studies are two disciplines that are normatively oriented toward interdisciplinary work. For example, any method and theory course taught in religious studies will typically examine theorists from a multitude of areas including, but not limited to anthropology (e.g. Clifford Geertz and/or Claude Lévi-Strauss), English (e.g. Northrop Frye and/or Judith Butler), sociology (e.g. Emile Durkheim and/or Karl Marx), psychology (Sigmund Freud), philosophy (e.g. Paul Ricoeur and/or Michel Foucault), or linguistics (e.g. Ferdinand de Saussure). This kind of interdisciplinarity operates between disciplines drawing data and theory from a number of areas of study for the purposes of teaching and research. There are very few 'pure' theorists of religion, other than Mircea Eliade and those who closely follow him.

A clear recognition and deployment of the interdisciplinary nature of religious studies would I think strengthen the standing of field in the university. Although yes, there is resistance to an interdisciplinary orientation, in the last decade there has been a general shift toward a reserved acceptance of interdisciplinary work. The durability of any pedagogic newcomer can be ascertained in some measure by its reception, particularly by the sciences, and interdisciplinary work has gained some legitimacy there. Yes, there continues to be the view that interdisciplinary work is something one engages as a sideline to one's disciplinary-oriented work. And certainly the tendency has been to discourage graduate students in particular from this kind of work:

> As I have told quite a few students who wanted to work within the kind of interdisciplinary approach I have been defending, choosing an interdisciplinary research topic at the doctoral stage involves serious career risks. Also, it is much harder to get a proper training without investing all of one's energy into one discipline, or rather sub-sub-discipline.[21]

But the potential that may well reside in interdisciplinary work remains intact.

It is difficult to say if interdisciplinary work is the wave of the future, but certainly interdisciplinary 'teams' of researchers are becoming more frequent. For example, I am currently on one project that involves a broad spectrum of researchers including those from the faculty of Arts, e.g. psychology, sociology, women's studies and economics, and from the faculty of social work, and I am a part of another group of researchers that includes, thus far, myself and two geographers. This project is oriented toward outcomes and adaptations regarding climate change in Ghana. My positioning within both women's and religious studies, as well as being adept in theories from both locations, was in this instance, and others I believe, a strength.

6 LOOKING TO THE FUTURE OF RELIGIOUS STUDIES IN CANADA

Certainly I am no prophet, nor do I desire to be one, but I think I can say one or two things about the future of religious studies in light of past and current trajectories. I think first and foremost that postcolonialism and globalization are having, and will continue to have, a significant effect on religious studies. The kinds of effects will be varied, but certainly politics and policy development, and legal systems and justice are important areas currently developing in the field.[22] This kind of development also points to another shift; a shift away from an essentialized view of systems of belief and practice. Therefore, although certainly specialization in a 'religion' continues to be a significant orientation in religious studies, along with the development of areas of specialization such as philosophy, psychology and literature, nonetheless there has been a move toward a more thematic orientation; for example, religion and the law, religion and politics, religion and popular culture, women and religion, men and religion, or religion and healing.[23] It is this thematic orientation that is interdisciplinary and I suspect it will be one of the ways that interdisciplinary work will gain further respect in the field, at least from some.

At this time, however, the tendency is still to encourage students of religion to develop a field specialization, e.g. Buddhism, Hinduism and so forth (and with this a sub-field that often links nicely with the primary area of study, for example Taoism linked with Buddhism) and then subsequently add to this a thematic development such as law, politics, policy development or human rights. As Dan Sperber noted, although interdisciplinarity is given rhetorical support, when it comes down to it only well-established scholars can afford to take the risk. It is my hope that continued acceptance of interdisciplinary work will mitigate this and allow graduate students to develop their own good interdisciplinary projects. Such work, in my estimation, can only improve the perception of our field by our colleagues outside of religious studies, and increase the viability of the field itself. It has been my experience that many academics from a variety of fields do not understand the field and assume that religious studies is simply code for theology. In light of this, then, it is no surprise that excellent work done in religious studies is ignored and untapped by scholars in other areas of study.[24]

As for issues regarding race, power, gender and class, these categories continue to be underdeveloped in our field. Too many scholars in religious studies ignore these very important categories, thinking that they could not possibly be significant aspects of the study. However, if one is dealing with human beings and their social and cultural systems, then clearly they are important categories that are not only significant to data, but also to theory. In the past I have momentarily bracketed race, class or gender, but I have not ignored them, as they are too central to understanding systems of belief and practice.

In the end, I do believe that occupying women's studies and religious studies has been beneficial for me. This doubling up of areas of study brings a richness to my research and allows me to move into other fields to learn just a little more. When I began my journey in academia, I did so because I loved to read, to learn and to think. However, from the outset I was not thrilled by disciplinary boundaries and it would appear that my career as a student and a faculty member reflect this resistance. For me, interdisciplinary labour allows for breathing space, and has ultimately expanded my opportunity to do what I like best: to read, learn and think.

12

Reflections on the Craft of Religious Studies

JON R. STONE (CALIFORNIA STATE UNIVERSITY, LONG BEACH)

Derrida is dead (to begin with). There's no doubt whatever about that. Unless this fact is distinctly understood, nothing wonderful can come of this story.

Derrida is dead. *Requiescat in pace.* Soon others will be uttering their eulogies over the remaining members of that generation of postmodern inter-preters, to whom ours had given such deference. And when, at last, they have absented themselves from view, yet another 'grand narrative'[1] to have inun-dated the Western academic world – including religious studies – in a stormy deluge will calmly recede. What new intellectual squall will rise in the wake of postmodernism, perhaps a blending of modern and postmodern narrative streams? Given our perspective, high atop this new century looking back upon the old, we see these previous trends, as one might look upon the waves washing across a beach, the surf lifting, swirling, rearranging and redepos-iting sedimentary sands of meaning, to little effect. Can one not make out the faint traces of tide lines left by earlier intellectual swells? As with all previous academic fads and fancies, this one – and the next one, too – shall pass.[2]

Scarcely a decade and a half ago, Tomoko Masuzawa keenly observed that 'in our time of the ubiquitous *post-*, the order of time itself has become some-what weird. We thought we were accustomed to living in terms of beginning, middle, and end, and we thought we always traveled in a passage of time as smartly as the pages between two hard covers; but now it looks like we are traversing a bad infinity which is, worse still, strangely convoluted.'[3] Yes, at the time, it did look as though we were 'traversing a bad infinity', but have we so easily forgotten that our own intellectual predecessors had been dazed by Nietzsche, who came as a madman holding a lantern as if to illumine the dawn? Except for those attuned to the spirit of their age, most had found them-selves blinded and disoriented by the bright searchlight of Nietzsche's work. '*We have killed him* [*God*] – you and I. All of us are his murderers,' Nietzsche's madman exclaimed in 1882. 'But how have we done this?' he enquired:

How were we able to drink up the sea? Who gave us the sponge to wipe away the entire horizon? What did we do when we unchained this earth from its sun? Whither is it moving now? Whither are we moving now? Away from all suns? Are we not plunging continually? Backward, side-ward, forward, in all directions? Is there any up or down left? Are we not straying as through infinite nothing?

And then, like hammer blows sealing shut a coffin lid, the madman declared: 'God is dead. God remains dead. And we have killed him ... What was holiest and most powerful of all that the world has yet owned has bled to death under our knives. Who will wipe this blood off us?'[4] But Nietzsche's madman had arrived too soon. The shaking of the foundations, the destruc-tion of the Western intellectual world, the death of God was yet to come.

1   MODERN VS POSTMODERN IN RELIGIOUS STUDIES

My graduate experience at Santa Barbara in the 1980s coincided with the high tide of the postmodernist and poststructuralist assault on modern rational thought. In between graduate seminars and shifts at a local market where I worked as a butcher, I imbibed Foucault and Derrida, supped on Lacan and Lyotard and picked at and puzzled over Barthes, Baudrillard and Bataille – and chased it all down with deep draughts of Jameson, Habermas and Heineken. While today, I still marvel at what this brilliant post-war critique of modernism had wrought upon the Academy, in terms of my own studies, I came away with a vague awareness that I knew less about 'religion' than when I had begun. In fact, the more I read and digested postmodern thought – to (re)mix metaphors – the more these intellectual currents carried me into deeper and deeper waters, and farther away from the theoretically certain shores of the social sciences where I thought I had found a safe harbour. Was not religion simply the 'audacious attempt to conceive of the entire universe as humanly significant', as Peter Berger had phrased it?; that religion, stripped of its sacred charms, 'implies that human order is projected into the totality of being'?[5] And as a social phenomenon, cannot religion be operationalized, quantified, measured?

When viewed through the fragmented prism of postmodernist/poststruc-turalist thought, the religious studies of Ninian Smart (PBUH), Mircea Eliade, Wilfred Cantwell Smith, Joseph Kitagawa and Charles Long, and the discipline they helped institute, had become, in a word, quaint. For to me, after studying these luminaries in our field, reading postmodernist critique was something akin to listening to the score of Stravinsky's avant-garde ballet, *The Rite of Spring* (1913), after hearing a recording of *The Nutcracker* (1892), and feeling embarrassment for Tchaikovsky, that hopeless romantic. While the postmodernist attack on the Enlightenment tradition certainly caused a stir within the humanities generally, unlike *The Rite of Spring*, postmodernism's own wild orgy of pagan rhythms did not touch off panic and rioting in the streets of Paris. In fact, it had been panic and rioting in Paris during the late 1960s that had led, among other things, to the postmodernist 'rethink' of modernity. Although it would bludgeon the Academy for two decades, as with Odysseus' childhood scar, the mark it left would later be touched by his nurse with many a tender recollection.[6] For my generation, the trauma has passed, but *cicatrix manet*, the scar remains. My fond memories of that period are a mix of certainty and uncertainty, of questions answered by questions that question what is behind a question.

While one may mourn the death of postmodernism, the end of its brief but terrific reign over many disciplines in the Academy signals a slow return of rational discourse and the eventual renewal of epistemic reliability grounded in the scientific method. But even if one returns from this wondrous postmodern journey, as with Odysseus' welcome return to Ithaca, will the academic world and the study of religion ever be the same again?

In many ways, it is as if my generation stood between two worlds – the modern and the postmodern. While our education was shaped and fashioned by our 'modernist' professors, our beliefs and opinions were fired in the kiln of postmodernist *simulacre*.[7] Ours is the first generation raised on television, a generation for whom the real is not the real, and electronic signals that display moving pictures on a 12-inch screen generated for us a hyper-reality. What was illusory became non-illusory and the firm belief that old rules no longer applied became the new rule to be applied. To know the self that could not be known, when joined with the postmodern critique of knowing and self-knowing, justified and reinforced our generation's self-absorption. This, in turn, produced a generation of maverick scholars who declared themselves not bound or bounded by time or tradition, but who, in consequence, to paraphrase my colleague Bradley K. Hawkins, tended to confuse cleverness and its attendant notoriety with seminality. To be sure, though 'a certain undesirable originality may be achieved without much trouble', to cite an 1805 review of Beethoven's *Eroica* Symphony, 'genius proclaims itself not in the unusual and the fantastic' – I might add, the grotesque – 'but in the beautiful and the sublime'.[8]

What is more, for our generation – or at least at my end of the baby boom – the postmodern world appeared to have collapsed into itself. The structures of meaning and the edifices of established systems of thought in which we had lived lay in ruins. It had been our self-appointed task to reconstruct a world of meaningful social experience. Indeed, the mood of our generation is captured in Marshall Berman's title, *All That Is Solid Melts Into Air*. As he writes, 'If we think of modernism as a struggle to make ourselves at home in a constantly changing world, we will realize that no mode of modernism can ever be definitive. Our most creative constructions and achievements are bound to turn into prisons and white sepulchres that we, or our children, will have to escape or transform if life is to go on.'[9] In fact, it was in the same section cited above that Nietzsche's madman 'entered divers churches and there sang his *requiem aeternum deo'*, and each time announcing, 'What are these churches now if they are not the tombs and sepulchres of God?'[10] What Otto Heller had said of Nietzsche nearly a century ago could also be said of the postmodernist project today. As Heller wrote:

> Nietzsche's merit consists not in any unriddling of the universe by a meta-physical key to its secrets, but rather in the diffusion of a new intellectual light elucidating human consciousness in regard to the purpose and end of existence. Nietzsche has no truths to teach, indeed he acknowledges no truth other than subjective ... His argumentation is not sustained and progressive, but desultory, impressionistic, and freely repetitional; slashing aphorism is its most effective tool ... [A]n implacable enemy of the *metier* ..., the formative and directive influence of his vaticinations, enunciated with tremendous spiritual heat and lofty gesture, has been very great. His conception of life has acted upon the generation as a moral intoxicant of truly incalculable strength.[11]

Interestingly, as a movement, postmodernism derived much of its thought and a good deal of its language and discourse from the writings of Nietzsche, as well as Marx, Freud and de Saussure. However, its application to the study of religion has been little different from Nietzsche's critique of religion, though no less insightful, when compared to earlier trends. The one thing that postmodernism seems to lack is a unifying system of thought. But, then, its aim has been to undermine the foundations of thought, not establish or support new ones.[12]

2   A METHOD/METHODOLOGY APPROPRIATE TO THE DISCIPLINE

Since the 1950s, religious studies has been desperately in search of a meth-odological approach – or rather *the* methodological approach[13] – to separate it from theology, its supposed ugly stepsister, and thus to give it credence and independent standing within the Academy at large. In effect, postmod-ernism, that 'endlessly engrossing territory of contemporary debate',[14] has been an illusory glass slipper that held out the promise of uniting a char-maiden with her fairy-tale prince charming. What living in the postmodern academic world has taught my generation is that there is no prince charming for religious studies, just as there will likely appear no grand theory unifying those who study religion today. Despite this illusion, there are still those who are convinced of the rightness of the postmodern approach as *the* method-ology most appropriate to the discipline, a philosopher's stone of sorts, which others before us had sought as anxiously as Malory's Grail knights in quest of Christ's sacred cup. But in the case of postmodernism, its quest has been in some ways similar to the 'righteous war' of Cervante's *Don Quixote de la Mancha* – 'de cuyo nombre no quiero acordarme/of which name I do not want to recall' – in full tilt against treacherous windmills posing as hulking giants.

Postmodernist ideas about and interpretations of literature and culture have certainly been interesting and insightful. And, in some cases, their proponents have offered useful correctives to the academic study of religion. What creates alarm is when these ideas become ideologies and when these ideologies become orthodoxies to be imposed upon scholars working in the field. Of course, the sad irony is that the post-war generation of the 1960s, a generation defined by its questioning of authority and pushing for revolutionary change, has set up altars to its own glorious past and demanded that their students and younger colleagues worship and revere them without question. Need one say it again?: Derrida is dead.

In fact, one needn't look too far to find examples of postmodern, or rather, anti-modern approaches being taken for gospel in religious studies, and being used in a crusade to root out methodological dissent. For instance, not long after the publication of *The Craft of Religious Studies* in 1998, a review appeared in the *Journal for the Scientific Study of Religion*. As with most book reviews, this reviewer took the opportunity to measure the worthiness of this collection of essays against current trends within the field. Though the purpose of the book was simply to present autobiographical profiles of scholars working broadly within the orbit of religious studies, the reviewer saw within it an agenda. 'Therefore,' the reviewer concluded:

> despite what seems on the surface to be its all too postmodern, self-reflexive approach, this collection's rationale is thoroughly modernist in its assumption that some sort of deeper, immaterial essence underlies the multiplicity of manifestations ... Having scholars of religion and religious scholars [viz., Jacob Neusner, Andrew Greeley, and Martin Marty] ... all grouped together in one volume, as if they were all involved in the common craft of religious studies, forces one to read 'religious studies' as both a field of study in the public university and a particular type of devotional practice, an all too crafty use of the adjective 'religious'.[15]

While I would not dispute that this collection was not without its flaws, or that '[t]ackling these essays requires a reader adept in mental, methodological, and institutional gymnastics',[16] I would point out that for a reviewer to make this kind of comment means that that same reviewer holds a decided *belief* about what 'religious studies' *is* and what true and faithful 'scholars of religion' ought to *do*. To my mind, charges of 'modernist' or 'essentialist' or 'reductionist' are merely ways of silencing dissenters, suppressing debate within a field, or otherwise trying to control academic discourse. Like grand inquisitors, many within my generation have made a career of policing other scholars' works in search of offensive modernist and essentialist language and approaches.

As academics (and presumably liberals and humanists), our conversation should welcome *all* voices – especially those voices excluded or ignored by traditionalist and modernist discourses – not quash them by means of postmodernist pogroms. Scholars and theologians, secular and religious, modernist and postmodernist are part of this field alike. In the end, we are all students of religion, however one might choose to define the field. And, in the end, whether religion is real or imagined, of human or divine origins, or true or false in its beliefs, the approaches we take and the methods we choose should be judged by one criterion: do our methods and methodologies teach us something, or reveal some new and interesting facet about *religion* as an aspect of human life and experience in the world? And what, in turn, does the study of religion teach us about the nature and character of humankind?

In its essence, then, research is the human mind (as) applied to the world, whether physical or social. In our case, it is the mind of the researcher (as) applied to the religious worlds created by men and women, past and present. To argue over the proper method to use or the correct methodology to employ only makes sense if our sincere aim is not simply to undermine someone's scholarly reputation, but to gain a clearer and more accurate understanding of those worlds. In my research, I have endeavoured to learn and apply some useful insight from everyone I have read and from every theory – new and old – that I have encountered. Thus, what was true for Terence over two millennia ago is likewise true for me: '*Humani nihil a me alienum puto*' – nothing that relates to humanity is foreign to me.

3   FROM POETICS (*SIC*) TO PRAGMATICS (*SIC*)

The reason for the very lengthy, and somewhat poetical, introductory section was to provide the reader with a perspective on the current methodological struggles within religious studies generally as well as to pique the reader's interest in the more practical and prosaic parts of this essay. Accordingly, the poetical will now give way to the practical in the form of guidance to graduate students from one who has travelled the same road and can therefore advise the 'tenderfoots' in our profession. The following observations that I make here, as well as the advice I give, are drawn from over 20 years of teaching, research and conference participation in the field of religious studies. Because I can only speak from my own experiences, my comments therefore should be read with that modest qualification in mind.

It was my fortune to undertake graduate work during the heyday of religious studies at the University of California, Santa Barbara. It was during this last decade of the Cold War that the balance of power in the field shifted westward toward Santa Barbara: Ninian Smart was dividing his time between Santa Barbara and Lancaster; Walter Capps was creating national interest in religious studies through his Vietnam War course; Robert Michaelsen, Phillip Hammond, and later Catherine Albanese and Wade Clark Roof, were defining new directions in the study of American religions; Birger Pearson and Kurt Rudolph (only briefly) were engaged in groundbreaking work in the Nag Hammadi library and in Jewish and Christian Gnosticism; Gerald Larson, Inés Talamantez, Raimundo Panikkar, Allan Grapard and several others were establishing a recognized centre for studies in Asian religions and indigenous traditions. As a native son of Southern California (Whittier/ La Habra), descended from pioneer orange growers and wildcatters, I had arrived at Santa Barbara (via San José and Ventura) with a background in Biblical Studies, intent on studying Jewish and Christian apocalyptic literature. But being at Santa Barbara tended to expand one's horizons and soon I found myself cobbling together a graduate programme that combined my work in biblical and extra-biblical literature with the current theoretical interests among social scientists in new religious movements, church and state relations, and resurgent fundamentalism – all of which offered utopian visions of a world that once was or a world that was to come.

All these combinations and recombinations made sense from a fragmented postmodern/poststructural perspective, and led to a commingling of ideas and approaches not previously imagined from a modernist theoretical or grand narrative perspective. This destabilizing of unified systems created 'little narratives' and, in turn, opened up new lines of enquiry for us graduates to follow. While some of my colleagues fell down the rabbit hole of postmodernist debate, I have been far less taken by trends in our field, and can rightly be criticized for my Brahmsian attempt to set new ideas in old forms, or to recover lost but useful ideas or methods of analysis that can be effectively applied to current research questions.

As a carpenter's son (my father was a master craftsman, no less), I have also been far less interested in critiquing theories and methods in the study of religion than I have been in using those theories and methods as the tools of my trade. I have kept those that work, and set aside those that do not or no longer work. With Rodney Stark, I would say that one's approach to the study of religion, and one's methods of research, should follow almost naturally from the question or questions one seeks to answer. As Stark advises, 'research questions must determine what method or methods are suitable – *how* to find out depends on *what* you want to know. When one's primary commitment is to a particular methodology, one's ability to pursue important questions is severely limited.'[17] Unfortunately for our discipline, there are many among us for whom one tool – a hammer or a crowbar – suffices for all projects. The researcher should learn how to approach theoretical questions and handle religious data with a certain measure of subtlety and finesse.

Accordingly, I would contend that graduate students enter their studies as apprentices to a profession, very much like artisans learning their trade from master craftsmen and craftswomen. Through their studies, these apprentices come to learn the *craft* of religious studies. The theories they use, and the methods they employ to address the problems presented to them, serve as their tools. Similarly, their teachers become their models for how scholars should ply their trade. The disposition or temperament of the craftsperson also influences their work. For me, that disposition has included an inquisitive mind, a limitless curiosity about the world, equanimity in handling conflicting information, an appreciation for differences of interpretation, and a dissatisfaction with the received tradition. In my own research and writing, I have sought to achieve clarity of thought, felicity of expression, and, above all, charity in my critique of the work of others. Much of this is dispositional, of course, but I had learned to be charitable by observing the collegial way in which my own professors treated each other, and especially the respect they showed toward those with whom they disagreed. This sense of fair play, also referred to more technically as 'structured empathy' by Ninian Smart, is undoubtedly an aspect of epoché that many in our field have striven to adopt as a preferred approach to religion (regardless of its connection to accursed phenomenology). As my revered teacher relates,

> [f]or me personally, this perspective came as a result of the influence of one of the few British values which I retain – no doubt caught from long years of playing beloved cricket, namely, the sense of fair play: the sense that our description of Buddhist or Hindu or other non-Western values has to be 'fair'. All this I characterize as 'warm neutralism'. Some of my critics say you cannot do it, that empathy without sympathy is a fraud. I, however, hold that while this is difficult to achieve in a pure sense, you can at least aim at it, aim at an approach to religions which is much better than aiming at unfairness, lack of empathy, and ignorance.[18]

Among the developments in the field over which Smart had expressed increasing alarm was the disposition or inclination toward 'specialisms'[19] or toward personal and political advocacy[20] that served only to fragment the field further and undercut the professionalism of the scholar.

As a result, much of what seems to pass for religious studies these days is little more than theology and apologetics in disguise. Though Timothy Fitzgerald would say that phenomenology, 'a contemporary style of [liberal] ecumenical theologizing',[21] has been bequeathed to us by Smart and his generation, despite the hiccup of postmodernist thought (or perhaps because of it), one trend within the academic study of religion that contributes to this 'theologizing' has been a growing parochialism within the subfields of religious studies.[22] While Smart and his generation were decidedly 'ecumenical', in most departments across the land today, we find Buddhists studying

Buddhism, Jews studying Judaism, Muslims studying Islam, Sikhs studying Sikhism, the mystically inclined studying mysticism, and Protestants and Catholics (including 'escaped' Evangelicals and 'recovering' Catholics) studying their respective branches of Christianity, etc. Even the recent movement of religious studies into 'area' and 'identity' subfields have followed this same trend. Women study women in religion; lesbian women and gay men study religion and (homo)/(bi)/(trans)sexuality; people of colour (!) study their respective racial or ethnic groups. Worse still, scholars from these subfields often reject as credible the work of someone who is not part of the religious or racial or gendered community which they are studying. In the end, everyone studies themselves, balkanizing the field even further. Doesn't anyone study 'religion' anymore? Are scholars of religion really content simply to study themselves or their own self-defined communities? What ever became of Max Müller's oft-quoted dictum, 'he who knows (only) one knows none'?[23] Is our field's current hyper-subjectivity and self-absorption the legacy of the 'me' generation or merely the offspring of its postmodernist fling? It seems to me that, as a discipline, we too have declared the death of objectivity (epoché) and, as with the old cliché, have thrown out the twin babies of self-discipline and self-reflection (or self-criticism) with the bath of the scientific method.

Related to the death of epoché, I would argue that subjectivity and self-interest have also opened the barn door to unbridled advocacy, which seems to be edging out our field's once rigorous research.[24] Advocacy is the claim to speak out in defence of a cause or on behalf of those who presumably cannot or will not speak for themselves. While advocacy certainly has its place in social and political discourse, I do not think that it should command the central place in one's research programme. Here is why: the work of advocacy is by nature ephemeral, changing itself and its focus with each new cause. Advocacy neither educates nor liberates truly; its aim is not to persuade but to coerce – by any means necessary. Because advocacy has little patience for persons or facts that might challenge its opinions – and these are opinions – it often ends up suppressing inconvenient facts, impugning the motives of its opponents, or in other ways destroying a climate of free and open enquiry that generations of scholars before us had sought to preserve. Of advocacy I would say: by all means, be politically active and fight for just causes – 'we all want to change the world'.[25] But, by all means, endeavour even more passionately to prevent one's personal and political causes from unduly influencing or otherwise determining one's study of religion. 'You better free your mind instead.'[26]

4   PUBLISH OR PERISH? CREATING A RESEARCH
PROGRAMME

Notwithstanding my foregoing remarks, I do believe that the scholar's life is a public life. Whether a person pursues a career in teaching or research – or schizophrenically in both – our professional obligation is the same: the scholar of religion must make his or her work public, and should make their published work accessible. Of course, for some scholars, their work may be specialized and therefore accessible to only a few; for others, their work may enjoy broader appeal. In either case, publish or perish is not a curse as much as it is a commission that we receive from the Academy. As academics – and most often as state employees – we have been granted extraordinary privileges in that our jobs allow us leisure to read, think, teach and write. It is our *dharma*, our duty, to publish our research findings in the appropriate forum. True, those of our colleagues at larger research universities have much more time and many more resources at their command. But the difference in one's professional assignments should not preclude anyone from developing an active research programme.

How, then, does one develop a research programme? While, traditionally, the doctoral dissertation has served as the point of departure for further research, a research programme is more than merely a continuation of what one has done as a graduate student. A research programme is a map of one's intellectual plans, a schematic of the questions one seeks to answer and the information one needs to know, the data one needs to collect, and the skills one needs to command to answer those questions. For instance, since my days as a graduate student, I have kept a notebook of questions about religious ideas and religious movements that I would eventually like to answer, and of some of the broader methodological concerns in the Academy that I would like someday to address. While I have selected topics and issues because they seemed to be interesting questions to me, I have also chosen my research questions for the simple fact that I wanted to learn something new. By contrast, Rodney Stark points out that he has 'selected research questions because of their theoretical importance' to the field,[27] while the British philosopher, John Hick, notes that many of his main research questions tend to be 'problem-driven, in a sense being attempts to contribute to the solution to acutely felt problems facing religious persons'.[28] Wendy Doniger, for her part, makes this interesting confession: 'Over the years people kept asking me why I did what I did, but I resolutely resisted all the requests to lay out my "method", for the very good reason that I didn't think I had one – several, maybe, but not one.' Earlier in her essay, she had admitted that 'I had always chosen topics that moved me'; the books she wrote were written 'not out of a desire to put in print what I understood, but, rather, in order to find out what I understood ... I have only known what I thought about many major issues by reading what I have written.'[29]

In terms of religious studies as a discipline, one question that has continued to intrigue me has been our field's continuing reliance on theories and models and typologies that were developed in the late nineteenth and early twentieth centuries, most especially those advanced by Marx and Weber, Freud and Durkheim, Jung and Eliade.[30] That is, the assumptions that have informed our field – at least among those of us who approach the study of religion from a secular, non-theological direction – have been based largely upon a perception of the world and a view of the world's religions that no longer hold true. Even modern scholars, such as anthropologists Clifford Geertz, Mary Douglas and Victor Turner, lived and wrote in a time very unlike our own. Rather than challenge these assumptions, many persons in our field seem content to hold onto and perpetuate theories and explanations of religion by individuals who could never have imagined life as now lived in the third millennium. Even controlling for modifications made by subsequent generations of scholars who have liberated the field and brought more diverse voices into the conversation, one still finds the assumptions behind these theories to be old-fashioned, reactionary, sometimes ridiculous or certainly out-of-step with the contemporary world.

As an example, Ivan Strenski recounts an episode early in his career in which he was lecturing to a class on 'Lévi-Strauss' structural approach to myth, and not doing a very good job convincing the students how wonderful it all was'. At a certain point, a 'somewhat perturbed young woman raised her hand in the middle of my lecture, stood up, and asked, "Why would *anyone* think about myth like that?!"' Strenski did not remember his reply but it gave him pause to reflect upon the fact that while he and other academics might take one theorist or another for granted 'as making total sense', at the same time, 'all attempted rationales for his [Lévi-Strauss'] method left my students dumbfounded. The genuine germ of wisdom and good sense contained in my student's question was to ask why otherwise equally intelligent, hardworking myth theorists had come up with such different methods of approaching myths, and more fundamentally different conceptions of what "myth" was.' A lesser scholar would have dismissed this student's question as a trifling nuisance. Instead, Strenski was inspired to investigate 'how and why a theory was formed in a particular way' and came to see theories 'as embodying various strategies and interests'.[31] To me, Ivan Strenski and many of my other mentors exemplify the intellectual derring-do that continues to give vitality to the craft of religious studies. They possess what I would call 'intuitive technique', following the observation of Jerome S. Bruner, who said: 'The shrewd guess, the fertile hypothesis, the courageous leap to a tentative conclusion – these are the most valuable coin of the thinker at work.'[32]

For most who are just finishing their graduate studies and embarking on their first year of teaching, revising the dissertation is typically the first place to begin when setting up a research programme. One strategy is to take two or three chapters of the dissertation and rework them into discrete articles for publication in journals. Another strategy is to spend one's first year after the PhD rewriting the dissertation to meet the style requirements of one or two university presses and then send it out for review by one or more of these target presses. Initial contact with editors can be made either at national conferences – they are always looking for new manuscripts – or by a query letter sent to the religion editor of the press. At times, established colleagues in the department may recommend editors with whom they have worked, and may even offer to send a query letter on your behalf, as several of my professors had done for me.

As an aside, let me offer this one bit of advice: whenever I have sent book manuscripts or articles to be reviewed for possible publication, I have always included the names and contact information of individuals who would be fair, if not favourably disposed to my work. This is not to say that I purposely 'stack the deck' in my favour, just that editors do not always know of the qualified individual in my area who might be willing to review my work. Because, most of the time, editors do not disclose the identity of the author to reviewers, providing names of would-be reviewers is neither a mortal nor a venal sin.

In addition, there may be opportunities to rewrite some sections of your dissertation in the form of encyclopedia articles for printed or online refer-ence sources. One of my earliest mentors in writing reference works was J. Gordon Melton, whose career was built on a mountain of superb reference works. Periodically, Gordon would ask me to write entries for one or another of his projects.[33] In fact, he gave me some of my earliest publishing oppor-tunities and taught me how to condense large amounts of material into 500–1,000 word entries, sometimes shorter.[34] I also owe a debt of gratitude to Gordon for commissioning my first book, *A Guide to the End of the World*, for his 'Religious Information Systems' series that he was editing for Garland (now part of Routledge/Taylor & Francis).[35] It was not my dissertation,[36] but it had been a project that I had been working on for several years as a graduate student. The idea for this book was first inspired in 1985 or 1986 by Walter Capps and Richard Hecht, the latter having asked me to do background research on fundamentalists' end-of-time interest in the nation of Israel for his monumental book with Roger Friedland, *To Rule Jerusalem*, which appeared a decade later.[37] Though I never published that paper in its original form, the essence of it became manifested in my *Guide*. As with this work, some of my other book projects likewise grew out of seminar papers, invited lectures,[38] informal suggestions from my professors, or as ways to exorcise the ghosts of my own ignorance,[39] heeding Dickens to 'beware this boy [ignorance], for on his brow I see that written which is Doom, unless the writing be erased'.[40]

Among the other more practical things that a freshly minted PhD can do to begin developing a record of research and publication, and get into the rhythm of scholarship, is to write book notes and book reviews. One venue for book notes is *Religious Studies Review*, which enlists the help of professors and some graduate students to read and review hundreds of books that are sent to its editors throughout the year. In addition to giving a young scholar a chance to participate in the larger conversation of the discipline, writing several reviews each year can give needed experience in meeting deadlines. It can also make it easier for a person to stay current with the research in his or her area.

Another way to help build one's research portfolio is by presenting papers at national and regional conferences, and by volunteering to organize sessions, chair discussion panels, or serve as a respondent. My practice has usually been to write an abstract for a topic that I would like to research and then submit it to one or another call for papers, which ever society's conference theme my paper seems to fit best. Finding a place on a national programme is at times difficult, but a person should be vigilant. But, because of the smaller numbers of submissions, regional conferences tend to be less selective than national conferences and usually have a place on the programme for nearly every paper proposal received. Either way, having my paper proposal accepted for a national or regional conference commits me to writing the paper and receiving helpful criticism from the respondent and from those who will attend the session. What is more, by the time I submit the paper to a journal for review, I have already received valuable feedback and have been able to address some of the problems that I might otherwise have overlooked.

5   AN ABRUPT ENDING ...

There is much more that I could say, but I realize full well that there is a limit to a reader's charity, especially when having to endure the counsel and advice of a scholar who has already come to the middle passage of his professorial voyage. And so, I will close these reflections on the craft of religious studies by inviting graduate students to reflect themselves upon the topics touched on above. Perhaps in 20 or 30 years time, another enterprising editor will ask you to offer your insights into a discipline that, one hopes, will remain far from the shoals of methodological shipwreck. By then, I will have passed into my nirvana, and your generation will be writing clever eulogies about ours.

13

Religion, Discourse and Hermeneutics: New Approaches in the Study of Religion

CHARLES H. LONG (EMERITUS, UNIVERSITY OF NORTH
CAROLINA, CHAPEL HILL)

We are all of us, and Eliade to the fore, would-have-been believers, we are all religious minds without religion.[1]

As for those subjects which might in principle become fields for disciplinary cultivation, but in which effective disciplinary development has scarcely begun, we shall speak of these as 'would-be disciplines.'[2]

1 INTRODUCTION: BACKGROUND

Some time ago at one of the periodic conferences that take place at the University of Chicago to discuss disciplines and methods I delivered a paper that traced the methodological history of the study of religion at the University of Chicago. The paper was published as an article, 'A look at the Chicago tradition in the history of religions: retrospect and future'.[3] In this presentation I gave an account of the methodological discussions centred on the study of religion at the university over a 60-year period. I chose to discuss the history of methodological discussions at the University of Chicago because it was one of the important centres for research and training of historians of religion and was self-conscious regarding the issue of method and theory for the study of religion.

I pointed out in my discussion that there had been a constant refrain over the years for the perfection of a systematic method for the study of religion and I concluded that such a method had not been forthcoming, and, in my opinion, was in fact, a false hope. I will state my conclusion at length:

The anticipation for a science of religion, a *Religionswissenschaft* has not been fulfilled; these expectations have been simply postponed from one generation to the next. One might wonder whether such expectations are legitimate. I am beginning to have my doubts. We all stand in appreciation and awe of the work that has been accomplished through making use of what we have learned from the history of our discipline. But is a 'science' in the Enlightenment sense a proper receptacle of these meanings? I am suggesting the human science that would be the proper receptacle will develop when the shadows surrounding the interpreter and the interpreter's culture as 'otherness' are made part of the total hermeneutical task. Our goal would then not be a science but a serious human discourse.[4]

In the Afterword of the Conference volume, the rapporteurs, Professor Joseph Kitagawa and Professor Gregory Alles, presented two responses to my paper. They suggested that in one sense my presentation in its concluding suggestion of a 'serious discourse' was reminiscent of 'inter-religious dialogue'. The other comment was expressed by Professor Benjamin Ray, my former student, who thought that my formulation of a 'serious discourse' was 'too sloppy'. I take as a point of departure this paper and the comments of my interlocutors.

2   THE CONSTRUCTION OF RELIGION

Scholars of religion were probably taken aback at Jonathan Z. Smith's oft-quoted statement that '... there is no data for religion. Religion is solely the creation of the scholar's study. It is created for the scholar's analytical purposes by his imaginative acts of comparison and generalization. Religion has no independent existence apart from the academy.'[5] The seeming radicality of this statement is matched by Michel Foucault's observation concerning the origin of the human sciences in general:

> The first thing to be observed is that the human sciences did not inherit a certain domain already outlined, perhaps surveyed as a whole, but allowed to be fallow, which it was their task to elaborate with positive methods and with concepts that had at last become scientific ... for man did not exist (anymore than life, or language, or labor); and the human sciences did not appear when, as a result of some pressing rationalism, some unresolved scientific problem, some practical concern, it was decided to include man (willy-nilly, and with a greater or lesser degree of success) ... they appeared [the human sciences] when man constituted himself in Western culture as both that which must be conceived and that which is to be known.[6]

While the rhetorical style of these statements might well shock humanistic scholars out of their doldrums and cause them to think seriously about method, both statements say at once too much and too little. Both statements help to disavow us of the notion that scholarly activity and research in the human sciences is merely the application of sophisticated methodologies to that which is 'naturally given' as social and cultural reality. Both statements emphasize the constructed nature of the data of the social and human sciences and the manner in which the epistemological problem involved in the creation of the data. Neither of the statements, however, places the origin of the construction or creation of these data within a proper temporal framework or situation. Foucault's notion of the *episteme* moves us beyond the automatic progressive notion of an evolutionary history of ideas but he fails to make adequate sense of the correlation of the *epistemic* structures to other levels of human reality. There is something to be said for Smith's notion that religion, insofar as it constitutes a datum for study, is created in the scholar's study but one must go a bit further and ask: 'Which scholars and in whose studies and for what reasons?'

In response to these issues I should like to understand the Enlightenment and the Enlightenment sciences against a background of the nascent mercantile theories and practices of the countries of the modern West. There is a relationship between the epistemological theories of mind and human constitution from Descartes to Kant and the English empiricists and the new notions of matter, materiality and its exchanges, though paradoxically these theories were not to be contaminated nor profaned by the numinous grossness or enticing fascination of the materiality and mercantilism that formed its context. This kind of methodological purity results in the 'ivory tower' construction of religion within the scholar's studies and the necessity for Locke and Hobbes to posit beginning stories within their philosophical treatises. This also accounts for Foucault's rendition of the rootless nature of these sciences.

3   THE ENLIGHTENMENT *ARCHE* FOR THE STUDY OF RELIGION

The study of religion growing out of the Enlightenment sciences was derived from a classification of the world into two major categories – the 'primitives', those cultures and peoples without written languages and cities, and 'Orientals', cultures outside the West that possessed written languages and lived in cities.[7] Much of the data for these categories grew out of the voyages of discovery beginning with the European 'discovery' of the new world and subsequently undertaken by most of the maritime nations of Western Europe. As a result of these voyages new kinds of relationships among and between human beings were made possible; a new and different kind of trade took place in every part of the globe. Another new and intense relationship among European powers ensued, prompted by their desire, possession and rivalry within the 'New World'. It was the ordering of these new data within the critical and creative orientation of those 'sciences' that presupposed the Enlightenment orientation that gave rise to new understanding of the 'human' and of religion.

Given the general ideology of the universality of what the Enlightenment considered to be reason, the strange and distant cultures that were now becoming known to the West were more often than not placed within the context of an evolutionary meaning of history. The actions, behaviours and customs of these other cultures were understood as embryonic growths of reason or reason, hidden or obscured by shadows of ignorance. From this point of view, religion as a category became the depository of a new form of *otherness* in a double sense. It was *other* in terms of a correlation between the valences of geographical distance and also in terms of the qualities of the foreign as awesome and exotic. I have coined the term *empirical others* to distinguish this meaning of alterity from the kind of alterity expressed in theories of religious experience in Rudolf Otto's classic.[8] Too often there has been an easy identity of Otto's *Wholly Other* of religious experience with the behaviours and practices of non-Western cultures. I have called this tendency to identify or correlate the meaning and nature of religion in the modern period a specific form of signification. The modern notion of religion as 'created in scholar's studies' or as emerging rootless from the inner epistemological consciousness of the modern West is directly related to the fact that religion as an authentic human mode has a direct relationship to those cultures that were 'discovered' and dominated by the West during the modern period. One might immediately raise the issue of those ancient Western cultures of the Near East or the Greeks or the Romans. In all cases the issue of distance is to the fore – either a distance in geographical space or in chronological time. In both cases this distance is a sign of passivity.[9]

With the end of the open practice and ideology of colonialism and imperialism we are confronted with a theoretical and practical issue of a different kind. The former 'sources of our data' have become interlocutors in the conversation about the human sciences, their origins, intent and meaning. The empiricity of their presence necessitates a rethinking of the categories. This other kind of difference must, however, be seen within the context of a world that has been subjected in a variety of ways with the sameness of a former colonialism and imperialism. In other words, we cannot authentically deal with this new situation by creating a binary composed of the meanings of the West on the one hand and the other meanings stemming from the cultures of the non-Western worlds. All cultures have experienced some form of colonialism whether as colonizers or the colonized. The former colonized for all sorts of reasons are forced to admit of this situation; the cultures of the colonial powers, having formally relinquished their rule, have not yet come to the intellectual and theoretical implications of this changed situation, especially as it applies to method and methodologies.

Dipesh Chakrabarty in several of his works has made this point in different ways. His clearest and most succinct statement of this point is,

'European thought is at once both indispensable and inadequate in helping us to think through the experiences of political modernity in non-Western nations, and provincializing Europe becomes the task of exploring how this thought – which is now everybody's heritage and which affects us all – may be renewed from and for the margins.'[10] It is thus not the intention of this new departure to substitute the opposite of colonialism as an alternative meaning of thought for what was the reigning content and style of thought of the cultures of the European colonizers. We should now raise issues from the kind of in-betweenness of time between the colonizers of the West and those who were dominated and colonized – from within the interstices of this contact situation.

It is well known that in the Enlightenment context of the human sciences the problem of the 'origins' of human institutions and modes of being provided an important take-off for investigation and research. The concern for origins included a search for the origins of language, marriage, society, religion and even the human mode of being itself. The quest for origins created speculative primordial and vague beginnings in some hoary past. So-called contemporary 'primitive' cultures were too often taken as approximation of these origins in the past.[11] This placing of cultures and peoples who are in fact contemporaneous with the West became a favourite modality within the human sciences. Johannes Fabian in his book, *Time and the Other*, is devoted to a discussion of this issue. He refers to this distancing within a contemporality as a denial of coevalness within the order of knowledge of the knower and the known. Fabian's statement to this point is as follows: 'The denial of coevalness ... can be traced to a fundamental epistemological issue. Ultimately it rests on the negation of temporal materiality of communication through language. For the temporality of speaking ... implies contemporality of producer and product, speaker and listener, Self and Other.'[12]

In the remainder of this paper I will discuss situations that have taken place as a result of colonialism and contact between the West and other cultures in the world: I will show how these situations could lead to another meaning of religion and its study.

4   A NEW *ARCHE* FOR THE STUDY OF RELIGION

4.1   *The origin of religion: the notion of the fetish*

At the present time the notion of the 'fetish' or 'fetishism' has been taken up in the sciences of psychopathology or is contextualized within a framework made famous by Marx's notion of 'commodity fetishism'. In the eighteenth century, fetishism was acknowledged by leading Western scholars as the 'origin of religion'. The term itself is derivative from the Portuguese, *feitico*, which is a form of the Latin, *facio, facere, factum*, terms having to do with making, doing or things made or accomplished. In Portuguese culture some form of these terms was used to designate witchcraft – extraordinary actions, usually evil or at least ambiguous, perpetrated by human beings. The word enters the scholarly lexicon not directly from the Portuguese, but from their settlements and relationships with certain Africans on the West coast of Africa. Though fetishism as the origin of religion lost its prominence in the early part of the twentieth century, its position being taken over by evolutionary and stadial notions, the residue of meaning contained in it continued to make it a concern for the social sciences.

William Pietz, in probing into this residual meaning of the fetish and fetishism, has revived the notion of the fetish in a new arena. In a series of brilliant articles published in the journal *RES* between the years 1985 and 1988, Pietz in a historical and analytical study brought about a new discourse about the meaning of the fetish for the methodologies of the social sciences.[13] Pietz discerned in his study that the discourse about the fetish emerged out of the cultural/social/commercial/sexual/linguistic contacts between the West and Africa and played a significant role in 'establishing certain preconceptions about human consciousness and the material world which became fundamental to the disciplinary human sciences that arose in the nineteenth century'.[14]

Pietz shows how the made or fabricated meaning of the fetish came from two sources. On the one hand the Portuguese traders as good citizens of a Catholic monarch asked the Africans, 'Who is your god?' The Africans replied by pointing to a talisman that they wore around their necks. Upon closer examination, the Portuguese discovered that many of these talismans were made of gold. They then enquired whether they would trade this 'god' for glass baubles or textiles. The Africans were willing to engage in such a trade. There is a second meaning attached to the notion of fabrication in the constitution of the fetish. The Africans with whom the Portuguese were dealing were members of what one might call a 'factory'. These factories were literally storehouses for captured slaves who were awaiting shipment across the Atlantic. Not only detribalized Africans from several different African tribes, but Europeans, former Muslims and Christians were residents of these factories. It was therefore these persons who no longer lived under the traditions of either African, European or Muslims traditions or orders of society. They were 'self-made men' whose major jobs was to reduce enslaved Africans from ordered societies into nondescript enslaved beings. The factories for the creation of slaves were the first step in the process of the social death of the enslaved persons.

Pietz offers a summarizing statement:

The first characteristic to be identified to the notion of the fetish is that of the fetish object's irreducible materiality. The truth of the fetish resides in its status as a material embodiment; its truth is not that of the idol, for the idol's truth lies in its relation of iconic resemblance to some immaterial model or entity ... second, and equally important, is the theme of singularity and repetition. The fetish has an ordering power derived from its status as the fixation or inscription of a unique originating event that has brought together previously heterogeneous elements into a novel identity ... the final two themes of the fetish are those of social value and personal individuality. The problem of the non-universality and connectedness of social value emerged in an intense form from the beginnings of the European voyages to sub-Saharan Africa.[15]

Pietz traces the history and literature related to the fetish from voyagers and discoverers from the seventeenth to the nineteenth century. Not only does he find that the notion of the fetish was being characterized as the general religion of the whole of Africa, it was taken up by Western scholars as the beginning and origin of religion itself. In addition, he finds that the notion of the fetish entered into Western scholarly and popular languages with no theological or philosophical discussion. The various descriptions in one of their forms were simply taken into the Western discussion concerning African religion in particular and the nature of religion in general. The notion of the fetish lies behind Kant's comment on Africa in his *Observations on the Feeling of Beauty and the Sublime* and Hegel's characterization of Africa in his *Philosophy of History*.

But something more sinister is going on in the meaning that is attached to the notion of the fetish. Obviously the Enlightenment had problems with the origin and beginnings of things and even more so with that meaning of transcendence that was related to a Creator of the world. In many traditions of the world, and especially in the Western religious traditions, the notion that a Creator God created the world gave assurance of an inherent value to the creatures of the world. The notion of the fetish, taking place within the interstices of the economic ordering of the Atlantic world becomes an almost perfect foil for the creation of a modality of matter that had no inherent value; the only value accruing to this form of matter was its exchange value. Now to be sure, one cannot place the total burden of the creation of this form of matter at the door of the fetish discussion. There is, of course, Max Weber's thesis concerning the role of the Protestant ethic and the creation of the Capitalist mode of production.[16] So while the meaning of the fetish is not the only cause, it is an important part of a constellation of meanings that have led to the disenchantment of the modern Western world.

It is interesting that this disenchantment of the world takes place within the orders of religious languages. Through the notion of the fetish, the inherent meaning of matter is debunked as a relic of a past age of ignorance. Nelson shows how the meaning of intimacy as an inherited modality of communal intimacy is given up for the overwhelming Calvinist emphasis on a High God whose relations to the world are inscrutable and unknown.

Along with other movements in the modern world the new form of matter that possesses no inherent value becomes matter as *the commodity*, whose value is realized only in exchange and it has the facility of being portable.

4.2   *The cargo cult*

The phenomenon that is called the 'cargo cult' was popularized through the work of an Australian government anthropologist whose professional responsibilities included keeping track of an area of New Guinea which was then governed by Australia. The anthropologist F. E. Williams made a report on strange new ceremonies taking place in neighbourhood of Vailala; this report was later published as *The Vailala Madness and the Destruction of Native Ceremonies in the Gulf District*. Here again is another scene of the encounter between the culture of the West and that of Papua New Guinea. In this case, the so-called 'cargo cult' centres around Western material commodities (cargo). From the original Williams' report we get this description: 'This movement involved, on the one hand a set of preposterous beliefs among its victims – in particular the expectation of an early visit from deceased relatives – and on the other hand, collective nervous symptoms of sometimes grotesque and idiotic nature.'[17]

K. O. L. Burridge tells us that these ceremonies revolve around mystical and messianic beliefs related to the veneration and expectation of Western commodity goods such as axes, knives, razorblades, coloured beads, tinned food, bolts of cloth, etc. This is why they are referred to as 'cargo' cults. Typically members of such a cult say that the commodities that have been brought to New Guinea by the Westerners were really in fact sent by the cultist's ancestors and were diverted en route by the Europeans.[18] As a matter of fact, the cargo cultists make it clear that from their perspective it is the Westerners who sacralize and venerate matter and materiality though they attempt to hide this fact from those whom they dominate. The Westerners tell them that their success is related to their God and their belief in Jesus Christ but the cargo cultists see in the Westerners' behaviour that they really in fact worship matter in the form of material goods – commodities which they have brought with them on great ocean ships.

Now it is clear that the natives of Papua New Guinea have a very different notion and meaning of exchange. At bottom their exchange system still carries with it notions of the gift and reciprocity. Furthermore, from their point of view, all the elements in the exchange, the object exchanged and the parties involved in the exchange are valorized; thus exchanges are always related in one way or another to some notion and meaning of community or the forms of intimacy related to communal life. It is clear that matter and materiality have not lost their inherent value for the cargo cultist; while dominated by Western power, they have not totally succumbed to the Western of abstract instrumental value as the reigning mode of exchange.

In addition, cargo cults often represent the only modes through which the natives of New Guinea are able to retain their identities. The cargo cult does not represent a simple binary with the natives on one side and the Westerners on the other; the relationship is more complex. As G. W. Trompf has noted, 'As we shall see, they symbolize the power available to whites; thus, with their hoped-for transference into indigenous hands, they amount to redemption from white domination and from the injustices of evident inequality or inaccessibility.'[19]

4.3   History and temporalities

In situations of colonialism, imperialism and domination, we are accustomed to hear some refrain on how the land was taken by the representatives of some Western power. Less often do we pay attention to the nature and meaning of time in a situation of this kind. The Enlightenment sciences present two interrelated views of temporality. From one point of view, time is understood as a variation of the Christian notion of time. In another version this Christian version is transformed into a secular abstract and neutral chronology based upon mathematical physical calculations symbolized by the Greenwich observatory. The change is designated as a change from AD, (Anno Domini, in the year of our Lord) to CE, (Common Era). In either case, the normative meaning of time is based upon a variation of the Western understanding of the temporal process. One of these variations of time is at work in defining the past, present or future or in universal terms; this time is also the basis for the periodizations of history, e.g. ancient, medieval and modern. Though the change from the qualitative Christian Western time of 'the year of our Lord' was changed to a neutral abstract notion of time, this same neutral and abstract time seemed to possess its own qualitative trajectory of progressivism. It is this qualitative trajectory that enables the social sciences almost unconsciously to carry on what Johannes Fabian has called the denial of coevalness.

A recent study of African American religion in Chicago is illustrative of this issue. What is striking in Wallace D. Best's work, *Passionately Human, No Less Divine: Religion and Culture in Chicago 1915–1952*,[20] a study of the migration of large numbers of African Americans from the rural South to the urban situation of Chicago, is the fact that at the University of Chicago was a Department of Sociology that was literally 'cutting its methodological teeth' on studies related to the nature of urbanity as a way of life. Wallace not only analyses and interprets the religious life of Black Pentecostal and mainline churches but also the meaning of the methodological impact of the Chicago School of Sociology. In addition, a number of the members of the 'Chicago School' were themselves African Americans.[21] For the most part, the sociologists defined the religious life of these migrant African Americans as an aspect of a bygone age and therefore would be ineffective as a meaningful structure in their adaptation to the urban situation. As Wallace's work shows, these migrants did not abandon their religion or their gods in the new situation – and their gods did not abandon them. As Wallace states at one point, 'The pervasiveness of a southern religious ethos over the entire religious scene and the cultural dominance of black southerners were intrinsic to that dynamic. The new urban religion ... had taken hold in Chicago during the migration era, even as important aspects of it eluded the view of some scholars.'[22]

The scholars of the Chicago school could not 'see' nor make sense of the urban situation of Chicago because they had decided that religion was not fitted for the modern urban situation and therefore any study of it as a creative form of cultural life would be ineffectual. This is as much an intellectual ideology as it is an ideology based upon the meaning and nature of temporality. There was the built-in sense that religion had no creative role in the temporality defined as the modern urban situation.

Karen Fields has raised similar issues in her studies of a religious prophet in colonial Central Africa during the early part of the twentieth century. There appeared in various villages in this area a prophet, one Shadrack Sinkala. Shadrack preached a radical iconoclastic message telling his hearers to stop the work of cutting trees, to leave their wives if they were polygamists – that they should not lie, cheat, steal or kill. The faithful must accept Christianity and be baptized. In addition, Shadrack preached that the faithful should not obey the colonial authorities, or the tribal chiefs or the missionaries; they should obey God only. His message had a very clear millennial intent; the kingdom of God was at hand! Fields attributes some of his doctrines to the missionary work of the Watchtower Society in this part of Africa but it does not account for the intensity of his message nor its effect upon all who heard him.

Fields' work operates on at least two levels. On the one hand it is a descriptive anthropological history of colonial Central Africa during the first 20 years of the twentieth century. Interwoven in this narrative is a running debate with her anthropological colleagues and interlocutors regarding the 'rationality' of millenarian prophecies of Shadrack. I cannot rehearse the entire argument here. Allow me to state a summarizing conclusion where Fields makes her case for 'rationality' of the religious prophet.

Thus anthropological thought about the colonial order could not surpass Shadrack's. In a fundamental sense, it could not even compete with Shadrack's, for it did not organize the facts of the whole society that he confronted with mind and body. He had no scientific theory that abstracted away the colonial reality. Anthropologists had. He lived within the colonial present; they within the ethnographic one. From his standpoint – of the whole, in the colonial present – the discoveries that organized anthropologists' passion for detail and their humane aspiration about ruling were neither here nor there.[23] The point of the argument was the insistence of her anthropological colleagues that because Shadrack expressed a religious and 'non-scientific' view of his situation it could be disregarded. In the first instance any religious view was an inadequate mode of interpretation for any modern social reality and it is clear that religion had no efficacious power to render any meaningful knowledge about social reality. Here again, the nature and meaning of a religious orientation is almost ruled out beforehand because of an ideology of the temporal sequences. There can be no efficacious meaning-attributed religion in the modern period.

In a book that is destined to become a classic, J. Stephen Lansing presents us with a study of the Balinese rice irrigation system.[24] The study is placed within the context of a methodological tradition that includes Wittfogel's *Oriental Despotism* and Marxian theories of production, nature and work. It, of course, draws upon contemporary anthropological studies of Bali. What Lansing discovers in his work is that the best mode of understanding and controlling the irrigation system of Bali is contained in and related to certain ancient rituals related to the temple structure of the old Bali kingdoms. After independence from the Dutch the Balinese did not return to these older structures, but saw independence as a signal for the importation of modern techniques of agronomy represented by the Green Revolution. The techniques of the agronomists of the Green Revolution could not sustain a reliable and consistent yield of rice. The discovery of the older temple rituals and ceremonies proved to be the most stable and reliable mode of the management of the irrigation system. No modern technique could approximate the deft and subtle manner in which the system operated.

Lansing tells us that, 'The images of society that the Balinese see in their terraced landscape do not reflect the progressive linear order that Marx and Hegel understood as "history".' He goes on to say:

> Instead, for the Balinese nonlinear patterns of temporal order emerge from the regular progression of natural cycles, the seasons of growth and change. When Balinese society sees itself reflected in a humanized nature, a natural world transformed by the efforts of previous generations, it sees a pattern of interlocking cycles that mimic these cycles of nature. Whereas Marx looked at nature and saw evolutionary progress, a Balinese farmer may look at nature and see the intricate patterns of the *tika* calendar or hear the interlocking cyclical melodies of a gamelan orchestra.[25]

It is instructive to note that Lansing's work is not a study of Balinese religion; it is rather a study of the nature and meaning of work as it is involved in the cultivation of rice. The methodologies employed are not those of the religious historian or investigator, and it is more dependent on Marx and Habermas than any well-known scholars of religion. Indeed, the *Afterword* of the text is written by his colleague, Valerio Valeri, who places Lansing's work under a most critical 'Marxist stare'. In his concluding statement,

Valerio Valeri states, 'He [Lansing] has brilliantly renewed Marx's theory of humanized nature and has forced us to see its strengths and limitations; and in the course of doing this he has shown, to paraphrase Kant, that production without ritual is blind and ritual without production is empty.'[26]

I have presented the examples above to show that the methodological presupposition of a 'progressive' linear meaning of temporality must be questioned in light of the data that appears. This presupposition concerning methodological temporality seems to be a supposition of much of what goes under the name of human sciences. The kinds of studies referred to above indicate the need for serious attention to the presuppositions of the meaning of temporality within the methodological epistemologies of our studies.

Kathleen Biddick has undertaken a radical critique of the presupposition of the Christian meaning of temporality as the normative meaning of historical time. I quote at length the manner in which she has raised this issue. She says:

> This study grapples with an unsettling historiographical problem: how to study the history of Jewish-Christian relations without reiterating the temporal practices through which early Christians, a heterogeneous group, fabricated an identity ('Christian-ness') both distinct from and superseding that of neighboring Jewish communities. These Christian temporal practices insisted on identiary time, by which I mean the assumption that time can be culturally identical with itself ... First, they posited a present ('this is now') exclusively as a Christian present. They cut off a Jewish 'that was then' from a Christian 'this is now'. They also imagined a specific direction to Christian time. They believed that the Christian new time – a 'this is now' – *superseded* a 'that was then' of Israel ... The purported 'secularization of modernity', I contend here, has never overtaken this core Christian conception of supersession. Supersessionary thinking and notions of modernity are closely bound, and, I argue, shape even the very terms of current debate among medievalists over the existence of Antisemitism in the Middle Ages.[27]

Biddick realizes that it is a false option to think that the alternative to this supercessionary history is a 'Jewish history'. One must rather find a strategy whereby the reality that occurs within such history can be interpreted in another manner. It is at this point that she suggests another mode of temporality. 'Indeed, this book is about the risk of thinking about "*unhistorical*" temporalities – ones not about divisions between then and now, but about passages, thresholds, gaps, intervals, inbetweenness. These unhistorical temporalities that do not use time as a utilitarian resource to ground identity are temporalities that can never be one.'[28]

Dipesh Chakrabarty speaks to this issue of the meaning of temporality as a methodological concern.[29] Chakrabarty's takes off on the issue of historicism and he raises this discussion through recourse to the scholarly text of three non-Western writers, Jomo Kenyatta, Anthony Appiah and D. D. Kosambi. He sets up the problem with Kenyatta's usage and admission of magical practices in his classic text, *Facing Mount Kenya*. This book had been the basis for Kenyatta's thesis with Malinowski and upon its publication he had asked Malinowski to write an introduction. It is clear that Malinowski is worried about the inclusion of Kenyatta's reference to his apprenticeship and practice of magic, especially now that he was a distinguished member of a social science discipline. Chakrabarty notes a 'doubleness' of voice in Kenyatta's text that is contrasted with a 'single-voice' disapproval and discomfiture in Malinowski's tone. Chakrabarty almost detects a double voice in Anthony Appiah's *In My Father's House*, where in an autobiographical section Appiah speaks of his father's communion with his ancestors by pouring a little gin on the ground. Appiah, the Ghanaian Cambridge-trained philosopher, glosses over this act of his father through some reference to anthropological literature by way of E. B. Tylor.

Kosambi is intrigued by the appearance of an ancient object, a saddle-quern, used to grind spices. It is clear that this is a very old Indian object but it is not mentioned or accounted for in any of the Hindu texts. The saddle-quern is the example of what Chakrabarty calls the 'timeknot'. Though the saddle-quern exists and is used now – sitting in a modern Indian kitchen – it still remains in another time for him. He can not ask the question about the relationship of the saddle-quern to the kitchen stove – though present together now, they are participating in two very different temporal modes.

Chakrabarty refers to this mode of understanding history as historicist and anachronistic. It involves the use of anachronism to convert objects, institutions and practices with which we have lived relationship into relics of other times. He goes on to say that, 'this capacity to construct a single historical context for everything is the enabling condition of modern historical consciousness, the capacity to see the past gone and reified into an object of investigation ... the modern sense of "anachronism" stops us from confronting the problem of the temporal heterogeneity of the "now" in thinking about history.'[30]

Chakrabarty's critique is directed mainly to situations, persons and cultures that are contemporary, whereas Biddick's focus falls primarily on the issue of Jews and Judaism, especially within medieval and modern Western history. In making clear the notion of 'unhistorical histories' she finds it necessary to bring to bear the meaning and nature of the fetish and fetishism in a fashion reminiscent of William Pietz's discussions.

5   CONCLUSION

I took as a point of departure for this paper the necessity to explain more
fully what I might mean by a 'serious discourse'. What I have done in the
above comments is to give examples of the kind of work I have implied.
I have introduced these examples and examples like them as the basis for
the kind of method that I think we might pursue in the study of religion.
My commentators felt that my remarks evoked a method involving 'inter-
religious dialogue'. There might have been echoes of this kind in my former
remarks, but that is not exactly what I have in mind. I would say that I
think that any future method must include the kinds of issues and questions
regarding the positing of data from scholars who are from other cultures.

My concern here is about what questions are asked and who asks these
questions. There is another issue having to do with matters related to
'the inter-religious'. I think that we must all admit that over the past 500
years every culture in the world has been affected by the West; the West is
everywhere. This 'West that is everywhere' is no longer under control of the
'original' Western culture; it no longer belongs to the West. This means also
that some form of the Enlightenment sciences are a part of the contemporary
scholarly world in every part of the globe.

This universal spread of the Enlightenment sciences is part and parcel of
the destructive and ambiguous symbolic constructions brought on by the
West over the past 500 years. Given the simultaneity of these sciences with
colonialism and imperialism, their clarity carries with them silences and
shadows and therefore one must practise them through a 'hermeneutic of
suspicion'. It is out this suspicious mode that I seek methodological moments
and rhetorical pauses in method. At one point I recommend that we need to
'crawl back through our disciplines'[31] so that we might experience another
modality of the temporality of these sciences.

While this paper has been critical of the practices of Enlightenment sciences, it does not shy away from the creativity and necessity of these sciences
in any discussion about human beings in any society or culture. Just as the
'science of religion' first drew its data from cultures, times and places distant
from the West, in too many cases the Enlightenment failed to exercise its
critical and creative role in the times and places where the West was in
control. All too often, other meanings from other sources were brought to
bear to fulfil the promise of the Enlightenment sciences.

I have attempted to bring a notion of 'matter' and 'materiality' back into
methodological discussions. By and large, notions of this sort are discussed
under the heading of 'materialism', which is an idealization of the meaning
of matter and often has no concrete referent since discourses flowing from
such idealization presuppose the abstract neutral time of the 'science' of
economics. Let me be clear at this point. I don't favour the expulsion of
the 'science' of economics nor any other of the Enlightenment sciences.
Rather, I recommend a critical discourse between these sciences and the

specific and concrete description of matter, its exchanges and meanings in specific situations of cultures and societies. If these exchanges are related in religious, ceremonial and symbolic modes, this does not mean that these realities simply refer to the secular order of an Enlightenment science. My comments can be summed up in Chakrabarty's apt statement: 'European thought is at once indispensable and inadequate in helping us to think through the experiences of political modernity in non-Western nations.'[32] I would expand this statement to include any situation on the globe.

14

A Student's Question: Religious Studies, Philosophy and the Examined Life

DONALD A. CROSBY (EMERITUS, COLORADO STATE
UNIVERSITY)

I was meeting with a student in my office one day at Colorado State University, where I taught for 36 years in the Department of Philosophy. The student was considering the possibility of continuing her studies after her philosophy major toward a doctorate in religious studies or philosophy with expectation of an eventual career as a college or university professor. She looked me in the eye and asked, 'If you had it to do over again, would you take up a career as a teacher of philosophy and religion?' I instantly answered, 'Of course I would.' I then began to reflect on my answer. I was somewhat surprised to note how spontaneous, unthinking and unequivocal it had been. But I then realized that my instinctive answer reflected the keen sense of excitement and satisfaction I have experienced throughout my career as a university teacher and researcher in the fields of philosophy and religion.

I devote this essay to relying upon my many years of working in these two fields in order to explain why I think it highly desirable and extremely valuable for teachers of religious studies to have as much acquaintance as possible with ideas, issues and thinkers in the field of philosophy, and for philosophy teachers to have a similar awareness of ideas, issues and thinkers in the field of religion. The fields have significant commonalities as well as differences, and I am firmly convinced that each can and does richly instruct and inform the other. By explaining why I believe this to be so, I can also give insight into why I have found teaching in these two disciplines to be so challenging and rewarding.

The philosophy department at Colorado State has a religious studies component, and a significant number of its students during my time there enrolled in an optional religious studies emphasis within the philosophy major. Earlier in my years at the university I regularly taught a sophomore level undergraduate course on Western religions (Christianity, Islam, Judaism, Zoroastrianism), and I taught an alternate year course in philosophy of religion up to the time of my retirement in December 2001. So although most of my teaching at Colorado State was in courses in philosophy

– from introductory logic and introduction to philosophy through upper-level courses and seminars for the MA degree – I also had a fair amount of experience there teaching courses in or related to religion (including some interdisciplinary courses). In addition, I have been the committee chair and principal mentor for many MA students who wrote their theses on topics that drew upon religious and philosophical sources and had relations to both fields.

Four of the six books I have written to this date and all of the three I have co-edited have focused on religious topics, as have many of the articles, chapters and reviews I have authored. I served as Assistant Professor of Philosophy and Religion (with teaching assignments in both areas) at Centre College of Kentucky before coming to Colorado State University, and have taught as an adjunct at Iliff School of Theology in Denver, Colorado, as well as being an adjunct instructor in the Philosophy Department at Florida State University. My doctoral degree from the joint programme at Union Theological Seminary and Columbia University is in religion (with an emphasis on philosophy of religion and ethics), and I took a sizeable number of courses in philosophy at Columbia as well. Finally, I hold a Bachelor of Divinity and a Master's Degree in American Church History from Princeton Theological Seminary. Therefore, I have an educational background in and experience of teaching in the fields of philosophy and religion. I feel fortunate to have had this kind of background and teaching career. My work in the histories and contemporary activities of these two often intersecting but also quite distinct fields has constantly reminded me of the crucial need for as much interdisciplinary breadth as possible to supplement disciplinary depth in university teachers' outlooks on the world and in the outlooks they seek to instil in their students.

Over the years I have observed that the interest students bring to the field of philosophy is often accompanied by, if not strongly motivated by, a strong interest in religious matters. Conversely, many of the questions students formulate in religious studies classes are probingly philosophical in character. Some of the questions they raise in both types of class are ones growing out of normal *intellectual* curiosity about the provocative topics and problems which the two fields bring forcefully to expression. But other kinds of question which students raise and with which they tend to become actively engaged are not merely intellectual or conceptual in character. They are *existential*, reflecting the students' deeply felt and sometimes even desperate searches for purpose and meaning in their lives.

I have tried in my teaching to give free rein to discussions of both kinds of questions because I am convinced that two tasks lie at the heart of education in all disciplinary areas. The first is to awaken a lively curiosity about intellectual subjects of various sorts and encourage the autonomous, self-directed intellectual development that grows naturally out of such awakened curiosity. The second is to find ways of providing motivation, guidance and support to assist students in the active formation of their personal characters, commitments and involvements in the world. The fields of philosophy and religious studies are admirably suited to the pursuit of these two goals. They can be especially effective in this pursuit when they are allowed to work together and to play a mutually critical and enriching role in the course of a student's education. In order for such a thoroughly interactive role to be possible in the college or university classroom, it is necessary that professors be familiar with and proficient in at least some basic aspects of both disciplines. I therefore strongly recommend to all who aspire to careers in either religious studies or philosophy that they endeavour to find out as much as they can about both disciplines and give sustained attention to ways in which they relate to one another.

What, then, do the disciplines of philosophy and religion have to offer and how can they be brought into relation with one another? By proposing answers to this question, I hope also to shed light on two others. Why is it essential in my view for prospective teachers in either field to be as knowledgeable as possible about the other field? And why have I personally found working in the two fields to be so stimulating and satisfying? In what follows, when I use the term 'philosophy', I shall usually mean Western philosophy since it is the kind of philosophy with which I happen to be most familiar. I do not mean for a moment, however, to suggest that the study of Eastern philosophical systems is unimportant. It would also be wise for prospective college and university teachers in the fields of either philosophy or religion to acquire as much acquaintance as they can with Eastern as well as Western philosophical traditions and writings. Once again, maximum breadth and variety in the two fields are highly desirable. I begin the development of my answers to the three questions raised above by considering seven important ways in which philosophy and religion have had both complementary and critical relations to one another throughout their respective histories.

1 COMPLEMENTARY AND CRITICAL RELATIONS OF PHILOSOPHY AND RELIGION

1   Philosophers often deliberately address religious questions as aspects of their philosophical investigations. Notable examples of such philosophers in the West are Plato, Plotinus, René Descartes, Benedict Spinoza, Immanuel Kant, Georg Wilhelm Friedrich Hegel and Alfred North Whitehead. Renowned Western religious thinkers have often been extremely competent philosophers as well. Examples are Philo of Alexandria and Moses Maimonides (Jewish); Augustine of Hippo, Thomas Aquinas and Friedrich Schleiermacher (Christian); and al Ghazzali, Avicenna and Averroës (Muslim).

2   Philosophy is especially noted for its conceptual rigour and careful

exploration of complex interrelations among key concepts, as well as for its respect for strictly logical modes of reasoning – although it admittedly has to rely at crucial points on models, analogies, metaphors and other kinds of more allusive, suggestive language. Plato's philosophy, for example, is highly technical overall, but it is couched in dramatic form and has recourse to story and myth at crucial junctures. Nevertheless, philosophy's typical mode of discourse is technical, discursive prose. Religion is especially noted for its keen sensitivity to imaginative symbols, metaphors, myths, parables, stories and rites as conveyors of meaning – although it has its more technical, discursive modes of elucidating meanings of these imaginative expressions as well, most notably in theological treatises or in systematic articulations of non-theistic religious outlooks such as the Indian philosopher Shankara's *Crest Jewel of Discrimination*. The extreme ends of the contrastive spectrum can be sharply drawn if we compare the chains of rigorous logical deduction that run throughout the philosopher Spinoza's *Ethics in the Geometrical Order* with the narrative vigour of much of the Hebrew Bible or the extravagant imaginative symbolism of the Hindu Bhagavadgita. Both characteristic modes of discourse, inquiry, expression and understanding are important. Philosophy can help to remind religion of the importance of the one, and religion can help to keep philosophy in touch with the importance of the other.

3   Both religion and philosophy investigate theoretical and existential issues, but philosophy tends to specialize in the theoretical ones and religion in the existential ones. The former tends to regard clarification, coherence and understanding as goods to be ardently sought for their own sake, while the latter focuses most typically on more practical goals as such as those of seeking inspiration, guidance and help for the whole of life and finding means for coping effectively with urgent threats to the affirmation of life, such as moral weakness and failure; the uncertainty of the future; feelings of aimlessness and despair; seemingly arbitrary, inequitable distributions of tragedy, suffering and sorrow; the grim menace of disaster and evil in all their forms; and the imminence of death.

The interplay between the two fields is a crucial contribution to life and learning, and each can assist the other in recognizing the importance and value of its special emphasis. As a rough analogy of the relation between the two, I suggest the relation of the theoretical and empirical aspects of the natural sciences – the one more abstract, rationalistic and cerebral, and the other more deliberately down-to-earth and in direct contact with obdurate facts. Each needs the other, and neither is complete without the other. Of course, religion also has its wide-ranging cosmologies and speculative visions, and philosophy can have its insistent practical ideals, applications and concerns. The movement known as 'existentialism' in twentieth-century philosophy is a good example of the latter, as are the social philosophies of Thomas Hobbes, John Locke, Jean-Jacques Rousseau, Karl Marx, John Stuart Mill and John Rawls. So the contrast should not be overdrawn. It is more one of characteristic or usual priority and emphasis, not one of absolute difference of approach, task or kind that admits of no overlaps or exceptions.

4   Philosophy can assist religion in the task of giving clear conceptual formulation and articulation to its outlooks and beliefs, and in making a convincing case for their reasonableness and importance. Religion can provide motivation and perspective for philosophical contemplation and articulation. Philosophy of religion is a subset of philosophy, akin to such areas within the discipline of philosophy as philosophy of science and philosophy of art. And religious philosophy stands on the border between the two fields of philosophy and religion. Philosophical assumptions, commitments and themes – implicit as well as explicit – are ingredients in particular religious outlooks on the world. In similar manner, significant religious elements have often been in the background if not the foreground of philosophical systems.

The two fields can and do complement one another, and have throughout much of Western history. In the East, what we in the West call philosophy and religion have generally overlapped with and interfused one another. The overlapping and interfusing have been so extensive at times in both the West and the East that it becomes difficult to tell where one leaves off and the other begins. In that case we can say that to study the one is also necessarily to study the other. This has been so in large measure in both the East and the West, at least until very recent times. The historical developments of Judaism, Christianity and Islam have been deeply influenced by and dependent upon patterns of thought in Greek and Roman philosophy, for instance, and the philosophies of the Medieval, Renaissance, Enlightenment and Romantic periods in the West have been conspicuously concerned with religious issues and shaped by prevailing religious ideas.

5   While philosophy inquires into the nature of morality, critically analyses moral claims, compares and contrasts moral claims with other types of claim, and proposes substantive moral theories and theories of social justice, religion's main business in this regard is its provision of motivation, strength, vision and hope for the development of individual moral characters, for success in building and sustaining basic moral principles in institutions and societies, and for working constantly toward a better world. Morality does not need to rely upon religion for its specific content, but it may find valuable inspiration, sources of hope and powers of transformation in religious views of the world. Both theoretical perspectives on moral issues and problems and

practical motivations for living morally are needed. Mind and heart need to work constructively together.

6   Religion's gravitation toward the practical rather than the theoretical and its sometime tendency to settle too easily for unexamined symbols, myths, stories and rituals can – if not counterbalanced by the critical perspectives and persistent questions characteristic of philosophy – lead to a dearth of creative thought, obliviousness to relevant new possibilities, and dogmatic fixation on outworn, inadequate categories of interpretation and understanding. The work of philosophers can help to make religionists more acutely conscious of the need for continuous discursive exploration and critical examination of the meanings of religious symbols. While such explorations and examinations should not pretend to exhaust the potential meanings of powerful symbols, they can perhaps find new kinds of meaning in them and new ways of applying them to the needs of the world. In this way, philosophy can help to give religion a critical cutting edge and adaptability to changing times and circumstances. It has done so in the past and can continue to do so in the future.

Religion, on the other hand, can remind philosophy continually of the practical needs, concerns and yearnings of human beings that cry out for address and resolution. Religious questions about the meaning of life; about sources of strength, courage and transformation in the face of suffering and evil; about the place of humans within and in relation to the cosmos as a whole; and about ultimate purposes and goals for human life will not go away. A *purely* critical, analytical or theoretical approach – such as that advocated by some philosophers and endorsed in some conceptions of the nature and methods of philosophical inquiry – cannot do justice to the existential urgency of these questions. Humans cannot live by theory alone. Knowledge and understanding are, to be sure, important goods in their own right. But they are not the only goods, nor are they even the most important kinds of good.

The intellect craves sustenance, but so does the whole person or soul. And the most important food for the soul is not mere knowledge, but wisdom; not mere conceptual understanding, but a depth of insight and awareness that cannot be reduced to clear-cut concepts or explicit theories. Religion at its best can help to awaken this insight and awareness through such things as meditation, prayer, worship, rituals, contemplation of the elusive but evocative meanings of religious symbols, reverence for the sacred, frank and humble acknowledgement of the profound mysteries of life, acting in a spirit of love to help those in need, forgiveness of those by whom one has been wronged, and other kinds of religiously inspired thought and practice. Religion can be justifiably critical of philosophy when it denigrates or ignores the importance of this crucial side of human existence. Philosophers who dismiss religion and the whole domain of religious questions and concerns out of hand, as some philosophers and philosophies unfortunately do, expose themselves as blind to fundamental, ineliminable dimensions of human thought and experience. Philosophy needs to cultivate its practical, existential side just as religion needs to cultivate its conceptual, theoretical side. Neither side is adequate without the other.

7   The last kind of inter-relation of religion and philosophy I want to talk about here centres on the two words 'faith' and 'reason'. Religious people sometimes claim that their religious outlook on the world does not rest on reason but solely on faith, and philosophers sometimes peremptorily dismiss religious claims from serious consideration on the grounds that, as assertions of mere faith, they are opaque to rational understanding or rational criticism. Religious people even go so far on occasion as to see philosophical thought as inimical to religious thought to the extent that it presumes to subject the latter to the scrutiny of the former. And philosophers sometimes assert that religion is mostly superstition and nonsense because its outlook is based on blind assent to authority, wishful thinking and mere credulity rather than careful critical thought and analysis. Faith and reason are thus sometimes set into total opposition to one another by proponents of religion and philosophy, and faith is said to be the province of religion while reason is said to be the province of philosophy. In this way of thinking, faith is the sworn enemy of reason, and reason is the sworn enemy of faith. It is thought to follow, then, that religion and philosophy should have nothing to do with one another.

To my way of thinking, this notion of the relations of faith and reason, and thus of the domains of religion and philosophy, is a grave mistake. Yet it is fairly common in our culture, and it is not without its serious proponents among advocates of religious or philosophical views. I find that some of my students have bought into it completely and uncritically when they begin their work in religious studies or philosophy. In place of this mistaken view, I suggest that we think in terms of what I shall call 'reasonable faith' and 'faithful reason', thus breaking down the assumed dichotomy between faith and reason I have been discussing. I contend that a so-called faith that is insulated from rational reflection, support and criticism is not only narrow and uninformed but can also become pernicious. It can be and often has been the source of fanatical prejudice, exclusivism and violence, as well as of twisted, constricted, inflexible visions of the world. This is so because such a view of religion and religious faith foolishly makes the two immune to rational criticism, ongoing empirical testing and learning from other points of view.

But by the same token, a conception of reason that claims to be wholly independent of faith is woefully misguided and misinformed. Philosophers who champion such a conception of the range and competence of reason fail to see how much of any general outlook on the world, whether philosophical or otherwise, rests upon aspects of hope, valuation, assumption and trust that cannot be made fully explicit or be made to follow strictly from rational analysis or theory. Philosophers must have hope of success in their work, for example, a hope that sustains them as they struggle with its demanding and often frustrating problems. They must value their work and regard it as important enough to warrant committing their lives to it and engaging themselves in it day by day. They must have confidence in the intelligibility of major aspects of the world, and they must trust their ability as human beings to decipher and defend, at least to some significant degree, that intelligibility. They must assume the most basic and general principles of logical reasoning in order to develop and defend more specific logical theories and systems. Even when they are sceptics in their philosophical outlook, they must trust at some level the reasoning and experience that lead them to sceptical conclusions. These elements of hope, valuation, assumption and trust are manifestations of faith. They lie behind explicit philosophical thinking as its tacit background. They are preconditions of philosophical inquiry, but they can also be tested and may be vindicated in impressive degree by outcomes of that inquiry. In these and other ways, faith and reason work together in philosophy. For gaining a fuller comprehension of how the two work together and how necessary they are to each other, there can be no better combination of resources than active study of the two fields of philosophy and religion.

2   THE VALUE OF STUDYING AND TEACHING PHILOSOPHY AND RELIGION

What these comparisons and contrasts of philosophy and religion, and these observations about the respective character of each of the two fields add up to, in my judgement, is the supreme importance of students in either of the two fields being as familiar as possible with work in the other field. And that means, in turn, the critical importance of teachers in the one field coming to know as much as possible about the other in order to guide their students in exploring the distinctive contributions of the one field to the other. Effective, persuasive teaching about the characters and relations of reasonable faith and faithful reasoning, as exemplified in both religion and philosophy, can do much to provide students with a sane and reasonable as well as a hopeful, trusting and enquiring attitude toward the world.

Faculty should not deliberately proselytise or indoctrinate students into their own personal religious or philosophical points of view. Their task is rather to make students aware of options and opportunities for the development of their own thought and for the direction of their own lives. Among the options that might well be pondered in classrooms, however, are the considered outlooks of teachers themselves in religious studies or philosophy, and these outlooks and the reasons for them can be openly shared with students by way of helping to illustrate the variety of such options and their different rationales. It is entirely appropriate, in other words, that professors have something to *profess* in their classrooms so long as they do so in the context of clear and adequate presentation of other related points of view. It is also appropriate for professors to alert students to their points of view so that students can be on guard against being unduly or unconsciously swayed by the professors' personal biases and opinions.

This is certainly true in religious studies and philosophy classes, but it is no less true in all types of classes in colleges and universities. All professors, whatever their disciplines, have debatable commitments, predilections and preferences that influence such things as the organization of their courses, their selection of reading materials, their interpretations of these materials, their responses to students' questions, and their ways of teaching. It is important that students know what their professors think and why and how they reason, and that the students be taught to understand in detail some of the relevant alternatives to their professors' particular outlooks and points of view. They should not be left with the impression that there is only one legitimate way of thinking about the complicated, many-sided problems and concerns of religion and philosophy. The subject matters of the two fields are profound and inexhaustible. They admit of no easy answers or of simple, single-minded approaches. If students fail to learn this fundamental lesson, they have learned virtually nothing about the character, content or focus of the two fields. Nor should students be left with the mistaken impression that there is or can be such a thing as a purely 'objective' kind of teaching, untainted, unaffected and unshaped by the teacher's particular backgrounds, assumptions, methods, interests and beliefs.

I was forcefully reminded of this illusion by an experience I had while team-teaching a two-semester Honors course on the Western Heritage. The other two teachers in the course were colleagues from the Departments of English and History. The English teacher and I were scheduled to lecture on the theologian-philosopher Boethius' book *On the Consolation of Philosophy*. We usually got together to discuss what each of us would talk about when we were interpreting a text for the class. However, my colleague from English came down with the flu, and we were not able to have our usual discussion. I went ahead and prepared my lecture and delivered it to the class. After doing so, I called him on the phone and said, 'I covered the whole text in my lecture. There's no need for you to worry about having to present a lecture on any particular aspect of the book.' He responded, 'Thanks, but I think I'll still take a shot at it.' He did so, and his lecture was deeply informed and explicated many important features of the text. However, it was almost totally different from my own lecture. And I thought I had covered the entire text, which was, after all, a text in my two fields of philosophy and religion! This experience made me deeply aware of how differently two or more teachers can go about teaching the same text. Both lectures were accurate as far as they went and dwelt interestingly and pertinently on aspects of the text. But both went off in almost entirely different directions because of the different backgrounds and interests of the two teachers. Of course, I am here talking about teachers from different disciplines. But the same sort of thing often takes place when teachers from the same discipline proceed to explicate common texts or lecture on common subjects. It is crucial that students understand this fact and the reasons for it. They have to learn to think for themselves because it is interpretation – and sometimes strikingly variable interpretation – all the way down.

It is important above all that classes in religion or philosophy not be allowed to degenerate into mere descriptions with no opportunity or incentive for students' active engagement in the issues raised, or into a passing parade of positions or practices simply to be memorized and recited in turn by the students. Competence in description and explication is necessary, of course, and curiosity about the details of and reasons behind what others think and believe is strongly to be encouraged. But students should also be invited to think both critically and constructively and to weigh the applicability of aspects of the various religious or philosophical outlooks to the development of their own outlooks and lives. It should be made clear to them that they are free to take issue with their teachers' outlooks, approaches, opinions and processes of reasoning so long as they endeavour to support their disagreements with relevant reasons of their own.

Students should regularly be assured that they are in no danger of grade recrimination for the *fact* of their disagreements with their teachers – such disagreements are welcome and appropriate aspects of students' learning how to think and dialogue about the issues involved – but it also needs to be explained to them that the quality, clarity and thoroughness of the reasons they present in support of their disagreements in essays or papers, as well as their accuracy and fairness in explaining the positions and rationales they are calling into question, will necessarily be subject to evaluation. This distinction and the need for it are not always understood by students. The basic point I am driving at here is that students should be taught to think, reason and experience at first hand for themselves as they wrestle with the issues raised in their classes, and that they should be led to understand that it is not sufficient just to memorize facts or parrot the views of others (including the views of their teachers), no matter how competently or accurately such memorizing or parroting may be done.

When they learn this lesson, the religious and philosophical traditions, systems, perspectives and claims under study can come boldly to life and begin vividly to reveal their inner logic and existential significance for those who profess them and live by them, as well as their possible relevance as stimulations and resources for development of the student's personal thought and life. Religion can complement and critique philosophy in this kind of continuing study, and philosophy can complement and critique religion – each abundantly informing and enlarging the vision of the other. Once again, however, this kind of mutual interaction of the two fields in the minds of students can best be guided and inspired by professors who have themselves learned to bring the fields into lively communication with each other in the ongoing dynamics of their own developing thought and experience.

3 WHY TEACHING IN THE FIELDS OF RELIGIOUS STUDIES AND PHILOSOPHY HAS BEEN PERSONALLY CHALLENGING AND REWARDING

Granted all that I have said about the importance, value and interest of studying interrelations of philosophy and religion, why have I focused on these two fields in particular and on their relations to one another? Surely there are relations of other fields that are of great interest and importance. The relations of philosophy to natural science, of religion to anthropology, of social philosophy to political science or of religion to art, and so on, are also intriguing fields of interdisciplinary study. I fully agree with this point, but I also contend that there is something special about the relations of philosophy and religion that is worth pondering. And I say this not only because I happen to have been educated primarily in these two disciplines and to have taught in them throughout my life.

What is special is that philosophy teaches us to search for the most comprehensive understanding we can gain of the universe as a whole, and religion teaches us to search for the most comprehensive vision possible of how we ought to live our lives. The crowning glory of philosophy as I view it is metaphysics. And I understand metaphysics to be the search for the generic (most general, indispensable) traits implicit in all types of experience and in each and every act of experience, and for the systematic ways in which these traits relate to one another. The central focus of religion is upon ultimate meaning, purpose and value, upon what is worth the reverence, loyalty, devotion and commitment of each person's whole being.

The history of philosophy offers many different metaphysical systems for our consideration, of course, and the history of religions presents us with many different visions of the religious ultimate and the transformative powers, purposes and values associated with it – transcendent God or Goddess, immanent God or Goddess, the Godhead, the One, the gods and goddesses, Tao, Brahman, Nirvana, Nature and so on. But philosophy in general urges us to think as comprehensively as we can about how and to what extent various fundamental aspects of the experienced world fit together, and religion in general urges us to think about and experience as deeply as we can what is of utmost value and importance in the world. And as I have already tried to illustrate, these two distinctive types of interest and inquiry have many kinds of intriguing and essential relations to one another.

In my view, the two disciplines are of central importance for our learning how to orient ourselves in the world and for learning how people in other places and times have oriented themselves in the world. Any so-called education that neglects, trivializes or sidelines these two areas of study shows itself to be a poor and meagre kind of education. Interdisciplinary work in other disciplines is undoubtedly desirable and worthwhile, and we ought to have much more of it in our educational institutions. But interdisciplinary work in the two fields of philosophy and religion is of particular value and importance. It strikes to the heart of what an education is all about, on both its theoretical and its practical sides.

At least I have found this observation to be so in my own experience as a teacher, and I am firmly convinced of its truth. It is gratifying to be able to teach in two disciplines that bear so deeply on what our curiosity about the world intensely seeks – a comprehensive, richly textured understanding of the world and our place within it – and what our hearts fervently yearn for – a vision of the source and substance of ultimate purpose, value and commitment we ought ardently to seek to attain, become and put into practice throughout our lives.

When she was a teenager, one of my daughters was talking to a male friend on the telephone. He asked her, 'What does your father do for a living?' She answered, 'He teaches philosophy and religion at the university.' He thought he had some idea of what religion is, but he had no clue about the nature of philosophy. So he asked, 'What is philosophy?' She said, 'I don't know either. I'll ask my dad.' She did, and after pondering her question for a moment, I answered, 'It's thinking deeply about the deepest kinds of questions.' My answer was far from being adequate, of course, but it seemed to satisfy her friend. The more I think about my answer, the more convinced I become that it's not bad. The only problem with it is that it does not clearly demarcate philosophy from religion. For in fact, both disciplines require deep thinking about the deepest kinds of questions.

But I want to continue to suggest that the philosophical questions are perhaps more theoretical or conceptual, and the religious ones, more existential or practical in character. The first has to do with the most intense kind of curiosity about the world as a whole, and the second has to do with the most intense desire to find saving value and meaning in the world. The two kinds of question are not unrelated, and this distinction between philosophy and religion (as well as the others I have drawn between the two disciplines) is sometimes blurred and cannot be made hard-and-fast. In any event, both disciplines require the deepest kind of questioning, thinking and investigating. To be able to involve students on a day-to-day basis in these two forms of persistent, demanding and deeply pertinent inquiry is a rare and inestimable privilege. It has brought great challenge, joy and fulfilment into my life. From the process of preparing, teaching, reflecting, puzzling, researching, writing – and especially interacting with my insistently questioning students over the years – I have learned much more than I could ever hope to put in words, even though I have been trying to put some of it into words all my life. The essay you have now finished is one feeble effort in this regard. But we experience more than we can know, and we know more than we can say.

Notes

INTRODUCTION

1 Stanley Fish, 'One university under God?', *The Chronicle of Higher Education*, 7 January 2005. http://chronicle.com/jobs/2005/01/2005010701c.htm. Regarding the supposed wake of 'high theory' and the dawn of 'post-theory', see also François Cusset, *French Theory: Foucault, Derrida, Deleuze & Cie et les mutations de la vie intellectuelle aux Etats-Unis* (Paris: La Découverte, 2003), as well as Terry Eagleton, *After Theory* (New York: Allen Lane, 2003).

2 This expression, '[i]t is a curse to live in interesting times', is an ancient Chinese saying, according to Jerome Kohn, which Arendt 'during the last eight years of her too short life, would cite as an aside in the midst of discussing the latest domestic disaster or international crisis'. See Jerome Kohn, 'Introduction', in Hannah Arendt, *Essays in Understanding: 1930–1954*, Jerome Kohn (ed.) (New York: Schocken, 1994), ix.

3 Older works, such as Paul Hazard, *La crise de la conscience Européenne* (Paris: Boivin, 1935), translated in English as *The European Mind, 1680–1715* (Cleveland: Meridian, 1963), or Frank Manuel, *The Eighteenth Century Confronts the Gods* (Cambridge, MA.: Harvard University Press, 1959), had begun to chart the early repercussions of European 'exploration' and conquest upon its worldview. In this respect, also see the very useful historical overviews and critical discussions of the changing European as well as Islamic, Indian, Chinese and Japanese 'xenologies' in Gérard Leclerc, *La mondialisation culturelle, Les civilizations à l'épreuve* (Paris: Presses Universitaires de France, 2000). According to Wilhelm Halbfass, the expression 'xenology' seems to have first appeared in M. Duala-M'bedy, *Xenologie. Die Wissenschaft vom Fremden und die Verdrängung der Humanität in der Anthropologie* (Freiburg/München, 1977). See Wilhelm Halbfass, *India and Europe: An Essay in Understanding* (Albany, NY: State University Press of New York, 1988), 507 n. 2; originally published as *Indien und Europa* (Basel: Schwabe, 1981). Such 'xenological' changes are in large part linked to the increasingly frequent and sustained contact between 'different' civilizations, cultures and religions.

4 W. C. Smith, *The Meaning and End of Religion* (San Francisco: Harper & Row, 1962), 18. Also cf. Talal Asad, 'Reading a modern classic: W. C. Smith's *The Meaning and End of Religion*', *History of Religions* 40, no. 3 (2001), 205–22.

5 'The simple act of comparing religions goes back quite far into history' (translation mine). Henri Pinard de la Boullaye, *L'étude comparée des religions, Son histoire en Occident*. vol. 1 (Paris: Gabriel Beauchesne, 1922), 1; the second volume to this critical study appeared as *L'étude comparée des religions, Ses méthodes*, vol. 2 (Paris: Gabriel Beauchesne, 1929).

6 'It must have imposed itself to some degree as soon as distinct cults found themselves side by side, as soon as a traveler left his or her village (or as soon as an indigenous person came into contact with a traveler), and could ascertain conceptions and practices different from those to which he or she had been accustomed. What behavior should one have in their regard? Why should one remain faithful to one and dismiss the other? These questions are so natural and of such gravity, that it was impossible to not give to them a response' (translation mine). Pinard de la Boullaye, *L'étude comparée des religions*, 1: 1.

7   Smith, *The Meaning and End of Religion*, 18.

8   Samuel P. Huntington, 'The clash of civilizations?', *Foreign Affairs* 72, no. 3 (1993), 22–49; and *The Clash of Civilization and the Remaking of World Order* (New York: Touchstone, 1997).

9   Edward W. Said, 'The politics of knowledge', in *Reflections on Exile and Other Essays* (Cambridge, MA: Harvard University Press), 372–85; the essay originally appeared in *Raritan: A Quarterly Review* 2, no. 1 (Summer 1991).

10 On the more practical side of things, the following are worth consulting: regarding academic life and work generally, Linda L. McCabe and Edward R. B. McCabe, *How to Succeed in Academics* (San Diego: Academic Press, 2000); regarding writing in general, even in our supposedly 'post-theory' age, Howard S. Becker, *Writing for Social Scientists: How to Start and Finish your Thesis, Book, or Article* (Chicago: The University of Chicago Press, 1986); regarding research and writing in religious studies more specifically, Dennis C. Tucker, *Research Techniques for Scholars and Students in Religion and Theology* (Medford, NJ: Information Today, 2000); Nancy J. Vyhmeister, *Quality Research Papers for Students of Religion and Theology* (Grand Rapids, MI: Zondervan, 2001); Scott Brown, *A Guide to Writing Academic Essays in Religious Studies* (London and New York: Continuum, forthcoming); regarding the dissertation more specifically, Joan Bolker, *Writing Your Dissertation in Fifteen Minutes a Day: A Guide to Starting, Revising, and Finishing Your Doctoral Thesis* (New York: Henry Holt and Co., 1998); Eleanor Harman, Ian Montagnes, Siobhan MeMenemy and Chris Bucci (eds), *The Thesis and the Book: A Guide for First Time Academic Authors* (Toronto: University of Toronto Press, 2003); William Germano, *From Dissertation to Book* (Chicago: The University of Chicago Press, 2005); and finally, concerning teaching generally, Anthony D. Smith, *Starting to Teach: Surviving and Succeeding in the Classroom* (London: Kogan Press, 1988); Peter Filene, *The Joy of Teaching: A Practical Guide for New College Instructors* (Chapel Hill: University of North Carolina, 2005); and more specifically, teaching in religious studies, see Mark Juergensmeyer (ed.), *Teaching the Introductory Course in Religious Studies: A Source Book* (Atlanta, GA: Scholars Press, 1991). More theoretically now, a better grasp of the history of the study of religion is invaluable *for the sake of* potentially adding to this purported sum. Therefore, the following also deserve attention: Robert D. Baird, *Category Formation and the History of Religion*, 2nd ed. (1971; repr., The Hague–Paris: Mouton, 1991); J. J. Waardenburg, *Classical Approaches to the Study of Religion*, 2 vols. (The Hague–Paris: Mouton, 1974); Eric J. Sharpe, *Comparative Religion: A History*, 2nd ed. (1975; repr., La Salle: Open Court, 1986); J. Samuel Preus, *Explaining Religion: Criticism and Theory from Bodin to Freud* (New Haven and London: Yale University Press, 1987); Walter Capps, *Religious Studies: The Making of a Discipline* (Minneapolis: Fortress, 1995); Frank Whaling (ed.), *Theory and Method in Religious Studies: Contemporary Approaches to the Study of Religion* (Berlin and New York: Mouton de Gruyter, 1995); Russell T. McCutcheon, *Manufacturing Religion: The Discourse on Sui Generis Religion and the Politics of Nostalgia* (New York: Oxford University Press, 1997); Mark C. Taylor (ed.), *Critical Terms for Religious Studies* (Chicago: The University of Chicago Press, 1998); Jon R. Stone (ed.), *The Craft of Religious Studies* (New York: St Martin's Press, 1998); Gavin Flood, *Beyond Phenomenology: Rethinking the Study of Religion* (London and New York: Cassell, 1999); Willi Braun and Russell T. McCutcheon (eds.), *Guide to the Study of Religion* (London and New York: Cassell, 2000); Hans Kippenberg, *Discovering Religious History in the Modern Age* (Princeton: Princeton University Press, 2002); Carl Olson, *Theory and Method in the Study of Religion* (Toronto: Nelson Thomson Learning, 2003); P. Antes, A. Geertz and R. Warne (eds), *New Approaches to the Study of Religion* (Berlin and New York: Walter de Gruyter, 2004); Philippe Borgeaud, *Aux origines de l'histoires des religions* (Paris: Seuil, 2004); Elizabeth A. Clark, *History, Theory, Text: Historians and the Linguistic Turn* (Cambridge, MA: Harvard University Press, 2004); William E. Deal

and Timothy K. Beal, *Theory for Religious Studies* (London: Routledge, 2004); Tomoko Masuzawa, *The Invention of World Religions* (Chicago: The University of Chicago Press, 2005); Michel Gardaz (ed.), 'Les Sciences religieuses au Canada/Religious Studies in Canada', *Religious Studies/Sciences Religieuses* 35, no. 3–4 (2006); 'Articles and essays on the future of the study of religion in the Academy', *Journal of the American Academy of Religion* 74, no. 1 (2006), esp. see Slavica Jakelić and Jessica Starling, 'Religious Studies: A Bibliographical Essay', *Journal of the American Academy of Religion* 74, no. 1 (2006), 194–211; and Robert Segal, *The Blackwell Companion to the Study of Religion* (Oxford: Blackwell Publishing, 2006); specifically regarding issues many of the essays in this collection also take up, namely those of 'identity politics', see José Ignacio Cabezón and Sheila Greeve Davaney (eds), *Identity and the Politics of Scholarship in the Study of Religion* (London and New York: Routledge, 2004); and finally, regarding the conflicted overlap between theology and religious studies, see the essays collected in Linell E. Cady and Delwin Brown (eds), *Religious Studies, Theology, and the University: Conflicting Maps, Changing Terrain* (Albany, NY: State University of New York Press, 2002).

CHAPTER 1

1 This chapter is a substantially revised version of a talk given at the Social and Political Thought Dissertation Research Workshop, York University, Toronto, 27 September 1996.
2 It covers, for the most part, the United States and Canada. In Great Britain and Ireland, check *Index to Theses* (www.theses.com). It features thesis abstracts only. The full text of most dissertations going back to the 1970s is available from the British Thesis Service (www.bl.uk/britishthesis). Depending on your topic, you may also want to check the Center for Research Libraries (CRL) (www.crl.edu). On CRL's home page, click on 'Collection Search Links' then 'Foreign Doctoral Dissertations'.

CHAPTER 2

1 A version of this paper was first presented at the Canadian Society of Biblical Studies annual meeting in Ottawa, 27 May 1998.
2 Anne Michaels, *Fugitive Pieces* (Toronto: McClelland & Stewart, 1996), 44.
3 CSBS 27 May 1996. Brock University; published in *The Council of Societies for the Study of Religion Bulletin* 26, no. 1 (1997): 12–17, www.ccsr.ca/remus1.htm.
4 University Affairs online, www.universityaffairs.ca/.
5 www.caut.ca/.
6 Chronicles of Higher Education online, http://chronicle.com/.
7 www.aarweb.org/publications/default.asp.
8 Canadian Corporation for the Study of Religion website, www.ccsr.ca.
9 www.aarweb.org/teaching/default.asp.
10 Mary E. Hunt (ed.), *A Guide for Women in Religion: Making Your Way from A to Z* (New York: Palgrave Macmillan, 2004); revising the Committee on the Status of Women in the Profession of the American Academy of Religion's *Guide to the Perplexing: A Survival Manual for Women in Religious Studies* (Atlanta, GA: Scholars Press, 1992); see my critique in the *Council of Societies for the Study of Religion Bulletin* 26, no. 2 (1997), 34–7.
11 www.cust.educ.ubc.ca/workplace/.

CHAPTER 3

1 Too many graduate students seem unprepared for what awaits them once they complete their dissertations. Sadly, in many cases their professors seem not to have considered it to be their responsibility to provide them with some of the tools necessary for navigating the job market. It is into this gap that the following theses – which have benefited from the comments of a variety of people at different career stages – are offered. I do so with a deferential nod not only to Martin Luther's 95 and Karl Marx's 91, but also the 13 offered more recently by Bruce Lincoln, 'Theses on method', *Method & Theory in the Study of Religion* 8 (1996), 225–7.

CHAPTER 4

1 A. K. Ramanujan's 'Is there an Indian way of thinking?' in *India Through Hindu Categories*, McKim Marriott (ed.) (New Delhi/London: Sage, 1990).
2 William Strunk Jr and E. B. White, *Elements of Style*, 4th ed. (1911; repr., White Plains, New York: Longman, 2000). Also consult the following: Jacques Barzun, *On Writing, Editing, and Publishing: Essays Explicative and Hortatory* (Chicago: University of Chicago Press, 1986); Casey Miller and Kate Swift, *The Handbook of Nonsexist Writing: For Writers, Editors, and Speakers*, 2nd ed. (New York: HarperCollins, 1988); Joseph M. Williams, *Style: Toward Clarity and Grace* (Chicago: University of Chicago Press, 1990); Peggy Smith, *Mark My Words: Instruction and Practice in Proofreading*, 2nd ed. (Alexandria, VA: EEI Press, 1993); Joseph M. Moxley and Todd Taylor, *Writing and Publishing for Academic Authors*, 2nd ed. (Lanham, MD: Rowman and Littlefield Publishers, Inc., 1997).
3 Rolf Norgaard, *Ideas in Action: A Guide to Critical Thinking and Writing* (New York: HarperCollins, 1994).
4 *Chicago Manual of Style*, 15th ed. (Chicago: University of Chicago Press, 2003); and The Chicago Manual of Style Frequently Asked Questions, www.press.uchicago. edu/Misc/Chicago/cmosfaq/tools.html. Similarly, see Joseph Gibaldi, *The MLA Style Manual and Guide to Scholarly Publishing*, 2nd ed. (New York: Modern Language Association, 1998).
5 *ATLA Religion Database* with Serials. Online database of publications on religion. Hosted by EBSCO Research Databases, http://web.ebscohost.com/ehost/search?hid= 109&sid=2bf2e334-3f74-43ff-a879-ce1cfdf889d6%40sessionmgr102.
6 *PapersInvited*. Online database listing call for papers, www.papersinvited.com/. Also see: *Journal of Scholarly Publishing* (University of Toronto Press), http://128.100.205.52/ jour.ihtml?lp=jsp/jsp.html. Ulrich's *Periodicals Directory*. Online directory of periodicals, www.ulrichsweb.com/ulrichsweb/default.asp?navPage=4&.
7 *Association of American University Presses Membership Directory*. Online database of university presses in the Americas, http://aaupnet.org/membership/directory.html. Also see *Selected Scholarly Publishing Bibliography*. Online database of materials on scholarly publishing, http://aaupnet.org/resources/bibliography.html.

CHAPTER 5

1 T. S. Eliot, 'Burnt Norton', in *A Little Treasury of Modern Poetry*, Oscar Williams (ed.) (New York: Scribners, 1952), 291.
2 Eliot, 'Burnt Norton', 289.

3 Harold Coward and Thomas Hurka, *The Greenhouse Effect: Ethics and Climate Change* (Waterloo, ON: Wilfrid Laurier University Press, 1993).
4 Harold Coward (ed.), *Population, Consumption and the Environment: Religious and Secular Responses* (Albany, NY: State University of New York Press, 1995); Harold Coward and Pinit Ratanakul (eds), *A Cross-Cultural Dialogue on Health Care Ethics* (Waterloo, ON: Wilfrid Laurier University Press, 1999); Harold Coward (ed.), *Indian Critiques of Gandhi* (Albany, NY: State University of New York Press, 2003); *Religion and Peacebuilding* (Albany, NY: State University of New York Press, 2004).
5 Harold Remus, William Closson James and Daniel Fraikin, *Religious Studies in Ontario: A State of the Art Review* (Waterloo, ON: Wilfrid Laurier University Press, 1992), 92 for Grant's vision.
6 Harold G. Coward, *Sacred Word and Sacred Text: Scripture in World Religions* (Maryknoll, NY: Orbis Books. 1988).
7 *Sphota Theory of Language* (1980; repr., Delhi: Motilal Banarsidass, 1986).
8 Regarding Professor Murti, see Harold Coward and Krishna Sivaraman (eds), *Revelation in Indian Thought: A Festschrift in Honour of Professor T. R. V. Murti* (Emeryville, CA: Dharma Press, 1977): his *Studies in Indian Thought: Collected Papers of T. R. V. Murti*, Harold Coward (ed.) (1983; repr., Delhi: Motilal Banarsidass, 1996); and *T. R. V. Murti* (New Delhi: Munshiram Manoharlal, 2003).
9 Harold Coward and John McLaren (eds), *Religious Conscience, the State and the Law* (Albany, NY: State University of New York Press, 1999); Harold Coward and Daniel C. Maquire (eds), *Visions of a New Earth: Religious Perspectives on Population, Consumption and Ecology* (Albany, NY: State University of New York Press, 2000); Harold Coward, John R. Hinnells and Raymond Brady Williams (eds), *The South Asian Religious Diaspora in Britain, Canada, and the United States* (Albany, NY: State University of New York Press, 2000); Harold Coward, Rosemary Ommer and Tony Pitcher (eds), *Just Fish: Ethics and Canadian Marine Fisheries* (St John's: ISER Books, 2000).
10 Paul Bramadat and David Seljak (eds), *Religion and Ethnicity in Canada* (Toronto: Pearson Longman, 2005).

CHAPTER 6

1 The traditional German 'Gymnasium' was a high school-cum-college with an emphasis on Latin and Greek, a nine-year course of studies after four or five years of elementary school. The alumni of the Collegio Germanico-Ungarico (founded in 1552) took their courses and academic degrees from the Gregorian University.
2 Paul Schebesta (ed.), *Ursprung der Religion: Ergebnisse der vorgeschichtlichen und volkerkundlichen Forschungen* (Berlin: Morus Verlag, 1960).
3 For some detail, see my short article 'Jacques-Albert Cuttat, a Pioneer of Hindu Christian Dialogue', *Hindu-Christian Studies Bulletin* 2 (1989), 4.
4 I published some personal reflections in an article 'Einübung des inneren Zwiegesprachs: zur Begegnung von Christen mit dem Hinduismus', *Kairos* VIII, no. 1 (1965), 54–61.
5 *Hindu and Christian in Vrindaban* (London: SCM Press, 1969): US edition: *In the Paradise of Krishna: Hindu and Christian Seekers* (Philadelphia: Westminster Press, 1971): and 'Remembering Vrindaban', in *Vignettes of Vrindaban*, A. McDowall and A. Sharma (eds) (New Delhi: Books & Books, 1987), 45–61.
6 'The *Bhaktirasamrtasindhubindu* of Visvanatha Cacravartin', *Journal of the American Oriental Society* 91, no. 4 (1974), 96–107.
7 *Hinduismus* (Koln: J. P. Bachem, 1965).

8   The issue attracted international attention when TIME magazine carried in its 4 March 1991 issue an item: 'Vrindaban: The Misery of the Chanting Widows'.
9   A third edition of *A Survey of Hinduism* is due to come out in 2007. For the prior edition, see Klaus K. Klostermaier, *A Survey of Hinduism*, 2nd edn (Albany, NY: State University of New York Press, 1994).
10 *Christ and Hindu in Vrindaban* (Koln: J. Hegner, 1968).
11 I wrote a brief report on this meeting in *Kairos* IX, no. 1 (1967), 142–4.
12 S. J. Samartha (ed.), *Dialogue between men of living faith* (Geneva: WCC, 1971), contains some of the papers presented at the conference. I published some personal reflection in an article, 'Dialog der Weltreligionen: Zur oekumenischen Studienkonferenz in Beirut', *KM* 4 (1970), 120–4.
13 'Findings of Bombay Consultation on the Theology of Hindu-Christian Dialogue', *Religion and Society* XVI, no. 2 (1969), 69–88, which includes a list of participants.
14 The preparations for, and the proceedings of, the consultation were published in a number of volumes by the organizers.
15 I recently discovered that the website of Mumbai (formerly Bombay) University is listing me among its 'prominent alumni' – in the company of Mahatma Gandhi and two dozen other notables, no less.
16 *Mythologies and Philosophies of Salvation in the Theistic Traditions of India*, Editions SR/RS 5 (Waterloo, ON: CCSR and Wilfrid Laurier University Press, 1984).
17 A selection of the papers presented were published in *Religious Studies: Issues, Prospects, and Proposals*, University of Manitoba Studies in Religion 2, Klaus K. Klostermaier and Larry W. Hurtado (eds) (Atlanta, GA: Scholars Press, 1991).
18 See my 'Inter-religious dialogue as a method for the study of religions', *Journal of Ecumenical Studies* 2, no. 4 (1980), 755–9.
19 Gordon Harland, 'The Department of Religion at the University of Manitoba', in *Religious Studies in Manitoba and Saskatchewan: A State-of-the-Art Review*, The Study of Religion in Canada 4, John M. Badertscher, Gordon Harland and Roland E. Miller (eds) (Waterloo, ON: Wilfrid Laurier University Press, 1993), 31.
20 Harold Coward, 'The contribution of religious studies to secular universities in Canada', in *Religious Studies: Issues, Prospects, and Proposals*, University of Manitoba Studies in Religion 2, Klaus K. Klostermaier and Larry W. Hurtado (eds) (Atlanta, GA: Scholars Press, 1991), 23.
21 Raimon Panikkar, 'The challenge of religious studies to the issues of our times', foreword to Scott Eastham, *Nucleus: Reconnecting Science and Religion in the Nuclear Age* (Santa Fe: Bear & Co., 1987).
22 Harland, 'The Department of Religion at the University of Manitoba', 32.
23 Theodore Roszak, *Where the Wasteland Ends* (New York: Anchor Books, 1973), xv.
24 Ibid.
25 In addition to the theoretical expositions in my major books I have expressed myself on some issues of method and theory in some articles such as 'From phenomenology to metascience: reflections on the study of religion', *Studies in Religion/Sciences Religieuses* 6, no. 4 (1977), 551–61; 'The Religion of Study', *Religious Traditions* I, no. 2 (1978), 55–66; 'Inter-religious dialogue as a method for the study of religions', *Journal of Ecumenical Studies* 21, no. 4 (1984), 755–9; 'Moksa and Critical Theory', *Philosophy East and West* 53, no. 3 (1985), 205–10; 'Religious pluralism and the idea of Universal Religion', *Journal of Religious Pluralism* I, no. 1 (1991), 45–64; 'All religions are incomplete', *Dialogue and Alliance* 7, no. 2 (1993), 66–76; 'Jnana – die Welt mit den Augen des Geistes sehen', *Religionen unterwegs* (Vienna) 4, no. 2 (1998), 4–9.
26 Resting on a too-literal translation of '*Religionswissenschaft*', an academic discipline founded by Friedrich Max Müller, the famous Indologist, and forgetting that in German '*Wissenschaft*' has much wider connotations than the English term *science* that is used nearly exclusively for the natural sciences. In German, 'Theology' is some-

times called '*Gotteswissenschaft*', i.e. 'Science of God', which sounds unacceptable in English.

27 *Eranos Jahrbuch* 1946, 491 ff. In a footnote Schroedinger quotes the first verse of the *Dhammapada:* 'All that we are, is the fruit of thoughts: it is based on thoughts, it consists of our thoughts.'

28 L. Feuerbach, 'Xenien' (*Gesammelte Werke*, Vol. 11), 188.

29 The expression was used by E. Schroedinger in an essay on 'The Nature of Science', in *Geist und Natur, Eranos Jahrbuch*, 1946.

30 I have expressed myself on this point in some papers such as 'A universe of feelings', in *Religion and Comparative Thought*, Billimoria and Fenner (eds) (New Delhi: Sri Satguru Publications, 1989), 123–39; 'Eine indische Wissenschaft der Gefühle', in *Indien in Deutschland*, E. Weber (ed.) (Frankfurt: Peter Lang), 137–50; 'Hridayavidya – A Hindu-Christian Theology of Heart', *Journal of Ecumenical Studies* 9, no. 4 (1972), 750–74.

31 David Suzuki, in a segment of his video series *The Sacred Balance*, looking back to the 1960s when he was a budding young scientist, remarks: 'We knew so much and understood so little! Later generations could well accuse us of mismanaging nature and natural resources, utilizing technologies based on a science that was utterly inadequate to deal with the intricate web of real nature.'

32 I published most of my seminar lectures in a volume *The Nature of Nature* (Adyar: Theosophical Publishing House, 2004). *The Theosophist* of Adyar/Madras had earlier published a number of individual papers, demonstrating the interest that Hindus especially take in science and religion.

33 This has been given even more emphasis by the recent establishment of a great number of coveted 'Research Chairs' that allow their occupants to devote themselves full time to research.

34 The expression is taken from *Dhammapada* I, 19: 'A mindless person reciting a large portion of scriptures but not heading its teaching is like a cowherd who counts the cows of others.'

35 I was particularly gratified by a review of my *Survey of Hinduism* by no less an authority than Arvind Sharma that appeared in *Studies in Religion/Sciences Religieuses* 25, no. 1 (1996), 111–12.

36 For Mahatma Gandhi *satya* and *ahimsa* were the two pillars on which his life and teaching rested – the two most central concerns in religion.

CHAPTER 7

1 David Chidester, *Word and Light: Seeing, Hearing, and Religious Discourse* (Urbana: University of Illinois Press, 1992), xiv.

2 Patti Waldmeir, *Anatomy of a Miracle: The End of Apartheid and the Birth of the New South Africa* (New York: W. W. Norton, 1997).

3 Adrian Guelke, *South Africa in Transition: The Misunderstood Miracle* (New York: Tauris, 1999).

4 Emile Benveniste, *Indo-European Language and Society*, trans. Elizabeth Palmer (London: Faber and Faber, 1973), 522.

5 e.g. David Chidester, *Savage Systems: Colonialism and Comparative Religion in South Africa* (Charlottesville: University Press of Virginia, 1996), 234; David Chidester, *Authentic Fakes: Religion and American Popular Culture* (Berkeley: University of California Press, 2005), 17.

6 Peter Biller, 'Words and the Medieval notion of "religion"', *Journal of Ecclesiastical History* 36, no. 3 (1955), 351–69; John Bossy, 'Some elementary forms of Durkheim', *Past and Present* 95 (1982), 3–18.

7   Peter Harrison, *'Religion' and the Religions in the English Enlightenment* (Cambridge: Cambridge University Press, 1990), 39.

8   David A. Pailin, *Attitudes to Other Religions: Comparative Religion in Seventeenth- and Eighteenth-Century Britain* (Manchester: Manchester University Press, 1984).

9   J. C. Warner, 'Mr Warner's Notes', in *A Compendium of Kafir Laws and Customs*, John MacLean (ed.) (Mount Coke: Wesleyan Mission Press, 1858), 57–109.

10   Chidester, *Savage Systems*, 73–115.

11   W. H. I. Bleek, *On the Origin of Language*, Ernst Haeckel (ed.), trans. Thomas Davidson (New York: L. W. Schmidt. 1869), xv–xvi.

12   Walter Cooper Dendy, 'Response to Henry Callaway', in *Proceedings of the Anthropological Institute* 1 (1872), 184.

13   Henry Callaway, *The Religious System of the Amazulu* (Springvale: Springvale Mission, 1868–79; repr. Cape Town: Struik, 1970).

14   E. B. Tylor, *Primitive Culture*, 2 vols (London: John Murray, 1871), 1: 380.

15   F. Max Müller, *Contributions to the Science of Mythology* (London: Longman, Green, 1897), 1: 204–5.

16   F. Max Müller, *The Question of Right between England and the Transvaal: Letters by the Right Hon. F. Max Müller with rejoinders by Professor Theodore Mommsen* (London: Imperial South African Association, 1900); also see David Chidester, '"Classify and Conquer": Friedrich Max Müller, Indigenous Religious Traditions, and Imperial Comparative Religion', in *Beyond Primitivism: Indigenous Religious Traditions and Modernity*, Jacob K. Olupona (ed.) (London and New York: Routledge, 2004), 71–88.

17   Desmond Tutu, *The Rainbow People of God: The Making of a Peaceful Revolution* (London: Bantam Books, 1995).

18   David Chidester, *Salvation and Suicide: An Interpretation of Jim Jones, the People's Temple, and Jonestown* (Bloomington: Indiana University Press, 1988; revised edition, 2003).

19   David Chidester, *Patterns of Power: Religion and Politics in American Culture* (Englewood Cliffs, NJ: Prentice Hall, 1988).

20   David Chidester, *Religions of South Africa* (London: Routledge, 1992).

21   LuLi Callinicos, *Oliver Tambo: His Life and Times* (Johannesburg: New Africa Education, 2004).

22   David Chidester, *Shots in the Streets: Violence and Religion in South Africa* (Boston: Beacon Press; Cape Town: Oxford University Press, 1991), 17.

23   Kader Asmal, David Chidester and Cassius Lubisi (eds), *Legacy of Freedom: The ANC's Human Rights Tradition* (Johannesburg and Cape Town: Jonathan Ball Publishers, 2005).

24   Chidester, *Shots in the Streets*, 7–8; Chidester, *Religions of South Africa*, 217–18.

25   David Chidester, 'Stories, Fragments, and Monuments', in *Facing the Truth: South African Faith Communities and the Truth and Reconciliation Commission*, James Cochrane, John de Gruchy and Stephen Martin (eds) (Athens, Ohio: Ohio University Press; Cape Town: David Philip, 1999), 132–41.

26   See Lourens Du Plessis, 'Freedom *of* or Freedom *from* Religion? An Overview of Issues Pertinent to the Constitutional Protection of Religious Rights and Freedom in "the New South Africa"', *Brigham Young University Law Review* 4 (2001), 439–66; Johan D. Van der Vyver, 'Constitutional Perspective of Church–State Relations in South Africa', *Brigham Young University Law Review* 4 (2001), 635–73.

27   Anonymous, 'Religions "Rebuilding SA" Mbeki', *Bua News*, 9 September 2003.

28   Naledi Pandor, address by the Minister of Education, Naledi Pandor MP, at the World Halaal Council AGM, Civic Centre, Cape Town, 13 September 2005. www.info. gov.za/speeches/2005/05091616151001.htm (accessed 26 October 2005); see David Chidester, 'Religion education in South Africa: teaching and learning about religion,

religions, and religious diversity', *British Journal of Religious Education* 25, no. 4 (2003), 261–78.

29   T. Dunbar Moodie, *The Rise of Afrikanerdom: Power, Apartheid, and the Afrikaner Civil Religion* (Berkeley: University of California Press, 1975).

30   Leonard Thompson, *The Political Mythology of Apartheid* (New Haven: Yale University Press, 1985).

31   Desmond Tutu, 'Archbishop Desmond Tutu's Address to the First Gathering of the Truth and Reconciliation Commission', 1995, www.doj.gov.za/trc/pr/1995/p951216a. htm.

32   Régis Debray, 'Marxism and the National Question', *New Left Review* 105 (1977), 20–42; see 26–7.

33   'The Freedom Park Heals and Reconciles the South African Nation', www.freedom-park.co.za/index.php.

34   Arjun Appadurai, 'Disjuncture and Difference in the Global Cultural Economy', *Modernity at Large: Cultural Dimensions of Globalization* (Minneapolis: University of Minnesota Press, 1996), 27–47.

35   Kalman Applbaum, 'Crossing Borders: Globalization as Myth and Charter in American Transnational Consumer Marketing', *American Ethnologist* 27 (2000), 257–82.

36   David Chidester, 'Credo Mutwa, Zulu Shaman: The invention and appropriation of indigenous authenticity in African folk religion', *Journal for the Study of Religion* 15, no. 2 (2003), 65–85.

37   Chidester, *Authentic Fakes*, 230–1.

38   'US Chat Show Host Could Be Zulu', http.//news.bbc.co.uk/2/hi/africa/4096706.stm.

39   Bruce Lincoln, 'Ritual, Rebellion, Resistance: Once More the Swazi Ncwala', *Man* 22, no. 1 (1987), 132–56.

40   Emile Durkheim, *The Elementary Forms of the Religious Life*, trans. Joseph Ward Swain (New York: Free Press, 1965), 62.

CHAPTER 8

1   Richard L. Rubenstein, *After Auschwitz: History, Theology and Contemporary Judaism* (Indianapolis: Bobbs-Merrill, 1966).

2   Richard L. Rubenstein, *The Cunning of History: Mass Death and the American Future* (New York: Harper and Row, 1995).

3   'Post-Holocaust Jewish Identity and the Academy: On Traveling the Diaspora and the Experience of the Double Standard', in *Identity and the Politics of Scholarship in the Study of Religion*, José Cabezón and Sheila Davaney (eds) (London: Routledge, 2004): 163–82.

4   For a more detailed analysis of Holocaust theology, see Marc H. Ellis, *Beyond Innocence and Redemption: Confronting the Holocaust and Israeli Power* (San Francisco: HarperCollins, 1990), 1–31 and *Toward a Jewish Theology of Liberation: The Challenge of the 21st Century*, 3rd ed. (Waco, TX: Baylor University Press, 2004). Also, see Michael L. Morgan, *Beyond Auschwitz: Post-Holocaust Jewish Thought in America* (Oxford: Oxford University Press, 2001).

5   Rubenstein, *After Auschwitz*.

6   David Horowitz, *The Professors: The 101 Most Dangerous Academics in America* (Washington DC: Regency Publishing Inc., 2006); Alvin H. Rosenfeld, *'Progressive' Jewish Thought and the New Anti-Semitism* (American Jewish Committee, 2006).

7   Shulamit Reinharz, 'Fighting Jewish Anti-Semitism', *The Jewish Advocate*, 21 December 2006.

8   Jimmy Carter, *Palestine: Peace Not Apartheid* (New York: Simon and Schuster, 2006).
9   Deborah Lipstadt, 'Jimmy Carter's Jewish Problem', *The Washington Post*, 20 January 2007.
10 Ilan Pappe, *The Ethnic Cleansing of Palestine* (London: OneWorld Publications, 2006).
11 See Jeffrey Goldberg, 'What Would Jimmy Do? A Former President Puts the Onus for Resolving Mideast Conflict on Israelis', *The Washington Post*, 10 December 2006.
12 Ethan Bronner, 'Jews, Arabs and Jimmy Carter', *New York Times*, 7 January 2007.
13 Michael Kinsley, 'It's Not Apartheid: Jimmy Carter's New Book About Israel', *Slate*, 17 December 2006.
14 Bob Thompson, 'Peace Provocateur: Jimmy Carter's New Hammer? It Looks an Awful Lot Like a Book', *New York Times*, 7 December 2007.
15 Benny Morris, 'This Holocaust Will Be Different', *The Jerusalem Post*, 18 January 2007.
16 Morris, 'This Holocaust Will Be Different'.

CHAPTER 9

1   This is a much expanded version of a presentation and process on 'Teachings of Blessing' at the Colloquium on Violence and Religion held at Purdue University in June 2002.
2   Thomas Mooren, 'September 11, 2001 and the Future of Monotheistic Religions', *Mission* 9, no. 1 (2002), 39–64.
3   Mark Juergensmeyer, *Terror in the Mind of God: The Global Rise of Religious Violence* (Berkeley: University of California Press, 2001).
4   Vern Neufeld Redekop, *From Violence to Blessing: How an Understanding of Deep-Rooted Conflict Can Open Paths to Reconciliation* (Ottawa: Novalis, 2002); P. Sites, 'Needs as Analogues of Emotion', in *Conflict: Human Needs Theory*, J. W. Burton (ed.) (New York: St Martin's Press, 1990), 7–33.
5   Following Steindl-Rast, I will capitalize 'religion' when it refers to the domain of Religion; please note: 'Religion, as I use this term, should be written with a capital R to distinguish it from the various religions. Religion in the full sense of the religiousness from which all religions flow, as from their source. Translated into everyday living, Religion becomes spirituality; institutionalized it becomes a religion.' Fritjov Capra and David Steindl-Rast with Thomas Matus, *Belonging to the Universe: Explorations on the Frontiers of Science and Spirituality* (San Francisco: HarperSanFrancisco, 1992), 13; regarding Religion's role in peacemaking, also see R. Scott Appleby, *The Ambivalence of the Sacred: Religion, Violence and Reconciliation* (Lanham: Rowan & Littlefield, 2000); Douglas Johnston and Cynthia Sampson (eds), *Religion: The Missing Dimension of Statecraft* (New York: Oxford University Press, 1994); David Steele, *Theological Assessment of Principled Negotiation as a Role Model for Church Involvement in the Mediation of International Conflict* (Unpublished, 1990).
6   Note that the Chinese character for conflict contains within it both 'challenge' and 'opportunity'.
7   For one example see Deuteronomy 28:1–14 where some form of *barak* is used 14 times; there is comprehensive empowerment in every area of life associated with living the Torah.
8   Walter Brueggemann, *The Land: Place as Gift, Promise, and Challenge in Biblical Faith*, 2nd ed. (Minneapolis: Fortress Press, 2002), 45–50; E. A. Martens, *God's Design: A Focus on Old Testament Theology* (Grand Rapids: Baker Book House, 1981), 102–8.
9   Genesis 48:3–4. Note that all biblical quotations are from the *Tanakh*.
10 Genesis 48:15–16.

11 Again see Redekop, *From Violence to Blessing*.

12 Psalm 103:1.

13 Exodus 3:14.

14 Psalm 103:2.

15 Matthew Fox, *Original Blessing: A Primer in Creation Spirituality* (New York: Jeremy P. Tarcher/Putnam, 2000), 42–56.

16 Redekop, *From Violence to Blessing*, 161–72.

17 René Girard, *Things Hidden Since the Foundation of the World*. (Stanford: Stanford University Press, 1987).

18 Redekop, *From Violence to Blessing*; namely the Oka/Kanehsatà:ke Crisis of 1990, 187–251. Also see Girard, *Things Hidden*, 416–31.

19 I use the word 'structure' in a manner similar to Girard. He would describe mimetic desire, scapegoating and related phenomena as diachronic structures. As such, there is conceptual space in his work for 'mimetic structures of violence'. However my development of this phrase goes beyond what Girard develops.

20 Johan Galtung, 'After Violence, Reconstruction, Reconciliation, and Resolution: Coping with Visible and Invisible Effects of War and Violence', in *Reconciliation, Justice, and Coexistence: Theory and Practice*, M. Abu-Nimer (ed.) (Lanham: Lexington Books, 2001), 3.

21 Janine Chanteur, *From War to Peace*, trans. S. A. Weisz (Boulder: Westview Press, 1992), 195–9.

22 Again see Galtung, 'After Violence', 3.

23 William Bole, S. Drew Christiansen and Robert T. Hennemeyer, *Forgiveness in International Politics: An Alternative Road to Peace* (Washington DC: United States Conference of Catholic Bishops, 2004), 7.

24 Again see Bole et al., *Forgiveness in International Politics*; also see John Paul Lederach, *Building Peace: Sustainable Reconciliation in Divided Societies* (Washington DC: United States Institute of Peace Press, 1997); Miroslav Volf, *Free of Charge: Giving and Forgiving in a Culture Stripped of Grace* (Grand Rapids: Zondervan, 2005).

25 Redekop, *From Violence to Blessing*, 255–83.

26 An observation pointed out to me by my friend Truda Rosenberg.

27 For a full development of this argument, see Vern Neufeld Redekop, 'The Centrality to the Exodus of Torah as Ethical Projection', *Contagion – Journal of Violence, Mimesis, and Culture* 2 (1995), 119–44.

28 Jacob Neusner, *The Way of Torah: An Introduction to Judaism*, 5th ed. (Belmont, California: Wadsworth Publishing, 1993), 7.

29 I am indebted to John E. Toews for many of these insights; see his *Romans* (Scottdale: Herald Press, 2004), 389–94.

30 A key text that talks about the components and purpose of *torah* is Deuteronomy 4:1–8, in which the components are listed as *hoqqim, mishpatim* and *mitzvot* – customs, judgements (I would suggest stories fit into this because of their casuistic nature) and commandments. For further conceptual development see Redekop, 'The Centrality of the Exodus'.

31 My thought here is influenced by Emanuel Feldman, *Biblical and Post-Biblical Defilement and Mourning: Law as Theology* (New York: Yeshiva University Press, 1977), in which he argues that the Torah reveals and emphasizes the life-orientation of God.

32 Rupert Ross, *Returning to the Teachings: Exploring Aboriginal Justice* (Toronto: Penguin Canada, 1996), 5; emphasis added by Ross; one of the best collections of aboriginal teachings is in *The Sacred Tree* (Lethbridge: Four Worlds Development Press, 1985); it results from a process of synthesizing oral teachings from Elders from a number of First Nations. Within the Mohawk tradition, a yearly recitation of the Kaianere'ko:wa, Great Law of Peace, is important. Among Mohawks there is ambivalence around this being written down.

33 Michael Polanyi, *Personal Knowledge – Towards a Post-Critical Philosophy* (New York: Harper and Row, 1964), 328–32, shows how within scientific disciplines there are rules of rightness that help to distinguish what is true and significant within the discipline. See endnote 5 regarding capitalization.

34 Free market economies still draw on normative concepts drawn from the work of Adam Smith. In addition there are customary rules of rightness that determine the parameters of business activity. This was brought home to me by émigrés recently arrived from the former Soviet Union in 1991. As they described the black market economy of Soviet-era Russia, rules of rightness within the Canadian economy came into clearer focus.

35 Muslims have a custom of whispering a teaching into the ear of a newborn baby. Toddlers who can understand but not speak are taught ways of behaving and respond to verbal directives.

36 Ken Wilber, *A Theory of Everything – An Integral Vision for Business, Politics, Science and Spirituality* (Boston: Shambala, 2001), 6–16, uses spiral dynamics theory to develop an understanding of levels of consciousness. Within the description of these levels one can see that different teaching may be operative at each level, but also the attitude and way in which teachings are used can change. See also the work of Robert Kegan and Richard McGuigan.

37 Polanyi, *Personal Knowledge*.

38 Note that within their respective traditions the teachings of Moses, Jesus, Mohammed and Buddha are totally wrapped up in their lives. Modern-day figures like Gandhi and Martin Luther King Jr had an impact because of what they said *and* what they did. The teaching of medicine became alive and more effective when making rounds with a mentor became central to the formation of physicians.

39 Gustave Le Bon, *The Crowd: A Study of the Popular Mind* (London: E. Benn, 1930), 141–7.

40 Anthony da Silva, 'Through nonviolence to truth', in *Forgiveness and Reconciliation: Religion, Public Policy, and Conflict Transformation*, S. J. Raymond Helmick and R. Petersen (eds) (Philadelphia: Templeton Foundation Press, 2001), 296–301.

41 Michael Battle, *Reconciliation: The Ubuntu Theology of Desmond Tutu* (Cleveland: The Pilgrim Press, 1997).

42 John Paul Lederach, 'Journey from Resolution to Transformative Peacebuilding', in *From the Ground Up: Mennonite Contributions to International Peacebuilding*, C. Sampson and J. P. Lederach (eds) (Oxford: Oxford University Press, 2000), 45.

43 This framework is developed in Vern Neufeld Redekop, *From Violence to Blessing*.

44 Exodus 20:10.

45 Deuteronomy 5:15.

46 Leviticus 25.

47 Please note here that I am lifting ideas from the story line; this does not imply a literal uncritical reading, as I argued elsewhere, even if these stories are retrojected back in time they still convey a particular approach to life.

48 See Kenneth D. Bush and Diana Saltarelli (eds), *The Two Faces of Education in Ethnic Conflict: Toward a Peacebuilding Education for Children* (Florence: UNICEF Innocenti Research Centre, 2000), which shows how education programmes can be used negatively to increase hostilities and social injustices or positively to reduce the negative impact of conflict, increase tolerance and orient people toward peace.

49 Daniel Bar-Tal and Gemma H. Bennink, 'The Nature of Reconciliation as an Outcome and as a Process', in *From Conflict Resolution to Reconciliation*, Yaacov Bar-Siman-Tov (ed.) (Oxford: Oxford University Press, 2004), 11–38.

50 Ross, *Returning to the Teachings*, 12–16.

51 Yaacov Bar-Siman-Tov, 'Dialectics between Stable Peace and Reconciliation', in *From*

Conflict Resolution to Reconciliation, Yaacov Bar-Siman-Tov (ed.) (Oxford: Oxford University Press, 2004), 69–75.

52 Within the Mohawk tradition Louis Hall put forward an interpretation of the Great Law that was oriented toward violence; in contrast, elders like Tom Porter interpret it ironically.

53 Polanyi, *Personal Knowledge*, 132–202.

54 Mary Clark, 'Meaningful Social Bonding as a Universal Human Need', in *Conflict: Human Needs Theory*, J. W. Burton (ed.) (New York: St Martin's Press), 34–59.

55 Paul Ricoeur, *Oneself as Another* (Chicago: University of Chicago Press, 1992), 115–25.

56 Kathy Van Loon, *The Golden Rule* (Toronto: Broughton's, 2000).

57 René Girard, *Violence and the Sacred* (Baltimore: Johns Hopkins University Press, 1988), 218–22.

58 Walter Harrelson, *The Ten Commandments and Human Rights* (Minneapolis: Fortress Press, 1980).

59 Mooren, 'September 11'.

60 Vern Neufeld Redekop, *A Life for a Life? The Death Penalty on Trial*, vol. 9 (Scottdale and Waterloo: Herald Press, 1990), 17–39.

61 In many seminars I have conducted on reconciliation, without fail a mimetic structure of blessing occurred such that participants could mutually contribute to their understanding of the topic and sense of wellbeing.

CHAPTER 10

1 Enrique Dussel has written extensively on how scholars in the hegemonic North overlook scholars in the global South. See Enrique Dussel, *The Underside of Modernity*, trans. Eduardo Mendieta (New Jersey: Humanities Press, 1996). Gregory Baum has highlighted that Canadian scholars face a similar silencing in the US.

2 Recent US legislation requiring a valid passport to cross the US–Canada border highlights the tension, raising the issue of who should issue passports to Mohawks as well as the issue of who may decide who belongs to the Mohawk people. While this question affects all Native Americans, it particularly affects the people of Akwesasne, whose territory is criss-crossed with white borders.

3 See Olivette Genest, 'L'interdisciplinarité. Mode d'emploi', *Resources for Feminist Research/Documentation sur la recherche féministe* 29 (2001–2002), 95–104; and Marie-Andrée Bertrand, 'La difficile pratique de la recherche féministe interdisciplinaire', *Resources for Feminist Research/Documentation sur la recherche féministe* 29 (2001–2002), 105–16.

4 Dorothy E. Smith, *The Conceptual Practices of Power. A Feminist Sociology of Knowledge* (Toronto: University of Toronto Press, 1990) and *Writing the Social. Critique, Theory and Investigations* (Toronto: University of Toronto Press, 1999).

5 Elisabeth Schüssler Fiorenza, *Rhetoric and Ethic: The Politics of Biblical Studies* (Minneapolis, Fortress Press, 1999), 22.

6 Dorothy E. Smith, *The Everyday World as Problematic: A Feminist Sociology* (Toronto: University of Toronto Press, 1987), 49–105. The original article appeared in 1977.

7 Smith, *The Everyday World as Problematic: A Feminist Sociology*, 51.

8 See Louise Melançon, 'Magistère théologie: Parcours et témoignage d'une théologienne', in *Des théologies en mutation. Parcours et trajectoire*, M. Beaudin, A. Fortin and R. Martinez de Pison (eds) (Montréal: Fides, 2002), 111–20.

9 See Schüssler Fiorenza's comments on the marginalization of feminist biblical studies, *Rhetoric and Ethics*, 43, 138, n.35.

226 *The Next Step in Studying Religion*

10 Sheila D. Collins, *A Different Heaven and Earth. A Feminist Perspective on Religion* (Valley Forge: Judson Press, 1974), 7. See also Katie G. Cannon et al., *God's Fierce Whimsy: Christian Feminism and Theological Education* (New York: Pilgrim Press, 1985).
11 Collins, *A Different Heaven and Earth*, 19.
12 Sherene H. Razack, *Looking White People in the Eye. Gender, Race and Culture in Courtrooms and Classrooms* (Toronto: University of Toronto Press, 2001), 169.
13 Musa Dube, *Postcolonial Feminist Interpretation of the Bible* (St Louis: Chalice, 2000), 39. See also M. Shawn Copeland, 'Christian Feminist Theology of Solidarity', in *Woman and Theology*, P. Kaminski and M. A. Hinsdale (eds) (Maryknoll: Orbis), 19–23.
14 Collins, *A Different Heaven and Earth*, 161.
15 Elisabeth Schüssler Fiorenza, *Wisdom Ways: Introducing Feminist Biblical Interpretation* (Maryknoll: Orbis, 2001), 118–34.
16 Razack, *Looking White People in the Eye*, 14.
17 See Hélène Pedneault, 'Entrevue: Simone de Beauvoir féministe', *Vie en Rose* 16, (March 1984), 25–36; and Nancy Huston, 'Les enfants de Simone de Beauvoir', *Vie en Rose* 16, (March 1984), 41–4. See also Toril Moi, *Sexual/Textual Politics. Feminist Literary Theory* (London: Meuthen, 1985), 98–9, 144–5.
18 Cf. Elisabeth Schüssler Fiorenza, *Rhetoric and Ethics,* 155. 'Western languages are androcentric … languages that claim to function as generic languages that include wom/men.'
19 Luce Irigiray, 'Frenchwomen, Stop Trying', in *The Sex which is Not One* (Ithaca, NY: Cornell University Press, 1985), 198–204.
20 Nicole Brossard, 'De radical à intégrales', in *L'émergence d'une culture au féminin* (Montréal: Éditions Saint-Martin, 1987), 171, translation mine.
21 In English, the normative maleness of human rights discourse is hidden by the seemingly inclusive usage, while in French, in spite of Québecois linguistic practices, *les droits de l'homme* dominates international usage, including at the United Nations. Even a journal such as *Concilium* favours this expression over the equally available *droits humains* or *droits de la personne*.
22 Monique Dumais, 'La théologie peut-elle être du genre féminin au Québec?' in *La Femme et la Religion au Canada*, E. Lacelle (ed.) (Montréal: Bellarmin, 1979).
23 Denise Couture and Marie-Andrée Roy, 'Dire Dieue' in *Dire Dieu aujourd'hui*, C. Menard and F. Villeneuve (eds) (Montréal: Fides, 1994), 133–46.
24 Elisabeth Schüssler Fiorenza, *Rhetoric and Ethic,* 126.
25 Luce Irigiray, *Entre Orient et Occident* (Paris: Grasset, 1999).
26 Smith, *Writing the Social*, 18–19.

CHAPTER 11

1 For example, see Darlene M. Juschka, 'A Nod in the General Direction of … Gender in the Study of Religion', *Studies in Religion/Sciences Religieuses* 30, no. 2 (2001), 215–22; and 'The Construction of Pedagogical Spaces: Religious Studies in the University', *Studies in Religion/Sciences Religieuses* 23, no. 1 (1999), 85–97.
2 Willi Braun and Russell T. McCutcheon (eds), *Guide to the Study of Religion* (London and New York: Cassell, 2000).
3 Willi Braun, 'Religion', in *Guide to the Study of Religion*, Willi Braun and Russell T. McCutcheon (eds) (London and New York: Cassell, 2000), 3–18; William Arnal, 'Definition', in *Guide to the Study of Religion*, Willi Braun and Russell T. McCutcheon (eds) (London and Now York: Cassell, 2000), 21–34.

4   Braun, 'Religion', 3–4.
5   Braun, 'Religion', 4–5.
6   See Arnal, 'Definition', 22.
7   Arnal, 'Definition', 31–2. The tendency to treat religion as something other than a concept is so embedded in the Eurowest, that to speak of it as a concept is to speak counter-intuitively. This suggests that religion is essentially a Eurowestern folk category; see Arnal, 'Definition', 31. For example, a recent archaeological dig in Botswana discovered 70,000-year-old spearheads that were apparently placed in close approximation to carvings on a snake-shaped rock. This they interpreted as 'the earliest evidence for ritual behavior, or what could be called religion'; see J. R. Minkel, 'Offerings to a stone snake provide the earliest evidence of religion', *Scientific American News*, 6 December 2001, www.sciam.com/article.cfm?chanID=sa027&articleID=3FE89A86-E7F2-99DF-366D045A5BF3EAB1. We see in this statement, then, a sui generis origin for religion, while religion is treated as a thing in and of itself. And then built onto these assumptions are a plethora of further assumptions: ritual behaviour is religious; placing spearheads near a snake-shaped rock is ritualistic; 70,000 years ago the shape of the rock was significant; and that the carvings (which of course cannot be dated) are ancient rather than modern.
8   The idea of religion as MacGuffin is a spin-off from J. Z. Smith's work, particularly 'Religion, Religions, Religious'; Jonathan Z. Smith, *Relating Religion: Essays in the Study of Religion* (Chicago: The University of Chicago Press, 2004), 179–96.
9   See Tomoko Masuzawa, *In Search of Dreamtime: The Quest for the Origin of Religion* (Chicago: The University of Chicago Press, 1993).
10 See for example Darlene M. Juschka, *Feminism in the Study of Religion: A Reader* (New York and London: Continuum Press, 2001).
11 Therefore, rather than focus on their theology and its viability, I examined how they used symbol, myth and ritual to develop a feminist the(a)ology. I did go on to discuss the problems of said the(a)ology in light of what I perceived to be theoretical problems, but these problems related to their conceptualization and use of symbol, myth and ritual.
12 Donald Wiebe, 'An Eternal Return All over Again: The Religious Conversation Endures', *Journal of the American Academy of Religion* 74, no. 3 (2006), 674–96; see 691.
13 Russell T. McCutcheon, *Critics not Caretakers: Redescribing the Public Study of Religion* (Albany, NY: State University of New York Press, 2001).
14 Certainly, I was given authors in a broad context from which their work emerged, for example, psychology, psychoanalysis, anthropology and so forth. But each of these areas was presented as monolithic and homogeneous and this obscures the actual theoretical orientation of the scholar under study. Questions that might be engaged are: what is the social and historical context (both broadly and intellectually) of the author and the work? How does the author understand religion as a general concept? And what other fissures and fractures might shape the work, such as gender ideology, issues of race, nationalism or class?
15 Certainly with this statement I have raised a universal, but there are some material universals that are functional, such as the warm-bloodedness of mammals or the use of language by human beings. I would argue that theorizing is one of these.
16 For an excellent critique of the category 'experience' and its problematic use in feminist theorizing, see Joan Scott, 'Experience', in *Feminists theorize the political*, J. Butler and J. W. Scott (eds) (New York; London: Routledge, 1992), 22–40.
17 One possible reason for the perception of theory and experience as antithetical could be that the category of universal is seen to converge with theory, while the category of the particular is seen to converge with experience. The opposition of universal and particular, then, is secondarily and problematically applied to theory and experience.

18 I am not advocating the dissolution of departmental boundaries, simply knowledge boundaries.

19 This is often where the category of experience is interjected and is made to play the role of both data and theory.

20 Darlene M. Juschka, 'Interdisciplinarity in Religious and Women's Studies', *Studies in Religion/Sciences Religieuses* 35, no. 3–4 (2006), 389–99.

21 Dan Sperber, 'Why rethink interdisciplinarity?' (2003), www.interdisciplines.org/interdisciplinarity/papers/1/21.

22 For example, see the work of David Chidester, *Savage Systems: Colonialism and Comparative Religion in Southern Africa* (Charlottesville: The University of Virginia, 1996); Tim Jensen (ed.), *Human rights, Democracy and Religion – in the Perspective of Cultural Studies, Philosophy and the Study of Religions* (Odense: University of Southern Denmark, 2005); and Winnifred F. Sullivan, *The Impossibility of Religious Freedom* (Princeton: Princeton University Press, 2005).

23 The thematic orientation in religious studies also takes the form of looking at particular concepts such as gender, experience, text, ritual and so forth. Work done that represents this kind of engagement, beyond those mentioned above, are Mark C. Taylor (ed.), *Critical Terms for Religious Studies* (Chicago: Chicago University Press, 1998); Malory Nye, *Religion: The Basics* (London and New York: Routledge, 2003); and John R. Hinnells (ed.), *The Routledge Companion to the Study of Religion* (London and New York: Routledge, 2005).

24 A good example of this ignoring of the field of religious studies is the recent work by Daniel Dennett, *Breaking the Spell: Religion as a Natural Phenomenon* (New York: Viking, 2006), who did not feel the necessity to read in the field. Dennett is certainly not the only scholar outside of religious studies to be ignorant of the field.

CHAPTER 12

1 On grand or great narratives, see Jean-François Lyotard, *The Postmodern Condition: A Report on Knowledge* (Minneapolis, MN: University of Minnesota Press, 1984), 31–8; and Paul Cobley, *Narrative* (London and New York: Routledge, 2001), 183–9; see also James A. Beckford and John Walliss (eds), *Theorising Religion: Classical and Contemporary Debates* (Aldershot, Hampshire UK: Ashgate Publishing, 2006), esp. Ch. 12 by James V. Spickard; Inger Furseth and Pål Repstad, *An Introduction to the Sociology of Religion: Classical and Contemporary Perspectives* (Aldershot, Hampshire UK: Ashgate Publishing, 2006), esp. Ch. 5.

2 For a history of intellectual developments within the field of religious studies since the nineteenth century, see Eric J. Sharpe, *Comparative Religion: A History*, 2nd edn (La Salle, IL: Open Court, 1986); for recent discussions and assessments of the academic study of religion in the West, see Donald Wiebe, *The Politics of Religious Studies* (New York: St Martin's Press, 1999); Hans G. Kippenberg, *Discovering Religious History in the Modern Age* (Princeton, NJ: Princeton University Press, 2002); and Daniel Dubuisson, *The Western Construction of Religion: Myths, Knowledge, and Ideology* (Baltimore, MD; Johns Hopkins University Press, 2003).

3 Tomoko Masuzawa, *In Search of Dreamtime: The Quest for the Origin of Religion* (Chicago: The University of Chicago Press, 1993), 13.

4 Friedrich Nietzsche, 'Selections from *The Gay Science*', in *The Portable Nietzsche*, ed. and trans. Walter Kaufmann (New York: Penguin Books, 1976), 95.

5 Peter Berger, *The Sacred Canopy* (Garden City, NY: Anchor Books, 1969), 28.

6 See Erich Auerbach, 'Odysseus' Scar', in *Mimesis: the Representation of Reality in Western Literature* (Princeton, NJ: Princeton University Press, 1953), 3–23.

7   For a discussion and critique of Baudrillard and 'simulacrum' and 'simulacra', see David Harvey, *The Condition of Postmodernity: An Enquiry into the Origins of Cultural Chance* (Cambridge, MA, and Oxford, UK: Blackwell, 1990), 300–3; and Madan Sarup, *An Introductory Guide to Post-Structuralism and Postmodernism*, 2nd edn (Athens, GA: The University of Georgia Press, 1993), 164–6.

8   Quoted in Artes Orga, *Beethoven: His Life and Times* (Neptune City, NJ: Paganiniana Publications, 1980), 89.

9   Marshall Berman, *All That Is Solid Melts Into Air: The Experience of Modernity* (New York: Penguin Books, 1988), 6.

10   Nietzsche, 'Selections from *The Gay Science*', 96.

11   Otto Heller, *Prophets of Dissent: Essays on Maeterlinck, Strindberg, Nietzsche and Tolstoy* (New York: Alfred A. Knopf, 1918), 115–16.

12   For more on postmodernist, post-structuralist and related intellectual developments, see Edith Kurzweil, *The Age of Structuralism: Lévi-Strauss to Foucault* (New York: Columbia University Press, 1980); Quentin Skinner (ed.), *The Return of Grand Theory in the Human Sciences* (Cambridge, UK: Cambridge University Press, 1985); David Harvey, *The Condition of Postmodernity*; Gianni Vatimo, *The End of Modernity: Nihilism and Hermeneutics in Postmodern Culture* (Baltimore, MD: Johns Hopkins University Press, 1991); Madan Sarup, *An Introductory Guide to Post-Structuralism and Postmodernism*; Homi K. Bhabha, *The Location of Culture* (London and New York: Routledge, 1994); and Pam Morris, *Realism* (London and New York: Routledge, 2003).

13   See Jerald C. Brauer, 'Preface', in *The History of Religions: Essays in Methodology*, Mircea Eliade and Joseph M. Kitagawa (eds) (Chicago: The University of Chicago Press, 1959), vii–x; for examples of more recent discussion and critique, see Gavin Flood, *Beyond Phenomenology: Rethinking the Study of Religion* (London and New York: Cassell, 1999); and Timothy Fitzgerald, *The Ideology of Religious Studies* (New York: Oxford University Press, 2000).

14   Masuzawa, *In Search of Dreamtime*, 14.

15   'Review of The Craft of Religious Studies', *Journal of the Scientific Study of Religion* 39, no. 3 (September 2000), 393.

16   Ibid., 393.

17   Rodney Stark, 'On Theory-Driven Methods', in *The Craft of Religious Studies*, Jon R. Stone (ed.) (New York: St Martin's Press, 1998), 175: see also, Rodney Stark, *One True God: Historical Consequences of Monotheism* (Princeton, NJ: Princeton University Press, 2001), 5 and 12–17.

18   Ninian Smart, 'Methods of My Life' in *The Craft of Religious Studies*, 22.

19   See Smart, 'Methods of My Life', 34–5.

20   See Wiebe, *The Politics of Religious Studies*, 130–5 and 285–91.

21   Fitzgerald, *The Ideology of Religious Studies*, 47.

22   For further discussion on phenomenology and phenomenology of religion, see Dermot Moran, *Introduction to Phenomenology* (London and New York: Routledge, 2000); Fitzgerald, *The Ideology of Religious Studies*, 10–15 and 33–4; Flood, *Beyond Phenomenology*, 18–28 and 225–30; and Wiebe, *The Politics of Religious Studies*, 109–13. Though not related to religion per se, a comment by Homi K. Bhaba, *The Location of Culture*, 4, is apropos of this point. He writes, 'if the interest in postmodernism is limited to a celebration of the fragmentation of the "grand narratives" of postenlightenment rationalism then, for all its intellectual excitement, it remains a profoundly parochial enterprise.'

23   Jon R. Stone (ed.), *The Essential Max Müller: On Language, Mythology and Religion* (New York: Palgrave, 2002), 81 and 112–13.

24   See comments and critique in Wiebe, *The Politics of Religious Studies*, 81–5, 109–13, 130–5 and 285–91.

25   Lyrics from The Beatles, 'Revolution', *Hey Jude* (New York: Apple Records, 1970).
26   Ibid.
27   Stark, 'On Theory-Driven Methods', in *The Craft of Religious Studies*, 175.
28   John Hick, 'Climbing the Foothills of Understanding', in *The Craft of Religious Studies*, 76.
29   Wendy Doniger, 'From Great Neck to Swift Hall: Confessions of a Reluctant Historian of Religions', in *The Craft of Religious Studies*, 47.
30   For a detailed examination of this issue, see Charles Y. Glock and Phillip E. Hammond (eds), *Beyond the Classics?: Essays in the Scientific Study of Religion* (New York: Harper & Row, 1973).
31   Ivan Strenski, 'The Rest is History', in *The Craft of Religious Studies*, 310–11; see also, Ivan Strenski, *Four Theories of Myth in Twentieth-Century History: Cassirer, Eliade, Lévi-Strauss and Malinowski* (Iowa City, IA: University of Iowa Press, 1987).
32   Jerome S. Bruner, *The Process of Education* (New York: Vintage Press, 1963), 14.
33   See J. Gordon Melton, Phillip Charles Lucas and Jon R. Stone, *Prime-Time Religion: An Encyclopedia of Religious Broadcasting* (Phoenix, AZ: The Oryx Press, 1997); in this instance, after Phillip Lucas and I had written the entire book, we then asked Gordon if he would write an introduction for it. Because Gordon had also helped us secure a publisher for our book, as a courtesy, Phillip and I were more than happy to place his name first on the title page.
34   See my entries in Larry G. Murphy, J. Gordon Melton and Gary L. Ward (eds), *Encyclopedia of African American Religions* (New York and London: Garland Publishing, 1993).
35   Jon R. Stone, *A Guide to the End of the World: Popular Eschatology in America* (New York and London: Garland Publishing, 1993).
36   Jon R. Stone, *On the Boundaries of American Evangelicalism: The Postwar Evangelical Coalition* (New York: St Martin's Press, 1997). This book is the revised version of my 1990 doctoral dissertation from the University of California, Santa Barbara. Inexplicably, the Library of Congress listed my PhD as having been granted from the University of California, Berkeley, where I was teaching at the time. By the way, when one of my former professors asked why it had taken me seven years to revise and publish my dissertation, I joked wryly, 'Because it took me that long to remove the advice of my committee.'
37   Roger Friedland and Richard Hecht, *To Rule Jerusalem* (1996: repr., Berkeley: University of California Press, 2000).
38   Jon R. Stone (ed.), *Expecting Armageddon: Essential Readings in Failed Prophecy* (London and New York: Routledge, 2000). This book grew out of a guest lecture that I gave for Phillip Hammond's Sociology of Religious Organizations course in January 1987. I presented a revised version of this paper at All Souls College, Oxford, in June 1993, and then reworked it for a lecture I gave that next week at the London School of Economics. I reworked the paper again in 1996 and then compiled and edited the accompanying readings while teaching an RS majors seminar in American Millennialism at UC Berkeley in Spring 1999.
39   Jon R. Stone, *Latin for the Illiterati: Exorcizing the Ghosts of a Dead Language* (London and New York: Routledge, 1996). This lexicon is largely the result of my longtime penchant for keeping lists of foreign words and phrases that I would encounter while reading, combined with bitter-cold winters that I endured during my temporary appointment teaching at the University of Northern Iowa from 1990 to 1993. With little else to do between classes, I began typing up my stack of lists and discovered that I had the makings of a useful little handbook. I finished the book in 1994 and, at the suggestion of Ninian Smart, I sent the manuscript to Routledge for review. They eagerly published it (my thanks to Marlie Wasserman and Maura Burnett). For nearly

a decade after its publication in 1996, *LFTI* was one of Routledge's bestselling books, the second best among its reference works.

40 Charles Dickens, *A Christmas Carol* (New York: Dover Publications, 1991), 49.

CHAPTER 13

1   E. M. Cioran, 'Beginning of a Friendship', in *Myths and Symbol: Studies in Honor of Mircea Eliade*, Joseph M. Kitagawa and Charles H. Long (eds) (Chicago: University of Chicago Press, 1969), 414.
2   Stephen Toulmin, *Human Understanding: The Collective Use and Evolution of Concepts* (Princeton: Princeton University Press, 1972), 379, emphasis added.
3   Charles H. Long, 'A Look at the Chicago Tradition in the History of Religions: Retrospect and Future', in *The History of Religions, Retrospect and Future*, Joseph M. Kitagawa (ed.) (New York and London: MacMillan, 1985).
4   Long, 'A Look at the Chicago Tradition in the History of Religions', 101–2.
5   Jonathan Z. Smith, *Imagining Religion: From Babylon to Jonestown* (Chicago: University of Chicago Press, 1982).
6   Michel Foucault, *The Order of Things: An Archaeology of the Human Sciences* (New York: Random House, 1970), 344.
7   This was, of course, a very rough categorization and represented the interest of the scholars involved and the availability of access to data. For example, no one knew where to place the Aztecs, Maya and Incas of the new world in this structure.
8   I refer here to Rudolf Otto, *The Idea of the Holy*, trans. John W. Harvey, 2nd edn, (London and New York: Oxford University Press, 1950).
9   See my discussion of 'empirical others' in the Introduction of Charles H. Long, *Significations, Signs, Symbols, and Images in the Interpretation of Religion*, 2nd edn (Aurora, CO: The Davies Group Publishers, 1999).
10 Dipesh Chakrabarty, *Provincializing Europe, Postcolonial Thought and Historical Difference* (Princeton: Princeton University Press, 2000), 16. See also Dipesh Chakrabarty, *Habitations of Modernity: Essays in the Wake of Subaltern Studies* (Chicago: The University of Chicago Press, 2002).
11 The search for origins was based upon a stadial notion of historical time. Ronald L. Meeks' study, *Social Science & the Ignoble Savage* (London: Cambridge University Press, 1976), is a lucid discussion of the beginnings of the four-stage theory of history and prehistory.
12 Johannes Fabian, *Time and the Other, How Anthropology Makes Its Object* (New York: Columbia University Press, 1983), 164.
13 See William Pietz, 'The Problem of the Fetish, I,' *RES, Anthropology and Aesthetics* 9 (Spring 1985), 5–17; 'The Problem of the Fetish, II: the origin of the fetish', *RES, Anthropology and Aesthetics* 13 (Spring 1987), 23–46; 'The Problem of the Fetish, IIIa: Bosman's Guinea and the enlightenment theory of the fetishism', *RES, Anthropology and Aesthetics* (Autumn 1988), 105–24.
14 Pietz, 'The Problem of the Fetish. III', 107.
15 Ibid.
16 See Max Weber, *The Protestant Ethic and the Spirit of Capitalism*, trans. Talcott Parsons (Charles Scribner's Sons, NY, 1958). Another take on the role of Protestantism can be seen in Benjamin Nelson's *From Tribal Brotherhood to Universal Otherhood* (Princeton: Princeton University Press, 1949): Nelson emphasizes the desacramentalizing of the world through Calvinism and he traces this process through a study of the practice of usury within the Calvinist tradition and its effect on the economic theories of modernity.

17   F. E. Williams, *The Vailala Madness and the Destruction of Native Ceremonies in the Gulf District*, Papuan Anthropology Reports, no. 4 (Port Moresby, 1923), 1.

18   See K. O. L. Burridge, *Mambu, A Melanesian Millennium* (New York: Harper and Row, 1970), xv ff.

19   G. W. Trompf, *Payback: The Logic of Retribution in Melanesian Religions* (Cambridge, UK: Cambridge University Press, 1994), 161. Trompf's work is the latest comprehensive study of Melanesian cargo cults.

20   Wallace D. Best, *Passionately Human, No Less Divine: Religion and Culture in Black Chicago, 1915–1952* (Princeton: Princeton University Press, 2005).

21   Some of the best-known African American intellectuals of this era were members of the 'Chicago school' of sociology. Among them were Horace Cayton, St Clair Drake, E. Franklin Frazier and Charles H. Johnson.

22   Wallace Best, *Passionately Human*, 34. Given the brilliance of the group of African American sociologists of this period and the creative vibrancy of African American religion during this same period, one is struck by the fact that none of them produced any major work on African American religion in Chicago.

23   Karen E. Fields, *Revival and Rebellion in Colonial Central Africa* (Princeton: Princeton University Press, 1985).

24   J. Stephen Lansing, *Priests and Programmers: Technologies of Power in the Engineered Landscape of Bali* (Princeton: Princeton University Press, 1991).

25   Lansing, *Priests and Programmers*, 133.

26   Lansing, *Priests and Programmers*, 142.

27   Kathleen Biddick, *The Typological Imaginary: Circumcision, Technology, History* (Philadelphia: University of Pennsylvania Press, 2003), 1.

28   Biddick, *The Typological Imaginary*, 2 (emphasis added).

29   See Chakrabarty, *Provincializing Europe*, 'Epilogue'.

30   Chakrabarty, *Provincializing Europe*, 243.

31   Long, *Significations*, 9.

32   Chakrabarty, *Provincializing Europe*, 16.

Index

AAR *see* American Academy of Religion
abortion 108
abstracts 181
academia 117, 140
academic positions 29
Acadians 149
accountability, graduate programmes 62
Africa 188, 189
  religion 189
African Americans 122, 191
African National Congress (ANC) 107,
  110, 111, 113
Aid for Scholarly Publication Program
  (ASPP) 57
America *see* United States of America
American Academy of Religion (AAR) 54
American Jewish Committee 123
American Theological Library Association
  (ATLA)
  databases 50
anachronism 195
ANC *see* African National Congress
anthropologists 93, 161, 179, 192–3
anthropology 85, 89, 94, 120, 163, 164–5,
  209
anti-Semitism 118, 123, 124, 126
anti-subordination 152
apartheid (South Africa) 102, 107, 109, 110,
  111, 113
applied research 63
Arab–Israeli War (1967) 121
art 209
articles, journal 52–4
arts *see* fine arts
ASPP *see* Aid for Scholarly Publication
  Program
ATLA *see* American Theological Library
  Association
Auschwitz 121
Australia 190
Autre Parole, L' 151

baby boom 171
Bali 193
  irrigation system 193
Bangalore
  Christian Institute for the Study of
    Religion and Society 81
barakat 130

Benveniste, Emile 102
berikah 130, 135
Bhagavadgita 202
Bible 91, 122, 124
  scholars 145
Bible, Hebrew 129, 130, 131, 132, 136, 137,
  140
bibliography 15, 17, 23, 26
blessing 129–46
blogs 47
Boethius 207
Bombay (Mumbai) 80, 81
  Tata Institute of Social Sciences 80
book reviews 29, 180
books 54
  proposals 55
Botha, Pieter Willem 108, 109
Brandeis University 124
British Empire 104
Buddhism 66, 96, 160, 166, 177
Bush, George H.W. 125
business 84
business studies 84

Callaway, Henry 105
Calvinism 189
Canadian Society for the Study of Religion
  (CSSR) 54
capital punishment 145
capitalism 92, 152, 189
cargo cult 190–1
Carter, Jimmy 124, 125
Catholic Church 76, 81
Catholic Theology Society of America 147
censorship 119
Central Africa 192
Centre for Studies in Religion and
  Society 70
Chicago, University of 183
  Department of Sociology 191
Christian community 122
Christian Institute for the Study of
  Religion and Society, Bangalore 81
Christian theology 137
Christianity 96, 119, 120, 121, 122, 133, 160,
  177, 199, 203
Christians 103, 126, 137, 188
class 152, 166
Classics 85